History of Delaware

FIFTH EDITION

John A. Munroe

A University of Delaware Bicentennial Book

Newark
University of Delaware Press

Associated University Presses
2010 Eastpark Blvd.
Cranbury, NJ 08512

The paper used in this publication meets the requirements of the American National Standard for Permanence of Paper for Printed Library Materials Z39.48-1984.

The Library of Congress has cataloged a prior edition as follows:

Munroe, John A., 1914–
    History of Delaware / John A. Munroe.—4th ed.
      p. cm.
    "A University of Delaware bicentennial book."
    Includes bibliographical references (p.) and index.
    ISBN 0-87413-772-1 (alk. paper)
    1. Delaware—History.   I. Title.

F164.M83 2001
975.1—dc21

                          2001027438

Fifth edition ISBN 0-87413-947-3   2006

To
the Munroes, the Dettlings, and the Levises
for their love and encouragement

Contents

Preface

For more than four decades students have been handicapped for want of a one-volume history of Delaware. Walter A. Powell's *History of Delaware,* published in 1928, has been out of print for more than four decades. Its place was filled for many years by a splendid book prepared by the Federal Writers' Project entitled *Delaware: A Guide to the First State,* originally published in 1938 and reprinted with minor revisions in 1948 and 1955. In this work an introductory section of over 150 pages included chapters on history, government, transportation, religion, agriculture, and so forth, that were generally an improvement on Powell's work, thanks to the competence of Jeannette Eckman, Anthony Higgins, and William Conner, who were editors of this guide.

Still, it was not primarily a history and made no effort to present a unified chronological account of the major developments in the history of Delaware. My colleague and teacher, H. Clay Reed, talked with me at various times of our eventually collaborating on a one-volume work when we were free of other pressing commitments, but, unfortunately, that time had not yet come when Professor Reed died in 1973. Meanwhile, he had edited a two-volume cooperative work, *Delaware: A History of the First State,* in 1947 (a third volume, entirely biographical, does not bear his name), and I had written a short (thirty-four-page) history of Delaware for a series of Students' Guides to Localized History issued by Teachers College Press of Columbia University and edited by Clifford L. Lord.

In the fall of 1974 I was approached by some members of the Delaware American Revolutionary Bicentennial Commission with the suggestion that I undertake to expand this brief sketch as a Bicentennial project. When I seemed receptive but pleaded the problem of time, the commissioners quickly arranged a year's leave of absence for me in the calendar year 1975, with

9

financial support shared by the commission and the University of Delaware. I am particularly indebted to the late John Mickey, then executive secretary of the commission; to Miss M. Catherine Downing, a member of the commission who, with Mr. Mickey, first broached the idea to me; to Dr. George H. Gibson, chairman of the commission's publications committee, who worked out details of the collaboration; and to Dr. E. Arthur Trabant, whose support of the project, as president of the University of Delaware and as chairman of the Delaware American Revolution Bicentennial Commission, was invaluable.

Any work like this history, covering a long period of time even though dealing with a small area, is bound to be based in great part on secondary sources—that is, on what has been written previously. Unfortunately, in Delaware historiography, as in the Arabian desert, there are "empty quarters," areas that have hardly been explored. Perhaps this presentation of a chronological account will stimulate new studies, particularly in areas previously unexamined. Such, at least, is the hope of the author.

Besides those institutions and persons already named, I acknowledge the assistance of C. A. Weslager, the late Thomas Herlihy, Jr., Carol E. Hoffecker, John C. Kraft, Norman B. Wilkinson, Francis Tannian, C. Harold Brown, Anna J. De Armond, Charles L. Reese, Jr., the late Ernest J. Moyne, John A. H. Sweeney, Anthony Higgins, Irving N. Morris, William P. Frank, and W. Emerson Wilson, some of whom have read portions of this work, while others have been helpful in answering questions and thus sharing their knowledge.

Harold B. Hancock, whose knowledge of the broad sweep of Delaware history is unexcelled, has my particular gratitude for reading this entire work as a kindness to me, saving me from several factual errors. I am grateful to members of the staff of the Eleutherian Mills-Hagley Foundation, the Historical Society of Delaware, and the State Division of Historical and Cultural Affairs for assistance at many stages of my work. Most of all, I am indebted to the staff of the Morris Library of the University of Delaware, where most of this book was written, for many favors. I am hesitant to mention individuals in these libraries and agencies for fear I would neglect someone. I am grateful to Betty S. Sherman for her care in typing my original manuscript and to Susan Stock Means for her efficient copy editing.

History of Delaware

1

The Dutch and the Swedes

The Land

The state of Delaware forms the western shore of the lower Delaware valley and a section of the Atlantic Ocean coast south of Cape Henlopen. It is roughly 110 miles long from north to south and shaped somewhat like a slipper sitting on its heel, its flat sole forming the western boundary with Maryland, while its tongue lies along the Delaware River and Bay. The width of the state varies from 35 miles at the southern boundary to 9 miles in central New Castle County. There are three counties: Sussex, the largest, to the south; Kent, in the center; and New Castle, which is the smallest, in the north.

Most of the state is part of the flat Atlantic coastal plain, but in the northwestern corner, on a line roughly from Newark to Wilmington, the plain gives way to the modest foothills of the Piedmont area. The most important geographic feature of the state is the river and bay for which it was named. This waterway brought the first European settlers to Delaware and furnished an avenue by which their products could be transported to the markets of the world. Its banks, however, are frequently sandy or marshy, and since silt hampers entrance to most tributaries, there are few harbors suitable for oceanic commerce, except in northern Delaware, where fast land borders the river at several places, notably at New Castle and along the Christina, the largest tributary of the Delaware in the state.

The ocean shore is a sandy beach from Cape Henlopen, at the mouth of Delaware Bay, to Fenwick (alternately pronounced *Finnix*) Island on the Maryland line. Behind this beach are three coastal bays. Two of them, Rehoboth Bay and Indian River

13

Bay, are connected with the ocean by the Indian River Inlet, north of Bethany Beach. (The location of the inlet, like the shape of Cape Henlopen, has changed over the years.) The third coastal bay, Little Assawoman, is west of the stretch of sandy ocean shore connecting Bethany Beach and Fenwick Island, which is not really an island.

Most of the small rivers and streams of Delaware flow eastward toward the Delaware Bay, the Delaware River, and the Atlantic Ocean, but in the south and southwest, streams like the Nanticoke and branches of the Pocomoke and the Choptank flow toward Chesapeake Bay. The interior of Delaware was once heavily wooded beyond the coastal marshes, with frequent ponds where drainage was poor, as in the great Cypress Swamp, about midway along the southern boundary.

All except the northernmost part of Delaware lies on what is now known as the Delmarva Peninsula, a tongue of land two hundred miles long that forms the eastern side of the Chesapeake Bay. Delaware occupies the northeastern third of this peninsula, which it shares with two counties of Virginia and nine counties of Maryland, these eleven counties commonly being called the Eastern Shore.

Though Delaware's longest boundary by land is with Maryland (on the south and the west), its closest connection historically and economically is with Pennsylvania. The short boundary between Delaware and Pennsylvania is part of the circumference of a circle with a twelve-mile radius based on the spire of the old New Castle Court House. This strange boundary was established in the grant by which King Charles II gave Pennsylvania to William Penn in 1681, but both before and after this grant Pennsylvania and Delaware shared some elements of government (the same governor, for instance) almost constantly until 1776. The eastern boundary separating Delaware and New Jersey was frequently a subject of dispute until a decision of the United States Supreme Court in 1935, which declared that the entire river lay in Delaware (to low watermark on the New Jersey shore) within twelve miles of New Castle. Farther south, through Delaware Bay, the boundary follows the main ship channel.

The southern boundary, surveyed in 1750–51, is a straight east-west line running halfway across the Delmarva Peninsula from Fenwick Island. Most of the western boundary is a straight line drawn northward from the halfway point (called the Middle Point) to make a tangent with the twelve-mile circle that forms the northern boundary. Beyond the tangent point, which is southwest of Newark, the western boundary follows the circle briefly (until exactly north of the tangent point) and then becomes a straight line running directly north to the southern boundary of Pennsylvania.

This western boundary was surveyed and marked in the years 1763–68 by Charles Mason and Jeremiah Dixon and is as much a part of the Mason-Dixon line as is the portion of the Maryland-Pennsylvania boundary that the same surveyors marked. A small triangular tract of land called the Wedge at the northern end of the western boundary and lying between the circle and the straight line drawn by Mason and Dixon was in dispute until 1893, when it was awarded to Delaware.

The Indians

When this state first became known to Europeans by voyages made in the early seventeenth century, it was populated mainly by an Indian people who called themselves the Lenni Lenape. English settlers called them the Delaware Indians, because they lived along both shores of the Delaware from the bay northward about two hundred miles. Their language was a version of the Algonkian (or Algonquin) tongues spoken by most of the tribes on the Atlantic coast; there were sharp dialectic differences, however, among different groups of the Lenape.

Politically, they were entirely decentralized, each village unit or community apparently running its own affairs. When first met by Europeans, the Lenape were under attack by the powerful central New York Indian confederacy called the Iroquois, and by another Indian tribe, the Minqua or Susquehannock, who lived in central Pennsylvania and, linguistically, were related to the Iroquois rather than to the Algonquin peoples of the coast. The Nanticoke, an Algonquin tribe, lived in Sussex County as well as on the Eastern Shore, and probably other Algonquin peoples, such as the Assateague and the Choptank Indians, lived in Sussex.

The Indians of Delaware lived by a combination of hunting, fishing, and farming. Of their scanty crops, the main one was corn, or maize, but they also grew beans and squash. They made their simple clothes of furs and skins, they fashioned boats (dugouts) from logs, and their dwellings were wigwams made of wood, reeds, and corn husks. Their history was recorded in a series of picture-graphs on painted sticks called the *Walum Olum;* from this mnemonic device Indian sages could recite the tale of their ancestors' migration from beyond the Mississippi to the Atlantic coast.

With only a few exceptions, the relations between Indians and the European settlers in Delaware were peaceful. At first the Indians were valued for the furs they could trade for European hardware and textiles. Soon, however, the Indians found their hunting area restricted by European settlements and gradually began to withdraw to the west and north. Most of the Nanticoke tribe left Sussex County in the middle of the eighteenth century, and by that time the Lenape had also withdrawn from Delaware.* Generally, the Indians of Delaware moved first into the Susquehanna valley of central Pennsylvania. From there, as settlement again pressed upon them, some moved into Canada; others went to Ohio and later moved again to the trans-Mississippi West.

Although the Lenape were a relatively peaceful people, oppressed by the stronger Iroquois and Minqua when the first Europeans found them, they acquired a military reputation as they moved westward, and eventually, before their final settlement in Oklahoma, they gained a reputation as one of the warlike tribes of plains Indians, providing a number of the Indian scouts employed by the United States Army.

Swanendael

It is surprising that the Delaware River, one of the major waterways of the East Coast, went unnoticed for more than a century after Columbus discovered America. It is quite possible, of course, that some early sailor entered the river in that period, but as far as is known its existence was a secret until 1609, when Henry Hudson, an experienced English sea captain commanding a Dutch ship, the *Half Moon,* entered Delaware Bay during his search for a northwest passage to China. On the same voyage he discovered the Hudson River, and after his return to Europe, Dutch vessels began to make frequent visits to what they called

---

* A small remnant of the Nanticoke keep their Indian heritage alive by maintaining a community center in Sussex County at Warwick, north of Indian River Bay.

the North River (the Hudson) and the South River (the Delaware), where they developed a profitable fur trade.

In 1610 Samuel Argall, an English sailor, had also found his
way into Delaware Bay, taking refuge from a storm that overtook
him on a voyage from Virginia, which had been settled in 1607.
Argall named the point at the entrance to the bay for Lord de la
Warr, the governor of Virginia, and the name soon was applied
by the English to the bay and the river, and finally to the land
on the western shore. A Dutch explorer, Cornelis May, gave his
own name to the capes at the mouth of Delaware Bay. The name
Cape May remained permanently attached to the New Jersey
side of the entrance, but Cornelis gave way to Henlopen as the
name for the cape on the Delaware side, though Captain May
had originally applied the name Cape Henlopen to a point
farther south, possibly Fenwick Island, which, because it was
wooded, in contrast to the sand dunes on either side of it, may
have looked like a cape from the sea.

The Dutch decided to solidify their claim to the Hudson
and Delaware valleys, which they called New Netherland, by
establishing trading posts. The first of these in the Delaware
valley was Fort Nassau, established approximately on the site of
Gloucester, New Jersey, but it was preceded in 1624 by a settlement of Walloons (French-speaking Belgians) on Burlington
Island. The Walloon settlement was apparently abandoned very
soon, but Fort Nassau was occupied intermittently for many years
before it was given up in favor of a Dutch post established at
New Castle in 1651.

Meanwhile, the Dutch West India Company, which was primarily interested in the profits to be made by raids on Spanish
and Portuguese possessions in America, opened the New Netherland colony to private enterprise, hoping to entice individual
stockholders into colonizing ventures. To this end, the company
promised to reward private initiative by handsome land grants,
along with various fringe benefits. For instance, if a stockholder
would settle fifty colonists in America, he could buy from the
Indians a tract of land running sixteen miles along a river bank
and as far inland as practical. He could fish and trade, except in
furs, all along the coast; he could guarantee his colonists freedom
from taxes for ten years; and he could rule them like a lord of
the manor, with the title of *patroon* (similar to *patron* in English), his settlement being called a *patroonship*.

The first European settlement in Delaware was a patroonship

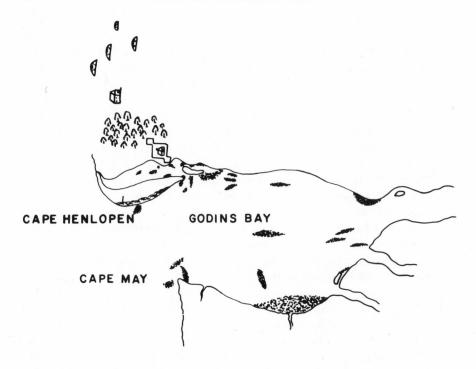

CAPE HENLOPEN   GODINS BAY

CAPE MAY

Adaptation of a map from the seventeenth century found among the papers of David de Vries. The Swanendael settlement on Lewes Creek is shown, as are shoals in the bay and, apparently, the wigwams of Indians. From The Evolution of Lewes Harbor, *by John C. Kraft and Robert L. Caulk, Technical Report no. 10 (College of Marine Studies, University of Delaware, November 1972), as adapted from C. A. Weslager and Arthur R. Dunlap,* Dutch Explorers, Traders, and Settlers in the Delaware Valley, 1609–1664 *(Philadelphia, 1961).*

founded by an Amsterdam merchant of Walloon origins named Samuel Godyn (sometimes written Godijn or Godin). As was customary, he made several other Dutch merchants his partners in the enterprise and included in the group a sailor named David Pietersen de Vries, who had wide experience in Dutch colonies overseas.

Acting through an agent named Gillis Hossitt, Godyn bought a large tract of land on the western side of Delaware Bay and dispatched settlers for his new possession on a vessel named the *Whale* (*Walvis*) commanded by Captain Peter Heyes. Heyes disembarked his passengers and cargo of provisions, building equipment, and livestock on what is now Lewes Creek in the early spring of 1631. Calling the settlement Swanendael, the thirty-two settlers constructed a brick dwelling surrounded by a wooden palisade and began to trade with Indians as well as to plant a crop. Hossitt was left in command when the *Whale* returned to the Netherlands.

A second expedition, commanded by de Vries, came to Swanendael in 1632, but even before it set out its commander learned that the colony had been destroyed and the colonists killed to a man. De Vries came to Delaware anyway and questioned the Indians to learn what brought on the massacre, which turned out to be the only case of a serious Indian onslaught upon Europeans in the history of Delaware.

It seemed that an Indian had stolen a tin coat of arms that the Dutch had set up on a stake by their house. All metals were fascinating to Indians, who were still living in the stone age, but the fuss the Dutch made about the theft as an insult to their country so impressed some of the Indians that they killed the thief. His friends, in turn, swearing vengeance, crept up on the unsuspecting Dutch when the latter were at work and killed them all.

The identity of the Indian tribe that perpetrated the massacre is not known. De Vries spent the winter of 1632–33 at Swanendael, attempting to establish a whaling enterprise on the bay, but the Dutch then knew little about whaling, and the enterprise was abandoned in the spring as a failure. No other expedition was sent, probably because the principal investor, Godyn, died in September 1633, two months after De Vries returned. An associate said that forty thousand guilders were lost on the colony, but, despite its failure, the brief existence of Swanendael furnished, many years later, an excuse for exclusion of Delaware from the grant of Maryland to Lord Baltimore, a grant made in 1632, one year after Gillis Hossitt and his Dutch settlers had landed on Lewes Creek.

New Sweden

The second European settlement in Delaware and the first that was permanent was made in 1638 on the shore of the Christina River, at a spot that is now on the east side of the city of Wilmington. The Christina settlers were Swedes, and their settlement was the foundation of a new colony, New Sweden, but it was a direct outgrowth of Dutch enterprise in North America.

The monopoly of the American trade enjoyed by the Dutch West India Company annoyed many Dutch merchants who disagreed with the company's policies, particularly its emphasis upon looting Spanish possessions. These were legal attacks, not piracy, because the Dutch war for independence from Spain (called the Eighty Years' War) was not officially terminated until 1658, and since the Spanish king had inherited the crown of Portugal too in 1580, Portuguese possessions were also a legitimate prey of the Dutch, who conquered most of Brazil. Since the Dutch had effectively secured their independence early in the seventeenth century, the prolongation of the war was of value to them chiefly as an economic opportunity to profit from the wealth of the American empire that the Spanish tried to keep to themselves.

To the Dutch West India Company, settlement of the New Netherland was a side issue, valued chiefly as a potential base for attacks on their enemies. Dutchmen who thought the company's policy shortsighted, favoring a greater emphasis upon settlement and the local trade with Indians and the neighboring English that it would facilitate, were forced to seek authorization from foreign nations for enterprises not approved by the company. Sweden was at this time a major military power and an ally of the Dutch against the Spanish. Swedish commercial life, however, was largely in the hands of foreigners, particularly the Dutch, and it was natural that Dutch merchants seeking authorization for overseas ventures (like a twentieth-century flag of convenience on a cargo ship) would appeal to the Swedes.

Gustavus Adolphus, the most distinguished soldier-king of Sweden, found Dutch proposals for a colonial venture attractive and chartered a company for this purpose. But the demands of his wars gave him no opportunity to develop his colonizing interests, and after his death in battle in 1632, the development of a Swedish overseas colony fell to the administration of his young daughter and successor, Queen Christina.

Chancellor Axel Oxenstierna, the dominant figure in Christina's government, took an active interest in a colonial venture; together with several other Swedish officials and a group of Dutch merchants, especially Samuel Blommaert, who was important in the Baltic trade and had been a partner of Samuel Godyn in the Swanendael patroonship, Oxenstierna formed the New Sweden

Company in 1637 and dispatched an expedition to America in November of the same year. Commanded by Peter Minuit, a German-born Dutch resident who was probably of French Huguenot ancestry, the expedition's two ships, the *Key of Kalmar* (*Kalmar Nyckel*) and the *Griffin* (*Vogel Grip*), delayed by storms, arrived in the Delaware River in March 1638, disembarking the first Swedish colonists in America on a ledge of rocks beside a stream that they named for their queen.

This expedition that founded New Sweden was a half-Dutch enterprise. Half the money that backed it came from Dutch sources, and a good part of the cargo was Dutch, as was part of the crew. The two vessels had Dutch skippers and Minuit, commander of the expedition, was a former director of the Dutch New Netherland. In fact, he had been director of the New Netherland when Swanendael was founded; it was natural that he would lead the expedition to an area he knew about—and that he knew to be unoccupied except for the small Dutch post at Fort Nassau.

It was the Swedish element in the enterprise, however, that persisted. The twenty-five colonists left behind on the Christina with Mans Kling in command when Minuit sailed off in June 1638 were Swedes, as were the ships that had brought them and the authority under which they planted their colony and erected what they called Fort Christina, the first permanent settlement in Delaware and, for that matter, in the Delaware valley.

Gradually, Dutch participation in the New Sweden Company declined, until it disappeared entirely. Minuit was lost at sea returning from the initial voyage, and, although his vessels returned safely to Europe, the expedition lost money. Another Dutchman, Peter Hollander Ridder, commanded the second expedition in 1640, but he was already serving as an officer in the Swedish navy, and Dutch participation this time was limited to half the cost of the cargo and provisions. In 1641 the Dutch stockholders sold out their interest, and the New Sweden Company became wholly a Swedish enterprise. Individual Dutchmen still played some part in it—for example, Ridder remained as governor of New Sweden until 1643—but the Dutch had infiltrated Swedish life at many levels. After 1641 the company was not only Swedish in direction; it was operated practically as an arm of the Swedish government because all but one of its principal directors were government officials.

Probably the first women and children came to New Sweden

This monument by Carl Milles stands at The Rocks, in Wilmington, as a gift to Delaware in 1938 from the people of Sweden in commemoration of the three hundredth anniversary of the first Swedish settlement in America. (Courtesy of the Historical Society of Delaware.)

with the second expedition in 1640. Nevertheless, the colony was not secure until 1643, when Ridder was succeeded as governor by an able, though arbitrary, soldier of enormous size named Johan Printz. Printz had been a college student, aiming to enter the Lutheran ministry, when he was shanghaied into the army. Military life, he found, suited him, and his experience in difficult commands prepared him for the situation he found in America.

The small Swedish colony on the Delaware to which he came in 1643 was challenged from two directions: by the Dutch, who regarded the Swedes as trespassers in New Netherland, and by the English, who claimed the whole Atlantic seaboard. Combining firmness in insisting on Sweden's rights with diplomatic tact in dealing with his more powerful Dutch and English adversaries, Printz maintained and strengthened his colony through the ten years he spent in America.

As New Sweden developed, it consisted of a string of small Swedish settlements on the west shore of the Delaware from below the Christina River to the area of Philadelphia. Governor Printz made his home on Tinicum Island north of Chester, and there were small communities around Fort Christina (Wilmington) and at Upland (modern Chester). A fort (Elfsborg) erected near the mouth of the Salem River in New Jersey was soon abandoned; many Swedes did move to the New Jersey side of the river but not until after the fall of New Sweden.

At its height New Sweden probably did not have more than one thousand residents. A good proportion of them were Finns, not Swedes, but the exact number of Finns cannot be estimated, because the records were kept in Swedish (a very different language from Finnish), and even men's names were written in Swedish forms. Finland at this time was ruled by Sweden, and many Finns had come to Sweden as pioneers in the largely unsettled forested country north and west of Stockholm, which they were often willing to abandon for the forests of America. One resident was an African servant (probably not a slave) acquired when a Swedish vessel visited the West Indies.

A Swedish Lutheran minister was sent to the colonies to serve the settlers as early as 1640. Though there were occasional periods when the Swedes had no pastor, the Swedish government continued to send ministers to the settlers on the Delaware for much more than a century after the Swedes had surrendered control of this land—until after the American Revolution.

The Swedes and Finns seem to have been remarkably well

suited for colonization in this area of North America. They were better prepared for the extremes of temperature found there than the English, who were accustomed to a milder climate, influenced by the ocean. Whereas wood was comparatively scarce in England, the Scandinavian immigrants came from a country where it was abundant. The log houses they built in New Sweden were better suited to this country than houses built by the English, who were initially more sparing in their use of wood. Travelers noted the greater warmth and comfort of the Swedish log houses, which became the prototype of the American frontiersman's abode.

As in house construction, so in clearing fields and in farming the Swedes and Finns adapted well to the new land. It was fortunate that they did, for after a few years they were neglected by their home government. Some of the Swedish officials interested in colonization died; others became distracted by pressing problems in Europe. From 1648 to 1654 no relief—not one ship—came from the old country.

Swedish trade with the Indians came to a halt as the supply of trading goods ran out. Only the formidable quality of the settlers themselves and the arbitrary, but able, leadership of Printz preserved the colony. English and Dutch complaints that the Swedes were illegal intruders became more pressing, but were withstood by Printz's careful diplomacy and by the hesitance of the English and Dutch governments in Europe to permit any offensive action harmful to their relations with Sweden.

The Dutch governor of New Netherland, Peter Stuyvesant, chafed at the restrictions placed upon him in dealing with settlers in an area the Dutch regarded as their own and where their post at Fort Nassau long predated Swedish settlement. In 1651 Stuyvesant, forbidden to attack the Swedes but directed to insist on Dutch rights to the Delaware, decided upon a new stratagem. He abandoned Fort Nassau for a new site, lower down the Delaware, at a place called the Sandhook (modern New Castle), where he built a post he called Fort Casimir. Fort Casimir was less well located for the Indian trade than a site up the river; its advantage was that it lay between New Sweden and the ocean. Potentially, it could control the trade of New Sweden, but only potentially, for Stuyvesant could not afford to garrison or arm Fort Casimir enough to make it an immediate threat.

Still, its very existence was galling to Printz, whose appeals to the Swedish government continued to go unanswered. At last,

Fort Casimir, erected in 1651 by the Dutch at New Castle. Adaptation of a sketch made by Peter Lindeström, a Swedish engineer, in 1654. (Courtesy of the Historical Society of Delaware.)

in 1653, he determined to return to Sweden and attempt personally to find relief for his colony. To return he had first to travel to Stuyvesant's capital, New Amsterdam (New York), and there take passage on a Dutch ship. The voyage was long and the experience must have been demeaning, but when Printz arrived in Sweden he found a strong expedition prepared and setting off for North America.

Its commander, Johan Rising, was previously an officer in the commercial department of the Swedish government. Apparently, he had little background for the governorship that was suddenly assigned to him on Printz's return. Arriving in America in 1654, Rising found Fort Casimir so weakly garrisoned that he captured it easily. But Rising's action gave Stuyvesant the excuse he was looking for.

The early forts built along the Delaware were intended only to withstand a minor attack by Indians or by marauders from the sea. Their walls and their armaments were never strong enough to resist an armed flotilla. After the Swedish fleet that brought Rising to America had departed, Stuyvesant prepared an expedition of several ships and several hundred men, a force strong enough to retake Fort Casimir and to establish his authority over New Sweden as well.

Coming to the Delaware, Stuyvesant landed soldiers between Fort Christina and Fort Casimir, preventing the Swedish garrisons in the two forts from joining forces. While the commander at Fort Casimir considered Stuyvesant's demand that he surrender, the one skirmish of the campaign occurred on the south bank of the Christina, where Dutch soldiers intercepted a small Swedish force headed for Fort Casimir and forced the Swedes to return to the shelter of Fort Christina.

Fort Casimir soon surrendered, and then Stuyvesant brought most of his men to the Christina, where he surrounded the fort there by land while his ships closed the mouth of the river. Rising, weakened by the loss of the troops in Fort Casimir, now found his situation hopeless. On September 15, 1655, he surrendered Fort Christina and all of New Sweden to the Dutch, who promised to respect the private property claims and the customs, including the religion, of all the settlers who wished to remain. Those who did not want to stay would be given transportation back to Europe with Rising.

At the moment of Stuyvesant's triumph he received disquieting news; Indians on the Hudson had taken advantage of his absence to attack the Dutch, loot their outlying farms, and threaten New Amsterdam itself. In his hurry to return, Stuyvesant made Rising an unusual offer. All of New Sweden would be given back to him except Fort Casimir; the situation on the Delaware would revert approximately to where it stood in 1654, before Rising's arrival.

Rising refused. He had not power, he declared, to make an agreement with the Dutch; he could not recognize their right even to Fort Casimir. Furthermore, the damage done by Dutch conquest was such that New Sweden was not prepared to sustain itself through the next winter. Apparently, Rising cared more about the strict legality of his position than he did about saving the colony for Sweden. The greater part of the New Sweden colonists refused to return to Europe with Rising and managed to get through the next winter on their own resources as they often had in the past.

The Dutch Again

Stuyvesant, distracted by problems elsewhere, had the good sense to leave the New Sweden colonists alone, despite advice from Europe that he should be wary of these foreigners and keep them under strict Dutch control. Their numbers were even increased by the arrival of some further Scandinavian immigrants who had prepared to go to America before news came of the conquest of New Sweden.

A year after the Dutch conquest, in August 1656, the Dutch West India Company sold part of their Delaware land to the City of Amsterdam. Merchants of that city, then in its richest period, were concerned about losing some of their foreign supplies because of wars in the Baltic Sea, an area where they normally had a prosperous trade. To make up for possible losses in Europe, these merchants (who controlled Amsterdam) began to develop a colony in Delaware south of the Christina. Its capital was New Amstel, the town that grew up around Fort Casimir, and though in some matters, such as defense and customs duties, it was still subject to the New Netherland government of Stuyvesant, in practice New Amstel was a separate colony.

Above the Christina the Delaware River valley remained entirely in the control of the West India Company; the residents of this area, mostly Swedes and Finns, were directly subject to Stuyvesant's government. Since most of New Jersey was still a wilderness, communication between the Delaware and the Hudson took place chiefly by sea. Stuyvesant therefore appointed a vice-director to represent him in the "Company Colony" on the Delaware. This official resided at Altena, as the Dutch renamed the village at Fort Christina, but most governmental problems were handled by minor officials chosen from among the Swedes and Finns.

One innovation that came with Dutch rule was the election of some officials at New Amstel. These were only minor officials, such as fence inspectors, but in their election in 1656 the Dutch introduced a practice that was continued in elections in Delaware even after the American Revolution. This was the system called double nomination, in which two people were named by the voters for every post to be filled; after the election final choice was made by the vice-director, who could appoint either of the two men (women were excluded) who had the highest number of votes.

The city of Amsterdam sent several cargoes of colonists to its New Amstel colony, but it had difficulty attracting the farmers and artisans who were most needed there. Such men found excellent opportunities in Amsterdam and its province, North Holland, where the movement to enclose and drain lands that were under water had recently begun. To secure labor, the Dutch began importing African slaves, often by way of the island of Curaçao in the Caribbean.

The Dutch also began to open a trade with the English in Maryland, from whom they bought tobacco to sell on the world market. The land in the interior of the peninsula was still unsettled, but gradually a road was developed through it along Appoquinimink Creek. Dutch settlers began to develop farms there, draining fields where necessary. They also established a new settlement at Lewes, near the site of old Swanendael, in approximately 1659.

In general, the merchants who directed affairs of the city of Amsterdam were pleased at the prospects they saw developing in their colony on the Delaware, especially their prospect of sharing in the lucrative Maryland tobacco trade. To simplify problems of administration, they arranged in 1663 to buy out the remaining interests of the West India Company in the Delaware valley and convert it all into the colony of New Amstel.

Officials of the Maryland colony were of two minds about the Dutch settlements on the Delaware. On the one hand, they regarded the Dutch as intruders on land to which they had a claim by virtue of their patent of 1632. On the other hand, they could not but be pleased at the opportunity of a second market for their tobacco that was afforded them by the proximity of Dutch settlements, particularly after English navigation laws sought to monopolize the tobacco trade for English merchants, forbidding colonists to sell directly to foreigners. But as long as there were Dutch settlements close to English tobacco plantations, these laws were very difficult to enforce.

2

The English

The Conquest

Between 1618 and 1648 most of the nations of western Europe were involved at some time or other in the Thirty Years' War. During this period, the English, while not always actively participating in the war, were generally in sympathy with the Dutch, who were at the same time fighting their war for independence from Spain. By the time the Thirty Years' War ended, the maritime power of Spain was drastically crippled, and a rivalry had developed between the Dutch and the English for commercial supremacy on the high seas.

During the Thirty Years' War Spain had still (as in the days of Queen Elizabeth and the Spanish Armada) seemed the chief foreign enemy of the English, who sent troops to the Netherlands to assist the Dutch in maintaining their independence. New Netherland, though planted in the center of an area England claimed, was temporarily safe from English attack because the English were hesitant to weaken their allies. But once this war was over, commercial rivalry between the Dutch and the English caused three Anglo-Dutch wars in the next quarter of a century.

The changed diplomatic situation opened the way for an English attack on New Netherland. Though this attack began in an interlude of peace just prior to the beginning of the second Anglo-Dutch war, it was approved by the highest authority, the king himself, for it was precipitated by a grant Charles II made to his brother and heir, the Duke of York. By this grant the king sought to reward his brother with potentially rich sections of the American coast, for the most part not yet settled by Englishmen, and at the same time oust the Dutch from North America and end their interference with English colonial trade.

There were two major areas in the grant given the Duke, one extending from the St. Croix River to Pemaquid, a large part of the present state of Maine, and the other from the Connecticut River to the Delaware, plus several offshore islands, including Martha's Vineyard, Nantucket, and Long Island. Probably the grant from the Connecticut River to the Delaware was intended to cover New Netherland, but the boundaries are strange. New Netherland had once claimed to extend east to the Connecticut, but the Dutch had been forced to withdraw somewhat after English settlements such as Hartford and New Haven were made to the west of this river. On the other hand, the Dutch had never recognized the Delaware as the western boundary of New Netherland: Swanendael, New Amstel, and all the area of conquered New Sweden testified to their interests west of the Delaware.

An English fleet of four vessels commanded by Colonel Richard Nicolls came to America in 1664 and captured New Amsterdam in August from an unhappy Peter Stuyvesant without a battle. After the surrender of the Dutch colonial capital Nicolls dispatched Sir Robert Carr with troops and two vessels to the Delaware River. When Carr reached the Delaware on September 30, 1664, he sailed upstream past New Amstel in order to negotiate first with the old settlers of New Sweden. They accepted the easy terms he offered, having no strong objection to exchanging Dutch for English rule. But when Carr approached the Dutch governor of New Amstel, Alexander d'Hinoyossa, he met a different reception.

D'Hinoyossa had apparently enriched himself by trade with Maryland while ruling his subjects on the Delaware harshly. He hoped that his diplomatic skill and his good relations with the English in Maryland would win him special consideration. When it became apparent that Carr would make no special concessions, d'Hinoyossa refused to surrender, and the English had to use force to capture the fort at New Amstel. Carr's two ships fired broadsides from the river and 130 English soldiers climbed into the fort from the rear, where it was weakest. Three of the 30 Dutch soldiers were killed and 10 were wounded. Possibly d'Hinoyossa had hoped for aid from settlers up the river and from some of the 90 male civilians in New Amstel; if so, he was disappointed.

The English leaders, including Carr and Nicolls, were well aware that the Duke of York's grant did not extend to the west side of the Delaware, but, as Englishmen, they felt it their duty to seize all the Dutch possessions in America. They were also aware that Lord Baltimore laid claim to this land, but they had no intention of turning the conquered area over to Maryland, particularly in view of the flourishing trade the Marylanders had carried on with New Amstel. Carr had some hope of securing a proprietorship of his own on the Delaware. When this failed, he reluctantly departed, leaving his relative, John Carr, in command by authority of Richard Nicolls, now governor of New York.

The Duke's Rule

For most of the eighteen years following the English conquest of October 1664, Delaware was ruled as part of New York. The one exception occurred in the summer of 1673, during the third Anglo-Dutch war, when the Dutch reconquered New Netherland. At this time the events of 1664 were almost exactly repeated, except that it was a Dutch fleet that came to New York (as New Amsterdam had been renamed), and it was the English who now surrendered the colonial capital because the strength of the attackers was overpowering. Again, as in 1664, part of the conquering force was dispatched from New York to the Delaware, but this time there was no resistance to the invaders.

The only violence arising from the Dutch reoccupation of Delaware occurred at Lewes in December 1673. Maryland authorities for several years had been insisting on their rights in this area, which they had incorporated into a Maryland county. After the Dutch reconquest, a Maryland force of forty men under Thomas Howell seized Lewes, captured the vessels in the creek, and burned every building in the town and its environs, except one barn, where the miserable inhabitants huddled for safety till the Dutch sent relief.

In 1674 the reconquest was ended, when a peace treaty terminating the war provided for a mutual restitution of conquests. Delaware and all of New Netherland were given back to the English—in effect, exchanged for Surinam (Dutch Guiana), which the English had captured.

Thereafter, as before the Dutch reconquest, the English governed Delaware as a part of New York. Even the Marylanders moderated their protests, because, although Delaware was not

Old Swedes (Holy Trinity) Church, Wilmington. Constructed in 1698 as a Swedish Lutheran church, Old Swedes became Protestant Episcopal in 1791 when no Swedish pastor was available. The tower and south porch are later additions to the structure. (Courtesy of the Historical Society of Delaware).

included in the Duke of York's grant, the duke's government exercised its powers in Delaware with royal approval. New Jersey had nominally been given away by the duke in 1664 to two friends, Lord John Berkeley and Sir George Carteret, but many years passed before a separate government was set up in this province.

New Castle, though a small town, grew in importance through these years as it continued to serve as a secondary capital to New York because of the geographic isolation of the Delaware valley. As a few settlers began moving across the river into New Jersey, they too came under jurisdiction of New Castle authorities. The beginnings of new counties, however, were marked by the establishment of courts at Chester and Lewes.

The English language and English institutions only very gradually supplanted Swedish and Dutch usages on the Delaware, the Swedes being long the dominant population element north of New Castle and the Dutch, to a slighter extent, below. In 1669 rumors of a plot among the Swedes and Finns led to the arrest of Marcus Jacobson, called the Long Finn, who was tried at New Castle by a commission from New York for causing dissension through tales of a Swedish naval expedition on its way to liberate the colony. Jacobson was whipped, branded, and sold into servitude in the West Indies, while his dupes or accomplices were fined various sums.

A new set of English laws, called the Duke's Laws, were approved by Governor Nicolls in 1665 for use in the English-speaking towns of Long Island. They were supposed to be introduced gradually in other parts of New York, but a decade passed before a copy of them ever reached the settlements on the Delaware. Meanwhile, however, the English element on the Delaware was slowly growing. New lands were being taken up in a rather haphazard fashion, with the government seeking an income from land, both by fees to confirm possession and by quitrents, modest annual charges upon landowners (usually one bushel of wheat per hundred acres) in lieu, theoretically, of services that might have been demanded of them.

Some of the new lands were taken up by old Swedish, Finnish, and Dutch settlers moving westward up the Christina or southward from New Castle. Of the English settlers, some came from Maryland, bringing slaves with them. The government sought to attract settlers on terms as favorable as in neighboring Maryland or in New England. In theory, a tract of fifty acres was assigned to each member of a family, but in actuality the grants seem to have been larger, varying from under two hundred to over one thousand acres.

As central Delaware was gradually settled, farmers on the St. Jones River appealed to the governor for a court of their own so they would not need to go to Lewes or New Castle to register deeds, probate wills, or settle disputes over land. They claimed to be one hundred tithables (taxable residents), which suggests a total population of at least five hundred in this area. In 1680 the governor approved their request, appointing justices of the peace and thereby creating the third Delaware county, called St. Jones. The court at Lewes had at first been called by a Dutch name, the Whorekill, but the name for the town and the county was changed in 1680 to Deal.

In 1674, when the Dutch surrendered Delaware to the English for the last time, the Duke of York secured a new grant to his colony, but once again, as in 1664, it did not include Delaware. In the next few years, some thought was given to having the grant rewritten to include Delaware, but the duke's advisers decided to let sleeping dogs lie. The Duke of York was a Roman Catholic and a great wave of anti-Catholicism swept England in the late 1670s, forcing the duke to leave London and live quietly in Scotland, out of public attention.

William Penn and Union with Pennsylvania

The northern limits of the future state of Delaware were established in 1681, when King Charles II created a province that he named Pennsylvania (Penn's woodlands) and gave it to William Penn, the son of Admiral Sir William Penn. Up to this time, the settlements in southeastern Pennsylvania, mainly Swedish and Finnish, had shared the same history as those in northern Delaware. English knowledge of American geography was inexact, so to be sure that New Castle town, which the king had no intention of taking from his brother, the Duke of York, was not included in Pennsylvania, the grant to Penn specified that his boundary would be twelve miles from New Castle. Thereby, the King created the unusual circular boundary that eventually became the permanent line between two states.

William Penn was an extraordinary man to be the proprietor of a large colony. Better educated and more idealistic than most colonizers, he was on very good terms with the royal family because his father had helped restore them to power in England in 1660 after they had lived abroad in exile for more than a decade. Thereafter, Admiral Penn and the Duke of York had together run the navy department, with the famous diarist, Samuel Pepys, as its secretary and their colleague. The king, who was usually in debt, owed Admiral Penn money, and it was this debt as well as a debt of friendship that he sought at least in part to repay by the grant to William Penn, after the admiral's death.

William Penn had requested the grant with two objects in mind: the reestablishment of the fortunes of his family, which he found in poor shape when, as the only son, he sought to settle his father's affairs; and provision of a place of refuge for those who were, like him, members of a new religious sect, the Society of Friends, scathingly called Quakers. The Quakers, founded by George Fox, who had visited America, were what is called a plain sect, eschewing what they regarded as vanities and seeking to lead humble Christ-like lives. Since all of the members at first were converts, they were very zealous about their convictions, arising in church to debate with the ministers, attracting crowds by preaching whenever and wherever the spirit moved them, and resisting authorities and laws they disapproved, even if this meant going to jail. They were fervent pacifists, they opposed taking oaths, even as part of legal procedures, and they refused to show special regard for one person more than another, avoiding many polite forms of language and customary gestures of respect.

Many of the practices of the early Quakers, such as dressing in plain colors, were abandoned by their successors, who decided that these practices attracted attention—and sometimes caused unnecessary expenditures—rather than having the opposite effect. But in Penn's day the Quakers seemed a very radical group and were often thrown in jail (as Penn was several times) for their refusal to conform. William Penn came under Quaker influence early, to the chagrin of his father, who resisted the temptation to disinherit him.

Most of the Quakers were artisans, farmers, or merchants. Because they worked hard, lived plain lives, and spent little money unnecessarily, they often became moderately wealthy. Several Quakers had settled in the colonies, and when the New Jersey proprietors, Berkeley and Carteret, divided their colony in two and then each sold his half, Quakers were the principal purchasers. Penn became interested in West Jersey, which led him to seek a colony of his own in Pennsylvania.

He was unhappy with his grant, however, because it did not

give him access to the ocean. Therefore, through intermediaries he appealed to the Duke of York to give him the land, now Delaware, between Pennsylvania and the sea. This the duke, who had as much reason as the king for gratitude to the Penns, agreed to do, and in 1682 he conveyed the Delaware counties to Penn by four separate documents.

The first of these was a deed to all the area within twelve miles of New Castle, and the second was a ten-thousand-year lease to the same property. The third document was a deed to the land from twelve miles below New Castle southward to Cape Henlopen, and the fourth was a ten-thousand-year lease to this land. Both the deed and the lease to the tract starting twelve miles below New Castle required Penn to pay the Duke one-half of all his income from this property.

Probably the Delaware counties were thus divided into two because the Duke of York did not want to interfere with Penn's use of New Castle but did hope for an income from the rest of the land. The only reason suggested for giving Penn both a deed and a lease is the doubtful nature of the duke's title. He administered Delaware as part of New York, with the king's evident approval, but he had no grant to Delaware; apparently, it was thought that the lease would be effective until the duke's title was proved in law. A provision in each deed required the duke, at the request and the expense of Penn, to make any further conveyances needed to assure Penn's rights to this property.

Shortly after these documents were drawn up William Penn arrived in America, and on October 28, 1682, he formally took possession of New Castle and the territory within twelve miles of it on the west shore of the Delaware. Ten days later on November 7, Penn's cousin William Markham represented the proprietor at Cantwell's Bridge (Odessa), taking possession of lower Delaware. In each case there was a ceremony called livery of seisin (delivery of possession), in which a piece of turf and a porringer of water were handed over by two justices representing the duke's government.

These ceremonies were wholly symbolic, but in a few days Penn took important innovative action, calling on the three Delaware counties to elect representatives to meet in assembly at Chester on December 4 with representatives of the three counties of Pennsylvania (Chester, Philadelphia, and Bucks). Penn changed the names of two of the Delaware counties, St. Jones becoming Kent and Deal becoming Sussex. Hereafter, the Delaware counties were called the Lower Counties (because they were lower down the river than Pennsylvania) or the Territories (as distinct from the Province of Pennsylvania). Occasionally, the name *Delaware* was used for them, but it was never official until after independence was declared in 1776. Before that time Delaware was a colony without a proper name except for the cumbersome "Counties of New Castle, Kent, and Sussex on the Delaware."

When the Delaware counties elected delegates to represent them in the assembly at Chester in 1682, it was the beginning of representative government for them, as it was also for Pennsylvania. The assemblymen at Penn's suggestion adopted an Act of Union, which theoretically united the Lower Counties and Pennsylvania. They also adopted a "frame of the government," a written constitution for the colony that Penn had prepared in England, as well as a series of bylaws establishing a remarkably humane, tolerant government, where, in Penn's words, "God may have his due, Caesar his due, and the people their due."

A Clouded Title

One reason Penn was eager to unite the Delaware counties with Pennsylvania was to protect them from Lord Baltimore, who was less hesitant to press his claims against a Quaker gentleman than against a royal duke. Boundary controversies quickly erupted on the fringes of the Delaware settlements, lasting for more than half a century and not finally put to an end, indeed, until just before independence. One of the more notable events of the boundary struggle occurred in 1683 when George Talbot, a cousin of Lord Baltimore, proceeded by order to settle Marylanders on lands on the edge of New Castle County. Talbot erected a small log fort on property of the widow Ogle near the community now called Christiana and kept it garrisoned for several years as a warning to Penn and his supporters not to settle land beyond that village.

But it was in England, not in America, that the contradictory claims of Penn and Lord Baltimore had to be adjudged before exact boundaries could be drawn. One of the major developments in establishing Penn's title occurred on March 22, 1683, when at long last King Charles II granted the Delaware counties, including the right to their government as well as to their soil, to the Duke of York. If the duke had then made a clear grant of these counties to Penn, much future controversy might have been avoided.

But Penn's advisers tried to get a slightly better grant for the Duke of York (and therefore eventually for Penn). A new document was drawn up providing, among other details, that the southern boundary would be set approximately at Fenwick Island, but Lord Baltimore protested, and the English government held up action on this grant (which never was completed) until both Baltimore and Penn could come to England and personally argue their case.

Penn returned to England in 1684, but before a decision was reached on revising the duke's grant, King Charles II died, on February 6, 1685, and the Duke of York became King James II. Now the duke's March 1683 grant could be revised, and, as king, he could give the Delaware counties to Penn—if they did not already belong to Baltimore. In the fall of 1685, the Privy Council acted decisively on Baltimore's claim. The Delaware counties, they said, were not part of Maryland because Lord Baltimore's grant was only to land hitherto uncultivated (*hactenus inculta*, in the Latin words of the grant). Since the Dutch had previously cultivated the soil at Swanendael, Delaware was excluded from Maryland. (The Indians were not considered to be nations having rights that could block the claims of European countries.)

This decision was followed by another settling the boundary, in general terms at least. The southern boundary was to be a line from Cape Henlopen to the middle of the peninsula, and the western boundary a line up the middle of the peninsula to the 40th parallel of latitude, the southern boundary of Pennsylvania. All land on the west of the peninsula would be Lord Baltimore's; all on the east, above Cape Henlopen, would be the king's, or Penn's, if the king wished.

King James had already indicated that he meant the Delaware counties to be Penn's. His reign was a troubled one, but in December 1688 he finally had a definitive grant made out to Penn for this area (called in this document Lower Pennsylvania). An important detail of this document was that King James excused Penn from all obligations, past or future, to share the revenues and named Penn true and absolute proprietor, free to merge this new province with Pennsylvania in one government under one set of laws if he wished.

*Map of New Sweden from the Dutch firm of Nicolas Visscher. A
Visscher map showing Cape Henlopen south of its present location
(as on this map) was used in settling the southern boundary of
Delaware. This map contains a mixture of Dutch, Swedish, and
English place-names and obviously dates after the founding of
Philadelphia in 1681, yet it does not show earlier English settlements
in New Jersey. Several details are incorrect, including the relative
distance from Swanendael to the mouth of the bay. From J. Thomas
Scharf,* History of Delaware, 1609–1888 *(Philadelphia, 1888).*

Unfortunately for Penn, the king had delayed too long. In this very month a revolution (called in English history the Glorious or Bloodless Revolution) forced James to flee the country, and the new grant never received final authorization. However, James had already given Penn a title that the courts eventually upheld against Lord Baltimore. A long suit between the heirs of these men lasted until 1750, when the Lord Chancellor decided in favor of Penn, declaring that the grant of March 22, 1683, to the Duke of York of lands he had previously deeded to Penn created an "estoppel," a bar to any other disposal of these lands by the duke, who was henceforth, as far as the Lower Counties were concerned, merely a trustee for Penn.

A Brittle Connection

Fifteen years passed between Penn's departure from America in 1684 and his return in December 1699. In this period his fortunes and those of his colonies experienced many changes. The overthrow of James II in December 1689 was followed by a period in which all of James's old friends were under suspicion and many of them, like Penn, were arrested and investigated by the new government of the joint monarchs, William III and Mary II. In 1691 Penn's proprietary rights were suspended; more than a year passed before this order was augmented in America, but finally in 1693, Benjamin Fletcher, already royal governor of New York, became governor of Pennsylvania and of the Lower Counties as well.

By 1694 a number of Penn's friends had risen to positions of influence in the court of William and Mary, and, investigations having failed to support such allegations against Penn as that he was secretly a Jesuit, plotting on behalf of his friend King James II, his rights were restored to him. He did not return to America, however, until December 1699, and in his absence relations between the Lower Counties and the province of Pennsylvania became strained. Basically the problem arose from seizure of power in Pennsylvania by the Quaker element, who conducted the government to suit themselves, with little regard to the wishes of either the Proprietor or the Crown.

Their policies annoyed the Lower Counties on several grounds. For one thing, Delawareans were generally members of the Church of England who spurned the Quakers as radical sectarians and were upset at their unwillingness to vote appropriations for military defense of the Delaware against enemy nations in wartime and pirates at all times. The Quakers also were newcomers, whose sudden accession to power rankled old settlers. The Dutch, for example, thought the Quakers had been too slow in acknowledging King William, who was Dutch stadholder before he was English king. There was also, particularly in the older town of New Castle, jealousy of Philadelphia and its surge to wealth and power.

In return, Pennsylvanians were increasingly disturbed by the power of Delawareans to block action by the General Assembly, in which all of the counties, the three in Pennsylvania and the three in Delaware, were represented equally. As the population of Pennsylvania increased, the people there were more and more insistent on an enlarged representation in the assembly. There were suggestions, for example, that Philadelphia City should have representation of its own besides the representation of Philadelphia County. Philadelphia, it was suggested, was worth more by itself than all of the Lower Counties.

Usually, the Pennsylvania Quakers had their way in the government because they had the ear of the Philadelphia-based executive, whether this was a council or a commission or a single governor or deputy, and because they usually could find a few sympathetic assemblymen from the Lower Counties—a Quaker from New Castle County, for instance, or a Lewes merchant with close ties to Philadelphia—who would give them a majority. Pennsylvania, increasingly demanding home rule in most particulars, came to look at the Lower Counties as a hindrance in the attainment of this goal. The friction between upper and lower counties upset William Penn, whose desire to unify the two areas arose chiefly from his fear that his title to Delaware (and his access to the sea) might not hold up unless he could tie this colony closely to Pennsylvania. For this reason, he was willing to accept almost any compromise that would preserve some relationship between the two.

In May 1691, for example, Delawareans, angered at the selection as deputy governor of Thomas Lloyd, the most bitter and uncompromising member of the Quaker faction, boycotted the assembly. Penn thereupon appointed his cousin William Markham, who was sympathetic to the Lower Counties and was not a Quaker, deputy governor of Delaware. For more than a year, until a royal governor took over, Penn's colonies had two governors and one assembly.

Benjamin Fletcher, the royal governor, being an Anglican,

was popular in the Lower Counties, especially since he appointed Markham, whose son-in-law became an assemblyman from Kent, his deputy when he returned to New York. And when the colonies were restored to Penn in 1694, it was Markham who served as Penn's deputy until he returned to America in 1699.

On several occasions, in 1684, 1690, and 1700, usually with Penn's encouragement, the assembly met in New Castle instead of in Philadelphia, which had early become its customary meeting place. Penn had also taken some of his councilmen to Lewes in southern Delaware in order to display his interest in the people there. And in several alterations in the charter (or frame of government), representation was always divided equally between Pennsylvania and Delaware. This was true even when the charter was suspended and the government was royal, as in 1693–94.

Yet the differences and dissatisfaction were growing and produced a final legislative schism in 1701. In the previous year, the assembly had met in New Castle and in a long session passed a total of 104 laws, many mere restatements of old laws that were feared to have lapsed in the troubled times. When the assembly met in Philadelphia in the fall of 1701, Pennsylvania delegates insisted they must confirm the laws passed in New Castle because otherwise they might not be valid in Pennsylvania. The Lower Counties were insulted, and a majority of their members walked out, declaring that if the two colonies were not united, laws passed in Philadelphia could not be valid in Delaware. Penn persuaded them to return for this session, but he yielded to their demand that he add a codicil to a final revision he had just made in the frame of government.

If within the next three years, the codicil declared, the majority of assemblymen from either Pennsylvania or Delaware informed Penn that they no longer wished to meet together in assembly, he would permit them to meet separately. In that case each Pennsylvania county could elect eight assemblymen and Philadelphia City two. The Lower Counties might determine for themselves how many members would sit in their separate Assembly.

This meant the separation of Penn's domains into two colonies, for two assemblies would mean two separate sets of laws hereafter, even if they continued to share the same governor and proprietor and, for that matter, the same king. The reason that Penn gave in on this point was that he was about to make another hurried trip to England. Again he was rushing back to defend his rights, this time against a bill in the House of Lords requiring that all proprietary colonies be turned over to the Crown. It did not pay him now to quibble over details of government when there was a good chance he would lose his colonies altogether. Knowing that some assemblymen in the Lower Counties were actively seeking royal government, Penn sought to leave America with all the popular support behind him that he could possibly win.

A Separate Colony

The threat of parliamentary action against Penn hung over him for years, but he had many influential friends and managed to cling to his possessions. In America, however, his attempts to reunite Delaware and Pennsylvania failed. In October 1702, the usual time of year for choice of assemblymen, the Lower Counties failed to hold elections. After the deputy governor, Andrew Hamilton, issued special writs, elections were held, but the elected Delaware assemblymen found legalistic excuses (they claimed not to have agreed to the new frame of government) not to meet with the Pennsylvania assemblymen. David Lloyd, a distant kinsman of and successor to Thomas Lloyd in leadership of the Quaker faction, saw in this recalcitrance of the Delawareans an opportunity to be rid of their interference in Pennsylvania politics. In the fall of 1703 Pennsylvanians took the option Penn had offered in the codicil to his 1701 frame of government, choosing eight assemblymen in each of their three counties and two more in the city of Philadelphia.

No assembly elections were held that fall in the Lower Counties. Governor Hamilton had died, and there was no one to urge Penn's wishes on them until Hamilton's successor, a young Welshman, John Evans, arrived in February 1704. Evans, as advised by Penn, appointed Delawareans to his council and persuaded the Lower Counties to hold assembly elections in the spring of 1704. These new delegates were willing to meet in assembly with the Pennsylvania members, motivated apparently by the failure of movements to establish a royal colony. But now they were repulsed; the Pennsylvania assembly, reorganized and enlarged by the terms of Penn's codicil, was unwilling to admit the Lower Counties on the old terms of equality, and the Delawareans would not enter a joint assembly on any other terms.

Nothing remained for the Lower Counties but to set up their own assembly. Governor Evans consented reluctantly, and the first separate Delaware assembly met in New Castle in the fall of 1704. William Rodeney, as he signed himself (*Rodney* is the more common spelling), was chosen speaker and presented to the governor, who came down from Philadelphia to give approval to the actions taken. Delaware was now for the first time a separate colony with a representative government, though sharing a governor with Pennsylvania, as well as a connection to the Proprietor and the Crown.

3

The Lower Counties on the Delaware

The Proprietors

After his hasty departure in the late fall of 1701, William
Penn never returned to America. His colonial interests had cost
him money rather than profited him, and finally he resolved to
sell the Crown the rights he claimed to govern both colonies,
though not his claims to the soil. Serious illness, terminating in
a stroke in 1712, prevented the sale from being consummated.
For the six years preceding his death in 1718, Penn was incapable
of any business. He had recovered sufficiently to get about and
seemed happy, but his second wife, Hannah Callowhill Penn, had
to perform all his business, getting his signature when she
needed it.

Penn was unfortunate in the choice of deputy governors who
represented him through these years. The first, Andrew Hamilton, died soon after his appointment. The second, John Evans,
was young and rash. The third, Charles Gookin, was erratic and
possibly mad. The fourth, William Keith, was conniving and
attempted to turn Delaware into a royal colony.

Fortunately for her family, Hannah Penn was both strong-
minded and resourceful. During William Penn's last years and
for the remaining eight years of her own life, she was, in essence,
though not in name, the true proprietor. In his will Penn had
passed over the son of his first marriage, William, Jr., who had
proved himself improvident, and deeded his colonial claims to
the sons of his second marriage. After a series of suits and negotiations, conducted skillfully by Hannah Penn, the inheritance

finally fell to her children, John, the eldest, who received a double share, Thomas, and Richard.

John remained a bachelor, and at his death in 1746 his share was left to his next brother, Thomas, who thereafter owned a three-fourth share in the proprietorship. At his death in 1775 his portion passed to a son who was still under age; for that reason and because the colonies were already in rebellion, this youth, John Penn, son of Thomas, is of little importance in the history of Delaware.

There is another John Penn, however, who did play an important role. John Penn, son of the junior proprietor, Richard Penn, came to America as deputy governor in 1763, returned to England when his father died in 1771, and came back to America as both deputy governor and junior proprietor (having inherited his father's one-fourth share) in 1773. The last colonial governor of Delaware and Pennsylvania, he spent the years of the Revolution in England but returned to Philadelphia with his American wife to make his home there when the war was over.

For a brief period following 1771, Governor John Penn's brother Richard also served as deputy governor. The title of deputy governor or lieutenant governor was used for the chief executive because the true governor was the proprietor—or, after William Penn's death, in 1718, the proprietors, for there were always more than one. After Penn's suspended proprietary rights were returned to him in 1694, the Crown refused to acknowledge his claim to the government of the Lower Counties; yet it allowed Penn and his heirs to exercise the power it never formally recognized. Every time Penn or his children appointed a deputy governor they had to acknowledge that the appointment, so far as the Delaware counties were concerned, was not to be regarded as impairing the claims to those counties of the Crown, which reserved the right to terminate the service of the governor when it chose. But the Crown never exercised the right to govern Delaware that it repeatedly reasserted. For all intents and purposes, Delaware was governed as a proprietary colony.

The claim of the Crown rested not merely on the deficiency in Penn's original title, given him in 1682 by the Duke of York, when the duke himself had no title to Delaware. Intermittently, another issue was raised—the fact that Penn had never made any payment on that one-half share of the revenue from lands south of the twelve-mile circle that he was pledged to pay the Duke of York according to the 1682 grant. This claim had become the Crown's after the Duke of York became king in 1685, but the duke, as King James II, planned to release Penn from any such requirement in the deed that was prepared, but not legalized, in December 1688. Penn's excuse thereafter was that the boundaries of the Lower Counties were never settled; in truth, he was in poor position to share his American income, for his debts exceeded his revenues to such a degree that he spent some time in debtor's prison. His obligation to share revenues would have been legally terminated had the sale he arranged in 1712 not been canceled after his stroke.

On several occasions attempts were made to remove the Delaware counties from the control of the Penns. For example, a Scottish lord, John Gordon, Earl of Sutherland, asked in 1717 that the Lower Counties be granted him in return for his services to the Crown. Later, in 1764, Benjamin Franklin, representing an antiproprietary party in Pennsylvania, urged that the Crown assume direct royal government of Delaware on grounds that the Penns had never paid the Crown any part of revenues that were, by this time, significant.

But the issue between the Penns and the Crown was never settled. The Penns had friends in court, the Delaware counties were of little significance in the total imperial picture, and it was easier for British administrators to live with the status quo than to change it.

Colonial Government

In fact, then, Delaware was governed as a proprietary colony, even if the Crown never entirely relinquished its claim to the government. After Penn's departure in 1701, a series of deputy governors, beginning with Andrew Hamilton and ending with John Penn, were appointed by the proprietors, confirmed, and, as far as the Lower Counties were concerned, given special approval by the Crown. The governor normally resided in Philadelphia, coming to the Lower Counties only for the meetings of the assembly in New Castle, which were regularly held in November, though often also, by adjournment or special call, in another season. The governor had an absolute power of veto over any bill passed by the assembly, but he was reluctant to exercise his power because he was dependent on the assembly for his salary. If the governor disapproved of a bill, a compromise could usually be worked out.

Once the governor approved a bill, it became the law without further submission anywhere. Legislation was not sent to England for approval or for review, either by the proprietors or by the Crown. In this respect, Delaware had almost unique powers of self-government for a colony—second only to Connecticut and Rhode Island, which elected their own governors. Pennsylvania, on the other hand, had to forward all its new statutes to England for approval or rejection by the Privy Council.

Besides his power of veto, the governor had important powers of appointment. He appointed—apparently, for such term as he chose—judges of the supreme court and justices of the peace. The latter officials, who were paid only by fees collected for services, had many administrative powers besides their judicial duties. They heard minor cases individually, and they served collectively on all county courts—the court of general sessions and gaol delivery, the court of common pleas, and the orphans court, to name but a few—usually on successive days. Acting as a court of assizes, they set many prices and rates, such as the price at which bread and beer should be sold. Acting as the levy court, together with the grand jurymen (appointed by the sheriff) and the assessors (elected in each hundred), they fixed the county property tax rate each year.

Although appointment of the justices was an important power of the governor, his hand in this respect was not entirely free. Certain people, men of significance and of interest in public affairs, expected to be appointed justices. If they were not, or if the governor dismissed them as justices, they might make trouble for him in the assembly. One of the reasons that Governor Gookin was thought to be mad was his dismissal of all the justices in New Castle County, coupled with his illegal attempt to dismiss the sheriff.

A sheriff and a coroner—the latter to investigate into all unnatural or unusual deaths, the former as man of all work in the county (jailer, deliverer of writs, judge of elections, and so on) — were elected in each county by the principle of double nomination. Each voter nominated (that is, voted for) two men; the governor chose the sheriff from the two most popular candidates. In practice, the more popular of the two was usually selected. Six assemblymen were also selected in each county to serve for one year. The assemblymen represented the county as a whole, and each voter listed six choices on a ballot that was written, but not secret. No ballots were printed and there were no formal, organized parties, but there were factions that often contested elections heatedly. One faction was called the "court party," normally the party that held office, and the other party was the "country party."

County elections were held only at the county seat, presided over by the sheriff, assisted by an inspector from each hundred. A voter had to own fifty acres of land, of which twelve acres were cleared, or have other property (for example, a mill, or tools, or livestock) worth forty pounds. Neither women nor blacks were specifically disfranchised, but (with possibly a few exceptions) they did not vote, though it is likely that by the end of the colonial period some widows and some free blacks could have met the property requirements.

"Little elections," as they came to be called, were held in the hundreds in September, a month before the county elections. A hundred is an old English subdivision of a county, its origin shrouded in mystery because the name is as old as the language and meant, in geographic terms, not much more or less when it was first used in this sense than it meant in colonial America. The name was used in many colonies but survived in America only in Delaware, probably because there the counties were all established so early—by 1680—that little reorganization was needed. In New England, the newer English term, *town,* replaced *hundred,* and in Pennsylvania and New Jersey the term *township* was adopted.

At the little elections the appointed tax collector presided, assisted by two freeholders of his choice, and the assembled voters chose an election inspector and (after 1766) an assessor. The inspector was needed at the county election to determine who was qualified to vote. Besides assessing the value of property for taxes, the assessor helped set the tax rate, but efforts to elect the entire levy court (as was done in Pennsylvania) were blocked by the governor until after the Revolution.

The general assembly in colonial Delaware was a very powerful body, since the bills it passed were reviewed by no one except the governor, who was eager to keep on good terms with this body. It was a unicameral body, a single house of representatives elected to one-year terms. After the separation from Pennsylvania in 1701, the governor's council, which was appointed, gradually lost responsibility for the government of Delaware. In the early eighteenth century, governors made it a point to have some Delaware residents on the council, but as time passed the Delaware representation was dropped except for one or two men,

View across the New Castle Green, showing, left to right, *the academy, Immanuel Church, Aull's Row (residences on Second Street), and the courthouse, the colonial capitol of Delaware. Watercolor sketch by Benjamin Latrobe, 1804. Original in Hall of Records, Dover.* (Courtesy of the Division of Historical and Cultural Affairs.)

like Benjamin Chew, who had property in both colonies. The president of the council did serve as acting governor if a deputy governor died or left his post, but he had no power to approve legislation, and in Delaware he was merely the presiding officer of a temporary executive committee that included the senior justice in each county and the speaker of the assembly.

Utilizing Proprietary Connections

During the eighteenth century the attitude of Delawareans toward proprietary government underwent considerable change. At the beginning of the century there was much suspicion of this government, so much that in 1708 half of the assemblymen signed a petition for direct royal government, which the speaker of the assembly himself took to England. In 1764, on the other hand, the assembly passed a resolution supporting proprietary government.

Suspicion of Pennsylvania and of the Quaker politicians there had not diminished. "At New Castle," wrote James Logan, the provincial secretary, early in the century, "they use the same language [in reference to Pennsylvania] that the Scots do in reference to England." In 1757, the Delaware assemblymen rebuffed a suggestion from the Pennsylvania assembly, declaring: "We are independent of them (which we esteem no small part of our Happiness) and will ever assert and support that Independency."

One reason for improved relations between Delaware assemblymen and the Proprietary, as the proprietors were referred to collectively, lay in their common interest in the military defense of the Delaware. The Delaware assemblymen were more willing to create a militia and to make appropriations for fortifications on the river than were their counterparts in Pennsylvania, who had religious scruples against war and felt some safety from naval attack by reason of the hundred miles of waterways separating Philadelphia from the ocean. The long coastline of Delaware on the ocean, bay, and river was exposed to attacks by pirates and by French and Spanish sailors. Pirates looted Lewes in 1698, and the French did the same in 1709. In 1747 marauders who were either French or Spanish attacked two plantations on Bombay Hook, at the head of Delaware Bay.

Proprietary governors and Delawareans were both eager for measures to stop such raids. Their cooperation included the issuance of paper money, especially in wartime, to meet the needs of defense as well as other financial problems. The first paper money was issued in the time of Governor William Keith, who sought to curry favor with the colonists by giving them a circulating medium they needed, since British money was in short supply. Delaware, like many colonies, issued paper bills of credit through a loan office in each county that operated as a land bank. A mortgage on the recipient's land guaranteed the repayment of the bills with interest, and the interest helped to take care of the financial needs of the colony.

The British government and the proprietors were opposed to colonial use of paper money for fear it would cause an inflation that would be damaging to British merchants. However, Delaware assemblymen issued these bills in moderate amounts and on such firm security that their value remained high. Furthermore, the lack of any review of Delaware laws in England meant that only the governor could check the assembly, and problems of defense led the governors to be reconciled to paper money.

In 1746, as requested, the assembly raised a company of soldiers that was sent to Albany for service in King George's War. In 1758–59, during the French and Indian War, three Delaware companies helped the British army under General Forbes that built a road through Pennsylvania on its way to seize Fort Duquesne (Pittsburgh). In the cooperation between proprietary governors and Delaware assemblymen on such military measures, it was important that a majority of both were members of the Church of England. So were most of the descendants of William Penn. (His son John Penn remained a Quaker, but the other younger sons and grandsons joined the Church of England or, as in the case of Thomas Penn, attended its services.)

In Pennsylvania, the Anglicanism of the Penns furnished one additional divisive factor between them and leading assemblymen. In Delaware, the reverse was true. An antiproprietary party in Pennsylvania tried to rouse support in Delaware and had some success, for there were always complaints to be found against the governors and their appointments. But, in general, proprietary support was strong in Delaware, where it was recognized that any change in the government was likely to weaken the semi-independent status of these three counties.

Another link between the proprietors and Delawareans was their common cause against the territorial pretensions of Lord Baltimore, who had regained his colonial possessions in 1715 after a long period when Maryland was ruled as a royal colony. Thereafter, frequent conflicts erupted along the uncertain borders over land titles and tax obligations. Residents of lands claimed by both colonies were sometimes thrown into a Delaware jail if they paid taxes only in Maryland, or vice versa. In 1732 an agreement was reached between Lord Baltimore and the Penns for the survey of boundaries of the Lower Counties according to the terms of the Privy Council decision of 1685, dividing the peninsula evenly north of Cape Henlopen. The map that was used in this negotiation showed Cape Henlopen not where it is today, but at Fenwick Island, lower down the coast and possibly the place where the name *Henlopen* had originally been applied.

Lord Baltimore soon regretted having ceded his claim to the Lower Counties and tried to upset the 1685 decision. The issue was taken to the English court of chancery, and only after its decision in favor of the Penns in 1750 was the marking of the boundaries begun. The transpeninsular line at the southern end of Delaware was completed by American surveyors in 1750–51, and only after they experienced difficulty with the tangent line on the western boundary were Mason and Dixon brought from England to complete the work. Their work on the Delaware line was finished in 1765, but the Pennsylvania-Maryland boundary survey kept them in America till 1768.

Royal approval of the new boundaries came in 1769, but the final step in the boundary settlement was not taken until 1775, for only then did the Delaware assembly order the boundaries of counties and hundreds, along with the jurisdiction of all governmental agencies, to be extended to the new lines.

Immigration

Completion of the boundary survey on a very favorable basis was the last major service of the proprietary family to the people of Delaware. The new boundary lay farther to the west, especially in Kent and Sussex, and farther to the south than Delaware authority had previously reached. On the south, two Anglican chapels of Maryland parishes (Prince Georges, at Dagsboro, and Christ Church, near Laurel) were found to be in Delaware. Many land grants made by Maryland authorities (the famous example is the large landholding of John Dagworthy) were now in Delaware, where these titles were recognized without difficulty as long as there was no contradictory land claim on the basis of a patent from the Penns.

So much land acceded to Sussex County that the new area was referred to for a while as New Sussex, and there was talk of forming a fourth county. In the long run, the enlargement of the boundaries did lead to the removal of the county courts from Lewes to a more central location (Georgetown), but not until 1791, after the Revolution.

One change made immediately by adjustment of the boundaries was an addition of a considerable number of Maryland natives to the population of Delaware. This, however, was no major innovation; for several decades Marylanders, white and black, had been moving into Delaware. The Eastern Shore of the Chesapeake possessed many inviting harbors, which encouraged settlement there before settlers came to the less inviting ocean shore of Sussex or, the environs of Lewes excepted, the shores of the Delaware Bay. As early settlers sought to acquire new property for their children or to replace land worn out by years of tobacco planting, they moved from the shores of Chesapeake Bay into Delaware.

During the eighteenth century there was a more or less steady stream of such migration from Maryland, and sometimes from the Eastern Shore of Virginia, into Delaware. John Dickinson's father, Samuel Dickinson, is the best-known example of these

The Dickinson Mansion, Jones's Neck, Kent County. Built by Samuel Dickinson, father of John Dickinson, in 1740, this was John Dickinson's home in his youth and again for a period during the American Revolution. (Courtesy of the Division of Historical and Cultural Affairs, Dover.)

migrants. He gave up his lands in Talbot County, Maryland, to the children of his first marriage and moved with his second wife to lands he had purchased on Jones's Neck (between the St. Jones River and Delaware Bay). The Rogers, Mitchell, Mifflin, and Burton families offer similar examples.

This transpeninsular migration particularly affected Kent and Sussex counties. At roughly the same time, another group of immigrants, the Scotch-Irish, were entering New Castle County. These people were the descendants of Scots who had been colonized in northern Ireland early in the seventeenth century, in the reign of James I, an English king who was a native of Scotland. They did not intermarry with the Irish, who considered them as interlopers, settled on confiscated lands, and were of a different religion, being Roman Catholics whereas the Scotch-Irish were Presbyterians.

After a century, many of the Scotch-Irish became dissatisfied with conditions in Ireland for various reasons—primarily economic, but also political and religious. Land rents were being raised by absentee landlords, usually English; English tariffs were costing the Scotch-Irish the market they counted on for such products as meat and textiles; they were required to contribute to a church they did not attend, the Church of Ireland, which was episcopalian and related to the Church of England. By 1720 several thousand men and women, most in their early twenties, were leaving Ireland each year for North America, and though they landed at many places in the colonies, their favorite destination was the Delaware valley, where they found good opportunities in a prosperous society that had no established church.

Though Philadelphia was the favored destination, many Scotch-Irish immigrants landed at New Castle, where vessels coming up the Delaware usually stopped to take on water and disembark travelers and cargo intended for the Chesapeake. Many of the Scotch-Irish immigrants could afford the trip only by indenturing themselves—that is, signing an agreement to work without payment for a limited period after their arrival, usually three to seven years. The ship captain was the other party to the indenture, taking his profit for their passage by selling the services of these passengers. Farmers or millers needing an extra hand could go to New Castle or, later, to Wilmington and buy an indentured servant.

Indentured servants could be of other nationalities than Scotch-Irish, but in Delaware the latter were most common. Some convicts were sent from England, sentenced to serve out their terms in labor in the colonies rather than in English jails. These men and women, though theoretically guilty only of minor crimes, were sometimes hardened criminals, like the fictional Moll Flanders of whom Daniel Defoe wrote. More of them were sent to the Chesapeake than to the Delaware.

Some of the Scotch-Irish who landed at New Castle eventually moved to the west, where cheap land was available in the foothills of the Appalachians. Others moved southward into Kent and, to a smaller extent, Sussex. But so many stayed in New Castle County that it came to assume a distinct Scotch-Irish coloration. Their Presbyterian churches became the most numerous in the county, and their members became very influential in its political, economic, and cultural life.

Some Scotch-Irish immigrants were better educated on arrival than were natives of America and found quick employment as schoolmasters. Unlike the German immigrants who were coming to Pennsylvania at the same time, the Scotch-Irish spoke the English language and were already subjects of the English king, so they had no problems of naturalization to face. Their quick progress in Delaware is illustrated by the fact that the first chief executive of the Delaware State (John McKinly), the first chancellor (William Killen), and the first commander of a Delaware regiment in Washington's army (John Haslet) were all Scotch-Irish immigrants.

The Scotch-Irish were almost all ardently anti-English in the period of the Revolution, because they arrived in America angry at the English government, which they blamed for their troubles in Ireland. On the other hand, their numbers, their ardor, and their success in political and professional life in Delaware helped raise a prejudice against them in the minds of other inhabitants, who regarded them as pushing newcomers, sources of discontent. By the time of the Revolution, Delawareans were speaking of an "Irish party" and a "Church party," referring by the latter term to members of the Church of England.

The Scotch-Irish immigration added to the diversity of New Castle County, which already had minorities of Swedes and Dutch, as well as a sizable Welsh settlement in a tract of land along the Maryland border below Newark. The difference in population and religion between New Castle County, on the one hand, and Kent and Sussex, on the other, became even more obvious as additional immigrants came to New Castle after the

Revolution and as the development of urbanization and manufacturing gathered force in New Castle County.

Throughout the state the largest minority group. was the African element, which grew in the early eighteenth century by immigration from Maryland, as slaves were brought to Delaware by their masters, and to a slight extent by the importation of additional slaves by sea. The emancipation of individual slaves began in Delaware before the Revolution and was quickened in that period by religious and political scruples. The maritime slave trade became obnoxious to Delawareans before slavery itself; bills to forbid further importation of slaves were introduced into the colonial assembly, but when such a bill was passed in 1775, Governor John Penn refused to approve it—possibly because of his sympathy for English slave traders. As soon as Delawareans renounced their English government and wrote their own constitution, in 1776, they included a clause forbidding the importation of slaves.

The life of a Delaware slave is related in the autobiography of Richard Allen, of Kent County, who bought his own freedom by extra labor and later became the founder of an independent denomination of black Methodists in Philadelphia.

Economic Life

Shortly before the American Revolution, New Castle was eclipsed in size by a new city called Wilmington, founded on the outskirts of the old Swedish community on the Christina River. Originally, the new community was called Willingtown, after Thomas Willing, an English merchant who settled there and began selling town lots in 1731 after marrying the daughter of a Swedish landowner, Andrew Justison. Willing saw the commercial advantages of locating a town on the banks of the Christina, where imported goods, obtained from Philadelphia, could be exchanged for the produce of farms in the interior of New Castle County and in the neighboring counties—Cecil, in Maryland, and Chester and Lancaster, in Pennsylvania. Because the new settlement was farther west than Philadelphia, it had the advantage of shorter roads to the interior.

When Governor George Thomas chartered the city in 1739, he named it Wilmington instead of Willingtown. Spencer Compton, the Earl of Wilmington, was an influential English nobleman whose influence at court the Penns were cultivating, and it seems likely that one of the proprietors, Thomas Penn, who was then residing in Philadelphia, was responsible for the name. Besides, Willing, who soon moved away, had been supplanted as the principal figure in the development of Wilmington by William Shipley, an English Quaker, and his wife, Elizabeth, a preacher and visionary.

Many Quakers from Pennsylvania followed the Shipleys to Wilmington, and the prosperity they created drew other settlers, particularly Scotch-Irish immigrants. The population doubled in size in a quarter century, from about six hundred in 1739 to over twelve hundred in 1775. The change in the nature of the population is suggested by the fact that whereas a Quaker, William Shipley, was chief burgess (the equivalent of mayor) in 1739, a Scotch-Irishman, John McKinly, was chief burgess in 1775. By this time, Wilmington, small as it was, was the largest city in Delaware.

The prosperity of Wilmington was enhanced by the development of mills on neighboring creeks, such as the Red Clay and White Clay, Mill Creek, and the Brandywine (then outside Wilmington), where water power was abundant. There were mills of various sorts, saw mills and grist mills particularly, throughout Delaware, but the flour mills near Wilmington on the Brandywine soon became the largest in the state and, by the 1790s, the largest in the new nation. Their advantage came from being in the heart of a rich wheat country, near navigable streams, and close to a large city, Philadelphia, from which flour could be exported to foreign markets.

Wheat and corn were the staple crops of Delaware, where agriculture was the primary concern of the people. Wheat was grown primarily in New Castle and Kent, but corn was grown all over the state. The flour and meal produced from these cereal crops found its chief market overseas, particularly in the sub-tropical sugar islands of the Caribbean, where it paid the planters to import foodstuffs while devoting their lands to the production of exotic crops that could not be grown in England.

Of course, Delaware farmers also grew various vegetables and fruits, but their market for such produce was limited; so was the market for livestock, though some meat was exported. There was, however, a thriving trade in lumber, particularly from the forests of Sussex County, where boards and shingles brought some landowners more income than the produce of their fields.

Land beside navigable water was regarded as most valuable, because the easiest, cheapest means of transportation was by shallops, small shallow-draft sloops, worked by a man and a boy, that could cross the silted mouths of the small rivers and creeks of Delaware and ascend them to landings where they picked up farm produce and unloaded goods from the city. The roads were generally poorly cared for, worked on when the weather made labor on the farms least necessary. Bridges, fords, and ferries were likely to be hazardous affairs. Roads offered the fastest travel, but the least comfortable and the most expensive for bulk goods.

The greatest landowners were the gentry, the men like John Dickinson and Caesar Rodney, who were sufficiently supported by the wealth of their lands to allow their attendance on public affairs. In colonial Delaware even the largest landholders did not approach the wealth of the gentry of Virginia or South Carolina, as the relatively modest home of Samuel Dickinson, the richest planter in Kent County, indicates. The yeomen farmers who

The Corbit-Sharp House, Odessa. Its construction in 1772–74 by the Quaker tanner William Corbit is described in Grandeur on the Appoquinimink *(Newark, 1959) by John A. H. Sweeney. It was restored and furnished by H. Rodney Sharp in the twentieth century.* **(Courtesy of the Henry Francis du Pont Winterthur Museum.)**

worked in their own fields were far more numerous than the gentry and cast the largest vote in county elections. Some farmers rented their land on shares, but hired men were hard to come by. Unfree labor consisted of two types, slaves and indentured servants, and it may be that the latter were as numerous as the former in the mid-eighteenth century. Some men, particularly in northern Delaware near the Christina and the Appoquinimink, were improving land by draining and banking it, because the proximity to the Philadelphia market made their lands more valuable than farms at a greater distance. Others, however, were being impoverished because their soil wore out from being planted year after year with the same crop, with no effort to enrich the land. It is probable that such uneconomical use of the soil caused the abandonment of tobacco, a valuable crop in lower Delaware in 1700 but practically unknown there by 1775.

An unusual product was the bog iron that was mined in small amounts in Sussex before the Revolution and was smelted in local furnaces that employed charcoal produced in the vicinity. An ore deposit was also found at Iron Hill in New Castle County. Throughout the state, ample fresh water, plus quercitron bark, encouraged establishment of tanyards, which were so numerous that it was necessary to import hides for their use. A people dependent on water transport naturally had to develop skills in shipbuilding; in this they were encouraged by plentiful supplies of lumber. But enterprises like shipbuilding, tanning, iron making, milling, and other kinds of manufacturing were all secondary in importance to agriculture. In colonial Delaware farming was king.

4

The American Revolution

Causes

Delaware was carried into the stream of the American Revolution not from impelling local motives but in the wake of neighboring colonies and from motives affecting Americans in general. The leaders of political life in the Delaware counties were, for the most part, third- or fourth-generation Americans, descendants of colonists who had come to America in the great English migration of the late seventeenth century. Though they spoke and wrote of themselves proudly as freeborn Englishmen, most of them had never even visited England. They were in fact Americans and, as such, ready timber to be lighted by a new nationalist fire.

One group of Delawareans, the Scotch-Irish, were immigrants or the sons of immigrants who arrived with an anti-English bias, blaming their misfortunes in Ireland on the Hanoverian monarchs and their parliaments. Men of this sort, like John Haslet and Thomas McKean, adopted loyalty to their new land with great fervor. A Scotch-Irish or Presbyterian loyalist in Delaware would be an anomaly.

Many of the most prominent Delawareans of the Revolutionary generation—George Read, for instance, and John Dickinson—were natives of another colony. This fact, however, and the likelihood that almost every Delawarean of any prominence would have close relatives living somewhere on the other side of Delaware's narrow borders only accentuated the tendency of Delaware to join with neighboring colonies in concerted action. Of all the outside influences affecting Delawareans, the greatest by far was the influence of Philadelphia.

It would be difficult to overemphasize the influence of Philadelphia on Delaware, for Philadelphia by 1775 dominated the economic and cultural life of the Delaware valley, its influence extending to Lewes, the home of Delaware River pilots, and to the St. Jones River and the Appoquinimink, where landings were loaded with produce bound for Philadelphia even more often than for New Castle and Wilmington. There was an area of southwestern Sussex where farmers had an easier commercial connection with the Chesapeake Bay than with the Delaware River, but even here the Philadelphia influence was not lacking, for the great families of the Eastern Shore of Maryland, like the people of Delaware, almost all had close Philadelphia connections.

Caesar Rodney went to school in Philadelphia. George Read and John Dickinson studied law there, and James Tilton medicine. Thomas McKean moved from New Castle to Philadelphia in 1774 but remained active in Delaware affairs. Even John Dagworthy, whose plantation was geographically as far distant from Philadelphia as landholdings in Delaware could be, had his close connections, for he was a native of Trenton, in the Delaware valley, and one of his daughters married a Philadelphian. Philadelphia newspapers and Philadelphia markets dominated their respective spheres of Delaware life.

If Philadelphians were upset by British revenue measures or by commercial restrictions, their fears were soon transmitted to Delaware. Tales of corruption in high places in Great Britain and suspicion of conspiracies against colonial well-being entered Delaware through the same channel.

By happy accident, the final settlement of the long boundary dispute with Maryland had occurred in 1775, just in time to free Delawareans from their long dependence on the Proprietary in this regard. There remained, however, a need to insist on their identity, to have a seat at intercolonial conferences, to demand an equal voice with other colonies.

The number of Delawareans so dissatisfied with the state of affairs as to participate actively in a war of rebellion was a minority, even of the free white inhabitants. Yet the number of loyalists so confirmed in their adherence to their monarch as to wish to dissociate their colony from its neighbors was apparently a smaller minority still. A significant number of the people were willing to allow themselves to be moved by events, day by day, to float with the American tide, causing little disturbance, accepting the inevitable. The rebels and the Tories made the most noise, because on one side or the other were ranged those who cared most about politics. But there was also a quieter element of humbler folk, like the Quakers and the Methodists, not to mention the more than 20 percent of the population who were black—a quiet element that cared little who won the war.

The happy situation of the Lower Counties at a semi-independent colony, an almost forgotten corner of empire, plus the small size of the colony and the consequent limited ambitions for its development, produced a situation where a moderate course would seem safest. Here in these Delaware counties the old order did not relinquish control. Gradually, not without occasional challenges from one side or the other, the colony was altered into a state. The colonial assembly, with some prodding, provided for a constitutional convention that the old, moderate leadership dominated and where an old society was reorganized under a new name: the Delaware State.

Congresses

The first opportunity Delawareans had to join with other colonists in protest against British policies was the congress that met in New York in October 1765 to deliberate on a colonial response to recent British measures, especially the Sugar Act of 1764, which strengthened parliamentary control over colonial commerce, and the Stamp Act of 1765, which sought to raise a revenue in the colonies by a tax on legal documents, playing cards, newspapers, and the like. Since the Delaware assembly was not in session to take action, the assemblymen in each county signed a letter appointing three delegates to the New York congress, one from each county. The Sussex member thus chosen, Jacob Kollock, apparently never went to New York because he expected to be reelected speaker of the assembly, which was due to meet in New Castle at almost the same time. The two delegates who did attend were Caesar Rodney, then thirty-seven, a well-to-do landholder in Jones's Neck of Kent County, and Thomas McKean, a thirty-one-year-old New Castle attorney.

Even Delawareans who, like Rodney, had worked closely with the proprietary government were sympathetic to the vigorous protests made against the Stamp Act, which was the work of Parliament, not the proprietors, and was therefore a setback to the Pennsylvania party led by Benjamin Franklin that advocated replacing the proprietary connection by direct royal government.

Franklin had secured the appointment of a Philadelphia friend as stamp agent for both Pennsylvania and Delaware, so there was no resident local stamp agent against whom Delawareans could express their anger.

In New York Rodney and McKean joined eagerly in the work of the convention, generally called the Stamp Act Congress, which recorded its opposition to taxation without representation (as the Stamp Act was regarded), to the recent commercial restrictions, and to their enforcement by trials in which juries were dispensed with. The Congress petitioned the king and Parliament for a redress of their grievances, and Delawareans rejoiced with other Americans when Parliament did repeal the Stamp Act in 1766.

In one more year, however, Parliament gave new cause for dissatisfaction by passing what were called the Townshend Acts, another effort to raise a revenue in the colonies, this time by import duties on glass, lead, paints, paper, and tea. Instead of sending delegates to a convention, the individual colonies kept in touch with each other by correspondence and in that way organized boycotts of British goods. Since very few imports from Britain came to Delaware except through Philadelphia, Delawareans opposing the new duties contented themselves at first with a petition of protest that the assembly sent to the king. Soon, however, a rumor arose that some merchants in New Castle County planned to supply themselves with new stocks of goods from Maryland instead of Philadelphia, because the nonimportation association entered into by Maryland merchants was less restrictive than the Philadelphia association. Friends of the Philadelphia connection then got to work, pledging Delaware merchants to support the boycott agreement entered into by the Philadelphia merchants. At a meeting in Christiana of representatives from several New Castle County communities, committees of inspection were set up for each town and instructed to watch for sales of embargoed goods and to report violations of the boycott to a general committee, of which George Read, New Castle lawyer and assemblyman, would be chairman. The general committee would be expected to extract a pledge of good conduct from the accused merchant and to sell any embargoed goods it found for the benefit of the poor fund of the county.

The Townshend duties, except for the tea tax, were repealed in 1770, and though this one tax remained, the colonists abandoned their boycott. Then in 1773 a new quarrel with the mother country broke out because Parliament gave the East India Company a monopoly on the sale of tea in America through its own appointed agents, who would be able to undersell all other merchants, even dealers in smuggled tea.

Americans decided to refuse to buy the East India Company's tea. A tea ship coming up the Delaware to Philadelphia was turned away by threats voiced at a mass meeting in Philadelphia, but in Boston in December colonists destroyed tea in an action famous as the Boston Tea Party. As punishment for this violence, Parliament passed a group of statutes that the colonists called the Intolerable Acts or Coercive Acts, closing the port of Boston and suspending the government of Massachusetts.

A committee of correspondence, created by the assembly, kept Delaware in contact with other colonies. When a new inter-colonial congress was planned, the committee organized mass meetings in each of the three county seats, where resolutions were passed in support of Massachusetts and the speaker of the assembly was urged to call the members together in informal session to select delegates to the Continental Congress, as the 1774 convention was called. The fact that the first of the county mass meetings, in New Castle, called for the assemblymen to meet there caused irritation in the other counties, which were not disposed to put up with domination by New Castle in the future.

Nevertheless, the meeting—which was extralegal because it was not at the usual time and not called by the governor—was held as planned in August 1774, and a three-man delegation, consisting of Rodney, Read, and McKean was elected to Congress. There they joined with other delegates in the two kinds of protest that had seemed effective in the past—petitions to the king and to Parliament and organization of a boycott of British goods.

This time the British did not give in, and a confrontation between British troops and colonial militia led to an outbreak of fighting in Massachusetts in April 1775. The next month the Second Continental Congress met in Philadelphia with the same three delegates representing Delaware as in 1774. They supported measures to create a Continental army commanded by Washington, while a revolutionary committee system gradually put Delaware on a war footing—to the discomfiture of some citizens. Committees of observation and inspection supervised enforcement of the new boycott, called the Association, while committees of safety began to gather arms and provide for military training.

In September 1775 a Council of Safety representing all three counties met at Dover to serve as an executive body for the military measures of the colony. In December Congress asked this council to raise troops for the Continental army, and in 1776 the first Delaware regiment, commanded by Col. John Haslet, was sent off to join Washington in time to participate in the battle of Long Island.

When independence was first considered in Congress in the spring of 1776, the Delaware delegates were still McKean, Read, and Rodney, who were under instructions from the assembly, as they had been from the beginning, to seek reconciliation, though they had full power to join in supporting any military measures. The official attitude of the Delaware assembly was that its actions were taken to protect the rights of freeborn Englishmen, upholding their ancient liberties and loyal to the king despite the mistreatment Americans were experiencing from his Parliament and his ministers. A similar attitude was popular throughout the Middle Colonies, where it permitted men of different minds, radicals and conservatives, to work together in these early stages of the Revolution.

But after a year of warfare this unity became increasingly difficult to maintain. On June 7, 1776, Congress accepted a motion for independence from Richard Henry Lee, but postponed debate on it to allow supporters time to persuade reluctant colleagues, both in Congress and at home in the assemblies. In Delaware a momentous decision was made in the assembly on June 15. A day earlier Thomas McKean presented a recommendation from Congress asking the colonies to suppress "every kind of authority under the . . . crown" and place government directly "under the authority of the people." The assembly took but one day to react as McKean wished, adopting on June 15 a resolution suspending all royal authority in Delaware and directing all officers to continue their duties in the name only of the three counties.

In operation the government of Delaware was unchanged, except that the legislature assumed all the powers of Governor John Penn. In theory the difference was enormous, for Delaware had severed its ties with Great Britain. On this same day, June 15, 1776, the assembly took another significant action, adopting new instructions for its delegates to Congress. All reference to reconciliation was dropped. There was no reference made to independence; the delegates were merely told to adopt whatever measures were necessary to promote the liberty and the safety of America. They were given freedom to decide for themselves how to vote on Lee's independence resolution.

Independence

When Lee's resolution was taken up in Congress on July 1, only two delegates, McKean and Read, represented Delaware. Rodney was absent because, after presiding over the assembly in New Castle, he had taken on another of his civic responsibilities. As brigadier general of militia he led an expedition into Sussex, where recent events had aroused such opposition that a group of loyalists had gathered under arms. They disbanded when the militia came, but the event kept Rodney from Congress as the discussion of independence began.

On July 1 the major debate occurred. Its exact details are unrecorded, but the principal speeches were made by John Adams, who urged passage of the resolution, and John Dickinson. Dickinson argued against declaring independence at this time, for he wished to preserve every possible chance of achieving a reconciliation and avoiding a long war. He was also aware that a decision for independence would divide Americans, turning their resistance to English authority into a civil war.

Dickinson's Quaker connections help explain his anxiety to avoid protracted war. Though Dickinson was not a practicing Quaker himself, his parents were birthright Quakers (his father had dissociated himself from Quaker meeting after being censured for allowing a daughter to be married in church), his wife was a Quaker, and his children were Quakers. But Dickinson believed that a defensive war—and such he considered the American Revolution to be—was a just war, and he was one of the few members of Congress at the time of the independence debate who served in the army himself.

In Congress each state had only one vote, though delegates were polled individually. After the debate, a preliminary vote revealed only nine states favoring independence. Delaware was not in this majority because the two Delaware delegates attending Congress on July 1 were divided on this issue, McKean voting for independence, and Read siding with his old and close friend

Dickinson (who was representing Pennsylvania) against independence. Before a final vote could be taken, a delegate proposed they wait over night to allow time for reflection.

When the final vote on independence was taken on July 2, the overnight delay had been used to good purpose. The resolution could have passed on a majority vote anyway, but its effect would have been diminished by the evidence that the Continental Congress was divided on this issue. The delay allowed three more states to be brought into the majority: South Carolina, because a delegate changed his mind or, at least, his vote; Pennsylvania, because two delegates in opposition (Dickinson and Robert Morris) stayed away; and Delaware, because Caesar Rodney appeared and joined McKean in placing his state in the ranks for independence. New York's delegates were still instructed to seek

James Kelly's equestrian statue of Caesar Rodney, in Rodney Square, Wilmington. This monument, which is wholly imaginative, commemorates the ride of Caesar Rodney from his farm in Kent County to Philadelphia on the night of July 1, 1776, to cast his vote for independence. **(Courtesy of the Historical Society of Delaware.)**

reconciliation and could not vote for independence, but they agreed not to vote at all on July 2 so that the resolution could be announced as carried by the unanimous vote of those states present and voting.

Caesar Rodney's hurried trip to Philadelphia to cast his vote for independence is one of the best-known events of Delaware history, but its significance is often misunderstood. He was not casting the decisive vote for independence, for the resolution would have passed even if he had not appeared. He was, however, casting the decisive vote in the Delaware delegation, allowing Delaware to join with the other colonies in making a united decision for independence. Rodney's devotion to duty can be best appreciated if it is remembered that he was absent from Congress not from self-indulgence but because of the heavy load of public responsibilities he bore as assembly speaker and militia general as well as Congressman; that he suffered from asthma and from a skin cancer on his nose that had been bothering him for more than ten years; and that the night of July 1, when he rushed from Kent County to Philadelphia in response to a summons from McKean, was an unpleasant one, full of thunder and rain.

Two days after Rodney's arrival at the Pennsylvania State House, where Congress was meeting, the decision of July 2 was embodied in the memorable words of Thomas Jefferson's Declaration of Independence, adopted without a recorded vote. The decision was now proclaimed to the world. Delaware, not without some reluctance at such an adventurous step, had cast its vote with its neighbors for independence.

The First State Constitution

The decision of Congress to declare independence made it clear that the action of the Delaware assembly in suspending government under the Crown on June 15 was to mean a permanent separation. A new organization of the government was called for. Consequently, the assembly met again in mid-July and passed an act providing for the election in August of a constitutional convention, with ten members from each county.

The convention that assembled in New Castle on August 27, 1776, and completed its work in less than a month produced not only the first state constitution for Delaware but the first constitution for any state that was written by a convention elected especially for this purpose. The convention did deal with some other business, but only minor matters that seemed pressing; for the main part, it stuck to its charge and completed its work in relatively short order.

George Read was chosen by the convention to be its president, and Thomas McKean was one of the most active members. Moderate to conservative opinion dominated the selection of delegates. There had been strong feeling in Delaware in opposition to any change in government; Thomas Robinson, a prominent Sussex merchant, claimed later that five thousand signatures had been collected on a remonstrance against change that had been seized and destroyed by advocates of revolution. While Robinson, who soon fled to a British ship, may have exaggerated the number of signatures to the remonstrance, the June 1776 loyalist uprising in Sussex, as well as the results of the August election, indicate that advocating an immediate declaration of independence was not the most popular course in Delaware.

Neither was Robinson's stern opposition to independence representative of Delaware feeling. George Read, elected president of the state constitutional convention, probably represented Delaware opinion more accurately than either Rodney or Robinson. He served as president of the council of safety, coordinating emergency military measures in Delaware, and yet in Congress he had voted against independence. Then, when the Declaration of Independence was adopted and time allowed for preparation of a fine parchment copy, Read signed it, along with McKean and Rodney. The moderate course Read followed, not a flaming advocacy of rebellion but resistance to British attempts at coercion and willingness to accept decisions of the majority, with all the risks these decisions entailed, probably suited the spirit of Delaware.

In the Delaware constitutional convention of August–September 1776, the predominantly conservative members wrote a constitution that was in keeping with the spirit of the times. The major foreign element in the colonial Delaware government had been the governor, with his power to appoint officials and veto legislation. He was therefore eliminated, replaced by an official called a president (one who presided, not governed), who had no veto power whatever and was required to share most of such powers of appointment as he retained with a four-man privy council, chosen, like the president, by the assembly.

The assembly, on the other hand, gained most of the power

THREE DELAWARE STATESMEN OF THE AMERICAN REVOLUTION

John Dickinson (1732–1808). Portrait by Charles Willson Peale. (Courtesy of the Independence National Historical Park Collection, Philadelphia.)

George Read (1733–1798). Copy by Thomas Sully of a portrait by Robert Edge Pine. (Courtesy of the Independence National Historical Park Collection, Philadelphia.)

Thomas McKean (1734–1817). Portrait by James Sharples. (Courtesy of the Independence National Historical Park Collection, Philadelphia.)

the executive relinquished. It elected the president, the privy council, and the judges, and the bills it passed became statutes automatically, without submission to anyone. The one notable change in this body was that it became bicameral, a conservative measure, substituting for a gubernatorial veto a check by each house on the other. The upper chamber, the legislative council, consisted of nine members elected to three-year terms; the lower chamber, called the house of assembly, had twenty-one members elected to one-year terms. All members were elected on a county-wide franchise.

There were no changes whatever in the qualifications for voting and only modest changes in the courts. Justices of the peace still dominated local government, but they were chosen now by the president and privy council from a list of double the necessary number nominated by the assembly. One notable clause in the constitution prohibited the importation of slaves. A bill of rights guaranteed freedom of press and of religion, but only Christians were promised the right to participate in politics. Nothing was said about freedom of speech, probably because of fear of loyalists. A new name, *the Delaware State,* replaced the awkward designations (such as *Counties of New Castle, Kent, and Sussex upon Delaware*) that had been used for the colony.

There is no indication that this convention gave any thought to submitting its work to the voters, for their acceptance or rejection. Instead, the new convention proclaimed that its handiwork would be put into effect after the fall elections of 1776, and so it was, but slowly, for though the new bicameral assembly met in the fall, it did not bother to elect a president until January 1777.

As the first chief executive of an independent Delaware, the legislature chose John McKinly, a physician and chief burgess of Wilmington. A critic, dissatisfied with the choice, wrote that McKinly was "a mere patch on the back" of George Read. His choice is an early example of a custom often followed in Delaware —the selection of a candidate who in many ways seems identified with the opposition party and can therefore either draw votes from it or at least help to modify party rancor. McKinly, an old militia officer in the French and Indian War, was a Scotch-Irish immigrant, and, as such, he represented the group most active in pressing the revolutionary cause. In its avoidance of extremes, the choice of McKinly is an example of Read's intelligent political management if it was Read, as is very likely, who brought about this election by an assembly that was dominated by conservatives from down state. This assembly had already infuriated the revolutionary element by its selection of a new congressional delegation, for it had dropped McKean and Rodney, the advocates of independence, while reelecting George Read and choosing as one of its new delegates John Dickinson, who was being charged in Pennsylvania, unfairly, with being a Tory because he had led the fight in Congress against declaring independence.

Dickinson, it turned out, refused to accept this election to Congress, though he appreciated the vote of confidence that his friends in Delaware, where he had been reared, had given him. It was obvious, however, that Delaware was entering the Revolution under a moderate leadership that did not want radical changes, except as the Revolution made them necessary. It was a leadership that would seek to suit its measures to the tone of the people of the state.

Invasion and War

Events in 1777 disrupted the placid way of life in Delaware. In the summer of this year, the British commander, Gen. William Howe, having been repulsed by Washington at Trenton and Princeton in a previous effort to take Philadelphia by marching across New Jersey, determined to move his army close to the largest American city, which was also the seat of Congress, by sea. Howe utilized a fleet of over 260 vessels to move an army of fifteen thousand men from New York, which he had captured in the summer of 1776, to Cecil County, Maryland, at the head of the Chesapeake Bay. He chose to approach Philadelphia by way of the Chesapeake rather than the Delaware because the Delaware had already been fortified below Philadelphia, and the only suitable landing places were so obvious that they could easily be defended.

After disembarking on the Elk Neck peninsula, Howe's army entered Delaware in two divisions, one marching up the Elk and through the town of Elkton, the other crossing the river from Elk Neck and marching east toward Middletown before turning north past Lum's Pond. The two divisions met at Glasgow, then called Aikentown.

To oppose the progress of the British, Washington had brought American troops from New York through Philadelphia and Wilmington to positions on the banks of the Red Clay Creek in the Marshallton-Stanton area. A chosen force of 720 infantry-men, taken from every unit and commanded by a New Jersey man of Scotch-Irish origin, William Maxwell, took positions in the woods above Glasgow. "Give them as much trouble as you possibly can," Washington instructed Maxwell. When the invading army, which included German mercenaries, met Maxwell's men, a hot battle broke out on the road skirting Iron Hill. Howe tried to surround the smaller American force, but Iron Hill on one side and Purgatory Swamp on the other prevented this maneuver.

Gradually, Howe's army pushed its way up the Newark-Glasgow road, where the Americans contested the advance with especial effectiveness at Cooch's Bridge, which gave its name to the battle. The fighting extended northward to the Welsh Tract Baptist Meetinghouse, which is still standing, before the Americans withdrew.

The British camped in the area of the battle from September 3 to September 6 before resuming their march. When they did move, it was in three divisions northward through Newark to Kennett Square, Pennsylvania. Washington, who had expected them to take the road to Christiana and Wilmington, kept his army between the British and Philadelphia, taking a new position at Chadds Ford, where the road from Kennett Square crossed the Brandywine.

The battle that followed on September 11, 1777, called the Battle of the Brandywine, was a major British victory. Outma-neuvering Washington, Howe brought most of his army quietly across the river at undefended fords to the north and surprised the Americans, who fought bravely but had to retreat. Following the battle, some British troops captured Wilmington without opposition, seizing President John McKinly, as well as the state treasury and many public records. For more than a month—to October 16, 1777—Wilmington was occupied by a Scottish High-land regiment and some German troops guarding a number of sick and wounded, while the invading army pressed on to Phila-delphia. Even when these last invaders left Wilmington, the state was still very close to the war, for the British fleet had sailed from the Chesapeake to the Delaware, where it finally forced its way through the river fortifications to reach Philadelphia and Howe's army in mid-November.

An American division commanded by William Smallwood and including the Delaware regiment garrisoned Wilmington from December 1777 to June 1778 while Washington's main army was at Valley Forge. The rest of Delaware lay at the mercy of the British, except for such defense as could be provided by the militia, who were called out at every hint of a British raid. In October 1777 the New Castle County elections had to be moved inland to Newark, because it was not safe for the voters to gather as usual at the courthouse, which was practically under the guns of the British fleet. Nor was it safe for the assembly to meet at New Castle, but fortunately provision had already been made in the spring of 1777 to move the fall session of the assembly to Dover.

The removal of the legislature from the old colonial capital was brought about by a voting combination of Kent and Sussex assemblymen, who were expressing some of the dissatisfaction felt downstate at the leading role New Castle County was taking in the politics of this period of upheaval. The upper house of the assembly met in Dover late in October 1777, but the lower house was unable to get a quorum, and the entire General Assembly did not meet until December, although even then most of the Sussex delegates were missing because a violent row in Lewes had interrupted the fall elections there.

Adoption of Dover as a permanent state capital was by no means certain at this time. After two years, in October 1779, a combination of New Castle and Sussex members passed an act allowing the assembly to meet at any place in the state it chose. For the next two years the legislature was in almost constant perigrination, rotating its sessions among all three counties and meeting successively in Wilmington, Lewes, Dover, New Castle, and in Lewes again, until it finally settled down permanently in Dover in October 1781. County rivalries had not disappeared, but Dover, near the center of the state, was an acceptable compromise location.

After President John McKinly's capture in September 1777, Thomas McKean and George Read, the presiding officers of the two chambers, each served briefly as acting governor. At that dangerous time, when it took unusual courage and devotion to the cause of independence to be chief executive of a state that was without a treasury and threatened at any moment by British naval power, the assembly chose Caesar Rodney as the second elected president. Rodney accepted the challenge and served as chief executive to 1782, through most of the remaining years of the war. He died in 1784, not long after his term ended.

The greatest danger for Delaware was over in June 1778,

when the British evacuated Philadelphia and their fleet left the river. However, a naval vessel generally remained on guard at Cape Henlopen, and small boats operating under its protection frequently crept up Delaware creeks to loot farms or seize goods at farm landings.

Another major problem of the Rodney administration was economic. To support the war, Congress issued so much paper money that it soon became nearly worthless, and since it was exchangeable at face value for state bills, the paper money of Delaware, which had been sound, also lost its value. A farmer who had produce to barter could make out without the paper money, but creditors were ruined, as were all who lived on a fixed income, like ministers and army officers.

The Delaware regiment through these difficult years was gaining an excellent reputation. Its first commander, John Haslet, had remained with Washington and been killed at Princeton after the terms of the first Delaware troops expired. David Hall commanded a regiment raised in 1777 until he was furloughed home because of illness in 1779, whereupon Joseph Vaughan took command. Under Vaughan and his successor, Robert Kirkwood, the soldiers of this regiment fought so well in the Carolina campaigns that they won the title "Blue Hen's chickens," after some gamecocks prized for their fighting qualities.

Delawareans who retained a sense of loyalty to the British government were less likely than the rebels to take up arms in order to have their way. The machinery of government, even when in the hands of moderates, was against them, for even moderates were eager to have Delaware keep in step with its neighbors in the Revolution. The most prominent Delaware loyalists suffered confiscation of their lands by statute. On several occasions loyalists did gather under arms, but they usually dispersed without a fight when opposition appeared, whether militia or, as happened at least twice, Continental troops sent by Congress. A band of loyalists led by Cheney Clow had a fortified headquarters in western Kent County that was captured by militia under Charles Pope in April 1778, though Clow himself was not taken until 1782. Pope also distinguished himself by commanding a small armed vessel that Delaware outfitted to defend river shipping against raids by loyalists operating from the British ships off Cape Henlopen.

5

The Constitutional Union

Ratification of the United States Constitution

In view of the eagerness of a small state like Delaware to keep
in step with its neighbors in the major events of the Revolutionary period, it seems at first view odd that Delaware should have
been the next-to-last state to ratify the Articles of Confederation,
which formed the first constitutional basis of the American union.
Although the Articles of Confederation did not go into effect
until March 1781, their preparation had begun in May 1776,
when a committee to draft them had been established by Congress at the same time that it established a committee to write
a declaration of independence. John Dickinson, as chairman of
this committee, drafted the first version of the Articles of Confederation, but they formed too centralized a government to
please most congressmen, and a revised version that was sent to
the states in the fall of 1777 was much weaker than Dickinson's
draft.

For the most part, the Articles of Confederation merely gave
legal basis to the existing alliance of thirteen states represented
in the Continental Congress. States like Delaware that had no
claims to lands west of the Appalachian Mountains feared that
large states with extensive claims, such as Virginia, in particular,
would have overwhelming influence in the new government. To
landless states, as the ones without extensive western claims were
called, it seemed that unsettled western lands ought to belong
to the union as a whole. Delaware and its neighbors, New Jersey
and Maryland, were encouraged in this opinion by land specula-
tors, primarily from Philadelphia, who had obtained claims to

77

some western lands from Indians but had no hope of having
these claims recognized by Virginia or other states whose citizens
were hoping to acquire the same lands.

Primarily because of their feeling about western lands, New
Jersey and Delaware, both of them later quick to ratify the U.S.
Constitution of 1787, were the eleventh and twelfth states, respectively, to ratify the Articles of Confederaion, which were
not to go into effect until ratified by all thirteen states. New
Jersey and Delaware ratified in 1779, but Maryland held out
until 1781. Though the Articles of Confederation were not
changed to suit the objections raised regarding the western lands,
the states with extensive western claims began making cessions
to the federal government, as Virginia did in 1784. If these cessions had not been made, the American system of admitting new
states on equal terms into an enlarging union might not have
developed as it did.

Under the Articles of Confederation, the United States
achieved several notable successes, bringing the Revolutionary
War to a victorious conclusion and establishing a system of land
survey and government for the West that provided for growth of
that area to statehood. But the Confederation government had
no power to raise money by taxation or to control commerce.
This weakness was particularly upsetting to Delaware, for it
saw its commerce controlled by Pennsylvania, which could collect
tariff duties on goods entering the port of Philadelphia even
though destined to be sold in Delaware.

Delawareans had also seen the proliferation of Continental
paper money, unsupported by tax revenues, destroy the value of
their state currency. They supported efforts to amend the Articles of Confederation to give Congress power to regulate commerce and raise money by tariff duties, but amendments needed
unanimous approval of the states, and since at least one state
opposed every attempt to strengthen the government, no amendment to the Articles of Confederation was ever adopted. In 1786
the Virginia legislature invited states to send delegates to a
convention at Annapolis, Maryland, to discuss the problem of
commercial regulations. Delaware was one of the states that
responded promptly to this invitation, but when the convention
met in September 1786, only five states were represented. John
Dickinson, who had recently moved back to Delaware from
Pennsylvania and was one of three Delaware delegates in attendance, was elected president of the convention, which decided

that because of its small attendance, it would postpone its deliberations in the hope that a convention it proposed for Philadelphia in the following spring would attract a larger representation. The spring convention, furthermore, would not restrict itself to commercial problems but would consider the general strengthening of the central government.

The Delaware General Assembly chose five delegates to go to the Philadelphia convention of 1787, which became known as the Constitutional Convention. They were John Dickinson, George Read, and Richard Bassett—who had attended the Annapolis Convention—plus Gunning Bedford, Jr., and Jacob Broom, who had also been named as delegates to Annapolis but had not attended. Richard Bassett was a wealthy landholder and lawyer, who was an enthusiastic convert to Methodism; Bedford, a Princeton graduate (and a younger cousin, not a son, of another Gunning Bedford, who was active in Delaware at the same time), was Delaware's attorney general; Broom was a young manufacturer from Wilmington; Dickinson, of course, was the most famous Delawarean on the national scene; and Read, though less well known nationally, was the most influential man in Delaware.

Read's influence was evident in the instructions the Delaware delegates carried with them to Philadelphia, for these instructions required them to insist on preserving for Delaware an equal voice with other states in Congress, no matter what other changes were made in the government. Read had served as chairman of the committee of the General Assembly that wrote these instructions. By inserting this insistence on an equal voice, he was providing the Delaware delegation with an excuse for resisting the arguments he knew would be presented in favor of making representation in Congress proportional in some way to the very great differences in size between states.

The Virginia delegation did open the convention with a plan that provided for proportional representation, which Delaware and other small states resisted vigorously. The insistence of the Delaware delegates that they had no power to accept such a plan helped bring about the great compromise on representation, whereby Virginia and the other large states got proportional representation in the lower house of the new Congress, while all states received equal representation in the Senate. This was, of course, something less than the strict letter of the Delaware instructions required. It demonstrates the political sagacity and standing of the Delaware delegates that they realized that this was the best arrangement they could hope for and that it would be understood and accepted at home. Once this compromise was arrived at, guaranteeing the continued influence of Delaware in national councils, the Delaware delegates supported almost every measure to strengthen the central government.

When the convention had completed its work and adjourned, ratification had been made to depend upon approval of the new constitution by special conventions in at least two-thirds (nine) of the states. The states near Philadelphia, the convention site, were the first to take action, partly because they were in closest touch with the proceedings of the convention. The Pennsylvania convention was the first to assemble, but while it was debating whether to adopt the constitution, the Delaware convention met in Dover on Monday, December 3, 1787. On Friday, December 7, 1787, it completed its meeting by ratifying the constitution by a unanimous vote. Thus Delaware (on a date that in subsequent years became known as Delaware Day) became the first state to ratify, the first state to enter the new constitutional union.

Although the designation as First State has been one of great pride to Delawareans ever since, the unanimity of the convention, when considered along with the absence of any strenuous opposition in the state, was at least as remarkable as the speed with which Delaware acted. It was a time when partisan feelings ran high in Delaware, when factions contested elections very bitterly. Yet on this issue they agreed. The one major item of debate at the convention seems to have been a disputed election in Sussex County. But friends of the defeated candidates there said they raised the issue only because there were other offices at stake. As far as the convention was concerned, they declared, it made no difference who was elected; all candidates favored ratification. New Jersey, another small state, was the third to ratify (Pennsylvania was the second) and did so by a similar unanimous vote in the convention.

To a small state like Delaware, union with its neighbors was of the greatest importance. Its only fear was the possible loss of its identity in a close federation with such comparative giants as Pennsylvania and Virginia. Equality in the United States Senate gave Delaware the assurance it needed. On that basis it could and did support a strong national union.

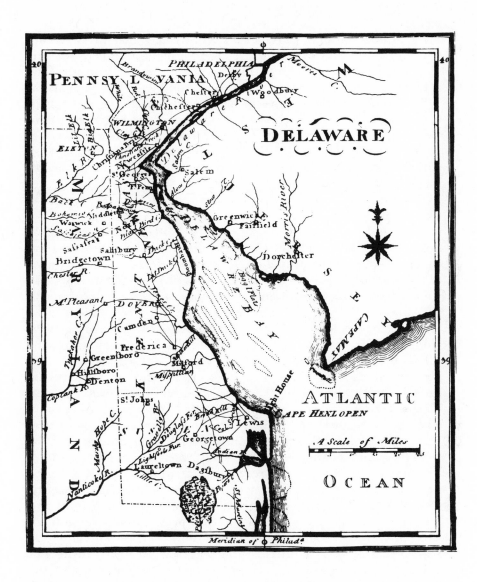

*Map of Delaware in 1800, showing new towns, such as Georgetown,
established after the American Revolution. An adaptation by Amos
Dolittle of the 1795 map by Joseph Scott. (Courtesy of the Division
of Historical and Cultural Affairs, Dover.)*

A New State Constitution, 1792

The new national government was inaugurated in 1789, and very quickly thereafter the Delaware assembly called for the election of a convention to rewrite the state constitution. The convention, which met in 1791 and completed its sessions in 1792, sought to correct several flaws in the hastily written 1776 constitution, to add provisions suggested by the experience of Delaware and the example of other state constitutions written in the intervening years, and to adjust state procedures and institutions to fit the framework of the new constitutional government of the union.

Meeting in Dover, the convention elected John Dickinson as its first president (he resigned the position later because of his health) and proceeded to make several changes that were merely nominal as well as a few that were substantial. Of the nominal changes, one was to drop *the Delaware State* as a title in favor of *the State of Delaware*. The two houses of the General Assembly were renamed the *Senate* and the *House of Representatives,* and the colonial title of *governor* was adopted in place of *president* for the chief executive. This official was given increased power, along with a measure of independence from the legislature, for the experiment of an executive council (privy council) was abandoned, and election of the executive henceforth was to be directly by the people at the same time legislators were chosen. The governor's powers of appointment (of judges and county officials) were increased, but he was not given the right to veto acts of the legislature, except constitutional amendments.

The numbers and terms of assemblymen remained as before, but new age and residence requirements were adopted. Twenty-four became the minimum age for representatives and twenty-seven for senators, with all legislators required to be citizens and inhabitants of the state for three years prior to election and inhabitants of the county from which they were elected for one year. Senators were required to be relatively wealthy—owners of two thousand acres or property worth one thousand pounds (the English term was still in use) in the county they represented; representatives were required only to be landowners, however small their landholding.

There were extensive alterations in the courts. Three state courts were established: the court of chancery, a supreme court, and a court of common pleas, these courts taking over much business previously left to justices of the peace in the county courts. A chancellor presided in chancery court, while each of the other two courts had a chief justice and three associate judges, one of whom, for each court, had to be resident of each county. (The practice of having a "resident judge" in each county was thus initiated.) Apparently, the growth of legal business had led to this change.

A major revision occurred in the franchise provisions that had been carried over unchanged from colonial times in the 1776 constitution. The requirement of possession of a specific amount of property was eased into a more democratic provision that the voter needed only to be a taxpayer. Since there was a capitation tax, the voter could be a poor man, without property. But at the same time that the franchise was liberalized in this regard, it was stiffened in other directions by a requirement that the voter be a free, white man. The obvious intent was to disfranchise blacks and women. Only white men had been voting (with a possible few exceptions), though the law had not previously restricted the ballot to them. Adoption of this new restrictive provision suggests that the status of women and of blacks was improving; however demeaning the new provision might be, it indicates that women and blacks were at least being thought of in relation to the franchise.

Religious liberty was advanced by a provision in the new constitution declaring that a person's religion could not be a reason for denying him any office in Delaware. This was an important provision, for although freedom of worship had existed in colonial Delaware, only Protestants could qualify for membership in the assembly. Alliance with France in the Revolutionary War had helped dispel the anti-Catholic bias most of the colonists brought with them to America. The new provision was specifically meant to open public service to Catholics; it also served Jews and other religious minorities.

Another modest change in the constitution that has important meaning was a change of wording, *every man* being substituted for *every freeman* in a provision promising the right to legal remedies against injustice. It is very doubtful that slaves did receive equal justice at law, but the change in wording suggests consciousness that they deserved consideration. Petitions from abolitionists asking that slaveholding be forbidden were rejected, and the provision of the 1776 constitution forbidding the importation of slaves was omitted, but since 1776 this constitutional provision had been given strength and made effective by laws setting heavy fines for the importation of slaves, including freedom for the persons imported, and there was also a law forbidding the exportation of slaves for sale. Though the constitution made no provisions to end slavery, these laws, which remained in effect, had practically banned the interstate slave trade from Delaware and in doing so contributed to the decline of slavery here.

Once again, as in 1776, the new constitution was put into effect without being submitted to the people. And once again, as in 1776, the dominant note in such constitutional changes as were made is their moderation. The changes did not drastically alter the political life of Delaware, nor were they intended to. The moderate politicians who had led Delaware into and through the American Revolution and who had helped write and ratify the U.S. Constitution remained in control of events.

George Read, who had signed the Declaration of Independence, though with some reluctance, and had played an important role in writing the U.S. Constitution, became a member of the first United States Senate in 1789 and continued there until he was appointed the first chief justice of the Delaware Supreme Court under the constitution of 1792. Richard Bassett, another member of the Constitutional Convention, also represented Delaware in the first United States Senate; at the end of his senatorial term, in 1793, he became chief justice of the new state court of common pleas.

Read and Bassett and their political allies found it possible to retain their influence in Delaware because they were generally wise enough to make needed changes in the government while avoiding extremes. The 1776 constitution had all but eliminated the power of the governor, who had generally been a foreigner and therefore suspect. The 1792 constitution reestablished a single executive with appointive powers but carefully avoided giving him the right to veto legislation. The assembly, though made bicameral in 1776, otherwise was changed very little, except for its greatly increased power. It was even chosen by the same electorate after 1776 as before, and the franchise changes of 1792 only made it more responsive to the free, white, male population of Delaware.

Slowly, gradually, the government of Delaware was becoming increasingly democratic. In the decade after adoption of the 1792 constitution, Delaware stood highest of all the states in the percentage of its free, white, male residents who actually participated in elections. Use of the qualifying adjectives *free, white, male* suggests, of course, what was true, that a majority of the adult inhabitants (the unfree, the black, and the female) were excluded from voting. But this was generally true in the United States of those early years. For conditions as they were in America, the state of Delaware exhibited a very high popular participation in government.

The Federalist Party

The enthusiasm Delawareans displayed for the new consti-tutional union in 1787 did not slacken in the years that followed. There never was a party in Delaware opposed to the U.S. Constitution, though there did develop different views regarding its interpretation and implementation. In the administration of President Washington, congressmen gradually separated into two parties, Federalists and Republicans, and a similar cleavage took place in Delaware, where, in general, the old court party, the Church party, the political moderates, identified themselves as Federalists, while the country party, the Irish or Presbyterian party, the most ardent in support of the Revolution, became the Republicans.

In the first decade of the new national union, the Federalists in Delaware ran affairs in their own way. They almost monopolized political offices of prominence, often moving from one office to another as if in a game of musical chairs. For instance, the last president under the 1776 constitution was Joshua Clayton, who became the first governor under the 1792 constitution and in 1798 was sent by the legislature to the United States Senate. Governor Clayton offered Senator George Read his choice of judicial posts under the new constitution. When Clayton's term ended, Read's brother-in-law, Gunning Bedford, Sr., became the second popularly elected governor.

Many other Federalists entered national politics by election to the federal House of Representatives and after a term or more moved to the Senate. John Vining, Henry Latimer, and James A. Bayard established this pattern, which was followed frequently in the early nineteenth century. Political posts were passed around not only within the party but also within certain families, like the Rodneys, the Van Dykes, and the Claytons. The longest of the Delaware political dynasties was established by a Federalist,

James A. Bayard, who was followed to the United States Senate by two sons (Richard and James), one grandson (Thomas) and a great-grandson (Thomas, Jr.). Moreover, the first Senator Bayard had been preceded in the Senate by his father-in-law, Richard Bassett.

Delaware Federalists found their basic support in the two southern counties, Kent and Sussex. Their appeal was apparently primarily to the rural Anglican and Methodist constituency of English background that was the dominant group in this area. This seems contrary to the common view that the Federalists were a mercantile party appealing to the commercial classes and that their opponents were the agrarian party, but in Delaware it was the commercial area, the city of Wilmington, in particular, where the Federalists were weakest. Delaware Federalism, though staunch in its support of the new nation, was in local matters based on support of the old order, represented better by the counties of Kent and Sussex than by New Castle, where life had been subjected to two major alterations in the eighteenth century. One of these alterations was demographic, the infusion of a large number of Scotch-Irish immigrants; the second was economic, a quickening of commercial life as typified by the growth of Wilmington.

The Federalist party also appealed to its clientele in Delaware because of its support of a strong union of the states; the small size and the close intercolonial connections of Delaware prevented the states' rights doctrines of the 1790s from having much appeal. As the pro-British and anti-French party during the wars of the French Revolution, the Federalists appealed to the natural prejudices of Delawareans, particularly of downstate Delawareans, who were predominantly of English stock. Federalist support of a strong navy was also a popular position with Delawareans, who feared in wartime for their exposed position near the coast.

Despite Federalist successes, an opposition party gradually grew in Delaware, basing its strength on the old country party and on the Irish Presbyterians, who were suspicious of any pro-British element. They were very critical of the Jay Treaty with Britain in 1794, of Federalist taxes and expenditures on the armed forces, and of the Alien and Sedition Acts of 1798, which they viewed as an attempt to enforce conformity of opinion. The greatest strength of this opposition party, which gradually became known as Republican and, still later, as the Democratic-

Republican party, was in New Castle County, where the Presbyterian element was largest; yet the greatest success of the party in state politics came when it ran a candidate from downstate, especially if he had a military reputation from the Revolution that would help him win votes from friends and neighbors that might otherwise go to the Federalist candidate.

John Patten, a Revolutionary veteran from Kent County who had married a daughter of the Presbyterian minister at Dover, was the first person elected to Congress who can be identified with this party. He was elected in 1794 after apparently winning the previous (1792) election, only to have the results overturned because many ballots had been marked incorrectly. The first Republican to be elected governor was David Hall, of Lewes, former commander of the Delaware Regiment. His election in 1801 followed the election to the presidency in 1800 of Thomas Jefferson, who had failed to carry Delaware. The second Republican governor, Joseph Haslet, also of Sussex and the son of Hall's predecessor as commander of the Delaware regiment, was elected in 1810. The second Republican congressman from Delaware, elected in 1802, was Caesar A. Rodney, nephew of Caesar Rodney, the Signer. Caesar A. Rodney also was the first Republican United States Senator from Delaware, but the fact that this election was not until the year 1822 indicates how hard it was for the Republicans to win control of the Delaware General Assembly, which elected senators.

Because they were challenging the established party, the Republicans found it necessary to develop an organization that would help them make the most of the strength they had. In the early 1790s a few people at each county seat had customarily agreed on a county ticket of candidates for the assembly, for sheriff, and for coroner. A clerk would write out many copies of this ticket and present them to the country folk as they arrived to vote.

The Republicans' first innovation was in calling a county mass meeting to make nominations. The first such meetings were apparently held in New Castle County, where the Republicans were strongest, at the Red Lion Tavern. Since some hundreds, particularly those at greatest distance, might not be able to get a large representation at the mass meeting, the practice developed of having a committee elected in each hundred at the September little elections. These committees would meet to form the county ticket, and the county meetings would appoint delegates to a state nominating convention in Dover. (Delaware was one of the first two states to develop a state nominating convention.)

The Republicans also sponsored newspapers and printed broadsides to popularize the claim that they were the party of the people and their opponents an aristocratic party that wished to rule like lords over peasants. "Do not offices run in the blood of families and descend from father to son?" argued a Republican, writing in an 1809 newspaper. "Have not most of the offices of this county for a long succession of years been confined to a few individuals? and were not the fathers, brothers, uncles, etc., of the present officeholders, officeholders also?"

After some initial successes by the Republicans early in the nineteenth century, the Federalists decided they must organize too. Soon they were holding mass meetings to choose county tickets, and before long they too were choosing hundred committees and county committees and holding a state nominating convention. They also had proved willing to adopt changes in the

Old Town Hall, Wilmington, built in 1798 and restored in 1927. The original architect was Peter Bauduy. (Courtesy of the Historical Society of Delaware.)

state government, as when the 1792 convention changed the franchise requirements to allow any taxpayer to vote. In 1793 the assembly, controlled by Federalists as it practically always was, provided for the election of the county levy courts, which established county tax rates and appropriated funds for county needs. In 1811 the party permitted district elections, a reform Republicans had long demanded. Until this time, voters had to go to the county seat for the election of all county and state officials, but after 1811 a polling place was set up in each hundred.

In American states generally, it was the Republicans who first developed party machinery, possibly because they were the more democratic party and, in theory at least, had the greater interest in involving ordinary folks in party affairs. Certainly, however, a major impelling motive to their organization was the fact that they began, in terms of the nation, as the opposition party and had to organize to elect congressmen with their point of view. What was unusual, possibly unique, in Delaware politics was the adaptability of the Federalists, who quickly copied new organizational techniques introduced by Republicans. The Delaware Federalists proved teachable, willing to adjust their methods to the needs of the times, as they also adjusted their policies. Although accused of being the aristocratic party, they ruled Delaware because they were solidly backed by the yeomanry of Kent and Sussex, and since at this time the three Delaware counties were approximately equal in population, Federalists had the support of a distinct majority of Delaware voters.

In the General Assembly in particular, Federalist majorities were hardly challenged for the first thirty years of the new government, for Kent and Sussex normally returned two-thirds of the legislators, even if New Castle usually voted Republican. So solid was this Federalist majority in the legislature, which chose presidential electors, that Delaware never cast a single ballot in the electoral college for Jefferson or Madison, the first two Republican presidents, and it voted for a Republican for the first time in 1820 only because President Monroe had no opposition in his contest that year for reelection.

Religious Revival

Aside from the political developments of the late eighteenth century, the most important movement in Delaware in this period was the Methodist religious revival. Methodism originated in England in the eighteenth century as a movement to revive faith and religious devotion. Its principal founders, the brothers John and Charles Wesley, felt that the organized Church of England, of which they were members, was not extending itself to reach dislocated English people who had moved from the parishes where they were reared to the new mill towns and the growing cities of England or to the colonies.

The earliest of the Methodists to come to Delaware was George Whitefield, an Anglican minister, who landed at Lewes in 1739. Although Whitefield, a fiery preacher, organized a short-

Barratt's Chapel, near Frederica, a Methodist meetinghouse built in 1780 by Philip Barratt, an early convert. It is known as "the cradle of Methodism" because in 1784 Francis Asbury met here with Thomas Coke, recently dispatched to America by John Wesley, and they planned the meeting in Baltimore at which the Methodist Episcopal Church was organized. Photograph by Edward Heite. (Courtesy of the Division of Historical and Cultural Affairs, Dover.)

lived society at Lewes that may have been the first Methodist group in America, his preaching on this continent was effective mainly among the Presbyterians. He emphasized enthusiasm rather than dogma and preached to large crowds on his several trips through Delaware, particularly in New Castle County; ten thousand are said to have gathered to hear him near the old White Clay Creek Presbyterian Church in December 1740, but it is likely that the estimate, Whitefield's own, is a bit swollen.

Whitefield's permanent effect in Delaware, however, was less than that of the next Methodist evangelists, who began visiting the Lower Counties in 1769. These men, many dispatched directly by John Wesley to preach the Gospel in the New World, were usually bachelors of limited education who had not been ordained but were regarded as lay preachers. In background, except that they came from England, they were not much different from the Delawareans of English stock to whom they appealed. The Delaware counties had never at any one time had more than five ordained Anglican ministers, and seldom so many. With the poor state of transportation, they could not travel far, nor could many people get to church on Sunday. Consequently, a large part of the population had no opportunity to go to church or to be attended by a minister.

The Methodist preachers went directly to these people. They preached anywhere they could find an audience, and in Delaware they worked on good terms with the Anglican clergy, attending an Anglican church themselves when near one and sometimes inviting Anglican clergy to their revival meetings. They did not come here as rivals to the Anglicans but to reach those out of touch with the Church of England. In most of their preaching in Delaware, they were not trying to win people from one denomination to another but simply to strengthen people's ancestral religious faith.

Being loyal Englishmen, all of the Methodist preachers returned to England when the Revolution began except Francis Asbury, the most important evangelist of them all. Asbury lived till 1816 and spent his life in perpetual itinerancy, constantly traveling through the American states and Canada. However, he spent more time in Delaware than anywhere else during the darkest period of the American Revolution because he refused to take an oath of loyalty that the individual states demanded, his objection being that it required him to swear to take up arms if called on. He found a haven in Delaware for twenty

Absalom Jones (1746–1818), born a slave in Sussex County, became a leader among the free blacks of Philadelphia and was ordained a priest in the Protestant Episcopal Church. Portrait by Raphaelle Peale. (Courtesy of the Delaware Art Museum, Wilmington.)

months, while friends in Kent County protected him from jail for refusing to take the loyalty pledge—though he said that the wording of the required oath in Delaware was so moderate that he might have taken it if necessary.

Despite the departure of the other Methodist preachers, their mission had been so successful that a group of Americans were quick to replace them. Unlike the Church of England, which required that its candidates receive a college education before being ordained by a bishop, the Methodists required only good character and zeal from their preachers, plus a willingness to work for almost no salary at all. Two techniques developed by these early preachers were the circuit and the camp meeting. The circuit was an area, often the size of a county, to which two preachers might be assigned. These men would constantly move around their territory, preaching in any convenient location and staying in the homes of friends whenever possible. As time passed, wealthy farmers built chapels (like Barratt's Chapel) in which services could be held.

The Methodist circuit rider solved the problem of making church services available to people on isolated farms by going directly to where the people were. The camp meeting met the same problem in a different way, by bringing the people to the preacher. Both devices were enormously effective in Delaware.

In 1784, after the Revolution had ended, John Wesley sent Thomas Coke to America to advise the American Methodists that they should form their own church. Coke met Asbury and gave him this advice at Barratt's Chapel, near Frederica, which has since been referred to as the cradle of American Methodism, for as a result of this meeting a conference was called in Baltimore at which the Methodist Episcopal Church was organized.

In its foundation, Methodism was closely linked to pacifism— or at least neutrality in the struggle between England and America—and to abolitionism. The preachers who came from England were all abolitionists and made a particular effort to preach to blacks as well as to whites. Their success was as great with Delaware blacks as with Delaware whites, and the early Methodist societies in Delaware had members from both groups. In time, however, as the Methodist church was Americanized, the blacks were made to feel uneasy in worshipping with whites (by being required to sit in the gallery, for example) and began to form their own churches. In some cases these churches of the blacks remained part of the Methodist Episcopal denomination. In other cases, black Methodists organized denominations of their own, as was true with Peter Spencer, a freeborn black of Wilmington, who organized what became the United American Methodist Episcopal Church,* and Richard Allen, a former Kent County slave, who founded the largest of the black denominations, the African Methodist Episcopal Church, in Philadelphia.

One native Delawarean, Absalom Jones, who was born a slave near Seaford in 1746, became the first black priest in the Protestant Episcopal Church. Jones, like Allen, had moved to Philadelphia and was associated with him there in the founding of one of the first organizations of blacks devoted to their own improvement, the Free African Society of 1787.

---

* Another denomination, the African Union Methodist Protestant Church, also traces its origins to Spencer.

Peter Spencer (1779–1843), a leader of the black Methodists who seceded from Asbury Church, Wilmington, in 1805 and later, in 1812, left the Methodist Episcopal denomination altogether to form a separate Methodist organization. (Courtesy of Mother U.A.M.E. Church, Wilmington.)

Protestant Episcopal was the name taken by American members of the Church of England when they set up their own church in 1786. This denomination was greatly weakened by the Revolution when many of their churches were closed and several of their priests, natives of England, had departed. One portion of the order of service requiring prayers for the king and royal family could not safely be followed in Revolutionary America, though the Anglican rector at Lewes thought he had neatly solved this problem by substituting for "O Lord, save the King," the words, "O Lord, save those who thou hast made it our especial Duty to pray for." His thoughts, he explained privately, were of the king, but members of his congregation might be thinking of the Continental Congress.

American Catholicism, on the other hand, was strengthened by the Revolution, as the French alliance encouraged respect for Catholics. There had been a few Catholics in Delaware, many of them landholders of Maryland origin, for a long time, but too few for a church. Priests from Maryland ministered to the Delaware Catholics until just before the Revolution, when a chapel was built at Coffee Run, in New Castle County. The immigration of Irish and French Catholics after the Revolution led to construction of a second Catholic church, St. Peter's, in Wilmington, but the great growth of Catholicism in Delaware, making it the major rival in size to Methodism, did not occur until the increase of immigration in the nineteenth century.

Presbyterianism in Delaware survived the Revolution with undiminished strength, but the decline of Scotch-Irish immigration and the antipathy these immigrants had aroused in Delaware by their political activities limited the expansion of their church. Presbyterians remained very influential in New Castle County, where they supported the academy that became the University of Delaware, but in the state as a whole the most popular faith of the common man, black or white, was Methodism.

6

The Old Order
and Some Innovations

Slavery

The forces of change that had produced a political revolution
and a religious revival in the late·eighteenth century had not
sufficed to rid the state of slavery, though the two decades following the American Revolution saw greater efforts to abolish the
evil institution than ever before—or after. In the middle of the
eighteenth century, it seems likely that over one-fifth of the population of Delaware were slaves. There are no worthwhile population statistics for this period, but the first federal census, in
1790, indicates that 21.6 percent of the population (12,786 out
of 59,096) were blacks. In 1790 almost one-third of the blacks
(3,899) were free, but it is likely that most of the free blacks had
gained freedom relatively recently.

The abolition movement that flourished in the years following the American Revolution was pervasive in its influence,
which stretched from Massachusetts to South Carolina. Men of
a generation that fought for liberty and freedom could hardly
ignore completely the condition of their compatriots of a different
hue. The 1776 Delaware Bill of Rights declared that "all persons professing the Christian religion ought forever to enjoy
equal rights and privileges in this state" and the preamble to
the constitution of 1792 stated that "through divine goodness
all men have, by nature, the rights . . . of enjoying and defending
life and liberty."

The men writing these documents may have given no thought
at all to the legal condition of blacks (or of women) in Delaware,
but repetition of such libertarian sentiments gradually led men

96

to think slavery an aberration in their political system. "Slavery in a republic or free government is a paradox," wrote a correspondent to the editors of a Wilmington paper, the *Delaware and Eastern Shore Advertiser,* in 1795.

Other men arrived at the same conclusions by religious, rather than political, arguments. "Slavery tends to destroy that free agency necessary to render a man accountable for his actions to a Supreme Being," declared a petition presented to the General Assembly in 1791. Ministers and other religious men of all denominations signed petitions such as this, but the Quakers and the Methodists were especially active. Spurred by a Quaker petition, the assembly considered an abolition bill in 1786 but tabled it. Richard Bassett, a leading Methodist, successfully introduced a bill to forbid the exportation of slaves for sale in 1787. Other laws passed at this time provided penalties for importing slaves, forbade the fitting out of ships for the slave trade, ordered trial by jury of slaves accused of capital crimes, and allowed free blacks under certain circumstances to testify in criminal trials. Of all the slave states, Delaware was the only one where a black was considered in court to be free unless proved to be a slave. Yet abolition bills, though considered in the legislature in 1796, 1797, and 1803, were always rejected.

At the beginning of the Revolution, slavery had existed in all of the thirteen colonies, but in these years when the subject was being agitated in Delaware, all the states to the north of Delaware were ridding themselves of slavery. The reason for the success of abolition to the north must have been in large measure economic; slaves were largely used as agricultural labor and, as such, were far more expensive to maintain in the North, where the growing season was relatively short and where provision of clothing and shelter was a greater problem than in the South. Perhaps Delaware, and Maryland too, offered a climate where the slave system had sufficient chance to prosper to give economic grounds for its retention. Such an argument would explain the strength of slavery in the southernmost Delaware county, Sussex, where in 1790 there were 4,025 slaves, as contrasted to 2,300 in Kent and 2,562 in New Castle.

But economic explanations are not the full story, as witnessed by the fact that Kent, an agricultural county that is south of New Castle, was the Delaware county where the largest number of blacks were free. The reason that almost two-thirds of the free blacks of Delaware were in Kent was probably the unique combination in this county of large numbers of Quakers and Methodists and a few individuals of exceptional influence. There were more Quakers in New Castle and a large number of Methodists in Sussex, but Kent was the home of influential members of both denominations. Richard Bassett, a Methodist convert who had a home in Dover, freed all his slaves, as did John Dickinson, who had close ties to the Quakers, though not himself a member of meeting. Many of the farms owned by Bassett and Dickinson were outside Kent, but Warner Mifflin, a Quaker from Camden, then called Mifflin's Cross Roads, and the most active of Delaware abolitionists, maintained a close connection with his Kent home to the end of his life. His influence, however, extended over a large area, for Mifflin traveled widely, particularly to urge his abolitionist views on Quaker meetings. He also prepared abolition petitions for legislative bodies, including the Delaware General Assembly and the Congress of the United States. Thanks to his reputation for pacifism during the Revolution, as well as his abolitionist activities, he gained an international reputation before his death in 1798.

Other distinguished Delawareans, including James Tilton, Allen McLane, Caleb Rodney, and Gunning Bedford, Jr., became members of abolition societies that sprang up in Dover, Wilmington, and Georgetown. Yet they never succeeded in bringing Delaware to the final step of adopting an abolition law. Perhaps the state was too much under the sway of the old order to adopt a policy that some citizens would have viewed as a radical step. Even the Quakers who signed an abolition petition in 1794 explained that they requested only gradual emancipation. "We wish not any sudden change in the established order of things," they wrote, "lest by benefitting a part, we should give a shock to the whole."

Some Delawareans attempted to defend slavery, and in the nineteenth century a reaction against abolitionism set in. Statutes were adopted limiting the rights of blacks, including free blacks, in many ways. They were, for example, forbidden to carry firearms, to intermarry with whites, or even to move into Delaware. Since Delaware slaves could not legally be sold out of state, where they were more valuable than at home, a profitable illegitimate business developed in the smuggling of blacks out of Delaware into Maryland for sale in Southern states. Most prominent in this business was a gang of cutthroats led by Patty Cannon from her tavern, strategically located at Reliance, on the state line. Finally arrested in 1829, Patty died in the Georgetown jail after indictment but before trial. Her story is thrillingly recounted in a work of fiction, *The Entailed Hat; or, Patty Cannon's Times*, written by George Alfred Townsend (1841–1914), a native of Sussex County who became famous as a correspondent in the Civil War.

Fears regarding the influence of free blacks, as expressed in the assembly, and that body's failure to pass an abolition law, did not prevent the work of liberation from proceeding gradually in Delaware. Manumission by individual slaveholders was encouraged by the easing of requirements that security be posted when slaves were freed; in 1819 all such requirements were abandoned, though the former owner was still liable for support of an aged or infirm black, a precaution that prevented a hard-hearted owner from abandoning a helpless, elderly slave after profiting from his labors during his physical prime. Besides a significant number of slave owners who freed all their slaves because of a conviction that slaveholding was wrong, there developed a custom of providing in a will for the emancipation of at least some favored slaves and of allowing others to buy their freedom by extra work. This work might mean permission to cultivate a private vegetable patch and sell the produce; in other cases, retired farmers rented out their slaves and allowed them to keep part of the profits of their labor.

Some slaves fled to the North, but in the first fifty years of the new nation it seems likely that more whites than blacks left Delaware. Statistics prove that free blacks found a place for themselves in the economic life of this state, for while the number of slaves declined drastically, the number of free blacks in Delaware rose even faster. Federal census figures are given in table 1 along with the percentage that slaves and free blacks formed of the total Delaware population:

TABLE 1

SLAVES AND FREE BLACKS IN DELAWARE, 1790–1840

Census Year	Slaves	Percentage of Population	Free Blacks	Percentage of Population
1790	8,887	15.9	3,899	6.6
1800	6,153	9.6	8,268	12.9
1820	4,509	6.2	12,958	17.8
1840	2,605	3.3	16,919	21.7

SOURCE: U.S. Census

The proportion of blacks in the total population, which increased steadily through these years (from 21.6% in 1790 to 25.0% in 1840) declined after 1840 because of the large immigration from Europe then underway.

Several Delawareans became well known for their part in helping slaves escape to northern states and Canada (the so-called Underground Railroad). Most famous of these "station agents," as they were called (from the railroad analogy), was Thomas Garrett, a Quaker iron merchant who had moved to Wilmington from his native Pennsylvania in 1822 and is said to have aided approximately three thousand fugitives. Eventually, in 1848, Garrett and John Hunn, a collaborator, were found guilty in federal court of damages against two Maryland slave owners. Though a very heavy fine was assessed against Garrett, he was not deterred. "Judge," he said, addressing Chief Justice Taney of the Supreme Court, who presided at the trial in New Castle while on circuit duty, "thou hast not left me a dollar, but I . . .

Thomas Garrett (1789–1871), abolitionist. Portrait by Bass Otis, 1838. (Courtesy of the Historical Society of Delaware.)

say to thee, and to all in this courtroom, that if anyone knows of a fugitive who wants shelter . . . send him to Thomas Garrett and he will befriend him."

Most of the fugitives Garrett aided apparently came from farther south than Delaware. The demise of slavery in Delaware seemed likely to occur by internal action. However, the devotion of the state to a policy of gradualism, to perpetuation of what could be salvaged of the old order, prolonged the legal existence of slavery.

The War of 1812 and the Federalists

The Federalist party, devoted to the maintenance of the old order, survived the challenge of war in the years 1812–15 better in Delaware than in most other states. Delaware Federalists, like most Federalists elsewhere, were opposed to what they called "Mr. Madison's war." Once the war began, however, they loyally supported the government, and their most distinguished statesman, Senator James A. Bayard, was chosen by the president to be one of his commissioners to negotiate a treaty of peace.

The safety of Delawareans was threatened during the war by a series of raids by the British navy on the Atlantic coast. In March 1813 a British squadron patrolling at the mouth of Delaware Bay threatened to destroy Lewes unless the townspeople sold them provisions. Instead of complying, Delaware authorities prepared to defend Lewes with a force of a thousand men commanded by Samuel B. Davis, a Lewes native and veteran of a long, adventurous career as a French naval officer and a merchant in New Orleans. On April 6 three British vessels began a twenty-two-hour bombardment, but they could not get close enough to Lewes to shell it effectively, and every attempt the British made to land men in the vicinity was repulsed by the Americans. After the shelling was over, Delawareans joked that

> The commander and all his men
> Shot a dog and killed a hen.

As the rhyme indicates, property damage was not great, and none of the defenders of Lewes was killed.

The British naval patrol off Cape Henlopen was more effective in stopping American commerce than it was in its attempt to force the people of Lewes to provide supplies. Occasional British forays inland resulted in destruction of American vessels off Reedy Island, near Duck Creek, on the Mispillion, and up Indian River. In 1813 British raiders in the Chesapeake Bay burned Havre de Grace and attacked settlements at the mouth of the Sassafras, as well as Frenchtown, a landing on the Elk River that was only sixteen miles from New Castle. These attacks led Delawareans to fear that British invaders might suddenly seize the mills on the Brandywine, particularly the du Pont powder mills, but the main British raids in 1814 were on the western shore of the Chesapeake, where British forces successfully marched on Washington but were repulsed when they attacked Baltimore.

A number of Delawareans won distinction in this war, including Dr. James Tilton, a Revolutionary veteran who became surgeon-general of the army, Jacob Jones, physician and naval officer, who captured the British vessel *Frolic,* and Thomas Macdonough, commander of an American flotilla on Lake Champlain that won one of the strategic battles of the war by halting a British invasion in 1814. Complaints about the Democratic-Republican administration's conduct of the war, especially its neglect of the navy and its failure to protect the coast, struck a popular chord of response and strengthened the Federalist opposition.

Although a Republican, Joseph Haslet had been elected governor in 1810, but once the war had begun Delawareans had returned to their Federalist habits, voting against Madison in the presidential election in the fall of 1812 and electing a Federalist to replace Haslet in the gubernatorial election of 1813. Federalist candidates were sent to Congress in 1812 and 1814, the election of the former year being remarkable because for the first time Delaware had two representatives to elect. In that year a new allocation of seats went into effect, based on the 1810 census; and for the ten following years Delaware had two members of the federal House of Representatives, both chosen at large. Reallocation after the 1820 census cost Delaware one of these seats, and since 1823 Delaware has had only one congressman, in addition, of course, to its two senators.

Delaware Federalists deplored the talk of secession that was common among some New Englanders of their party. They also lamented the sectionalism displayed in the Hartford Convention, which proposed constitutional amendments weakening the national government in 1814. Rejecting these proposals as vigorously as they had rejected the states' rights propositions of the Virginia and Kentucky Resolutions of 1798, Delaware Federalists came through the war without any taint of the disloyalty that was charged against the once powerful New England wing of their party.

In 1816 Delaware was one of only three states that supported the Federalist candidate, Rufus King, against James Monroe. Thereafter, the Federalists presented no more presidential candidates, but Delaware continued to elect Federalists in most elections as long as a Federalist ticket was presented. In the early 1820s the Democratic-Republicans won control of the legislature, but in 1823 the Federalists reestablished control and maintained themselves in power until they split into Jackson and Adams factions in 1827. The Federalist regime lasted longer in Delaware than in any other state.

The Development of Manufacturing

Under a veneer of constancy afforded by the continuance of Federalist government, Delaware was undergoing some changes in the early nineteenth century that were important in themselves but even more important in their consequences. These changes were primarily economic, and they involved the development of manufacturing and the improvement of transportation.

Manufacturing in colonial Delaware had decidedly been a secondary pursuit in the life of an agricultural society. Leather was made to clothe the farmer and to provide harness for his horses; lumber was cut and worked to give him shelter and to furnish his home; boats were built to move the products of his farm; and mills were needed to process his grain and prepare it for market.

By 1810 Delaware manufacturing was freeing itself from its dependence on the agricultural community. Grist mills were still the most important industry, but the largest mills in Delaware, those on the Brandywine, had come to be of more than local significance. They were regarded as models of their sort, equipped as they were with the laborsaving devices of Oliver Evans, who was born near Newport and became famous for his inventions of milling machinery, as well as of steam engines.

The Brandywine Mills below Market Street Bridge, with vessels bringing wheat or carrying away flour. Painting by Bass Otis, approximately 1840. (Courtesy of the Historical Society of Delaware.)

The best known of the flour millers were Joseph Tatnall and his son-in-law Thomas Lea, who bought grain in all the surrounding states, transported it to their Brandywine mills in their own sloops, and took the manufactured flour to Philadelphia for export. To protect the excellent reputation of Delaware flour abroad, the legislature in 1796 passed an inspection and grading law "to prevent the exportation of flour not merchantable."

The second most valuable product in 1810 was iron manufactures. Besides five forges in Sussex County, there were several rolling and slitting mills in New Castle County. Nails had been manufactured in Wilmington since at least 1789 because it was easier to take bar iron there and process it to fit local needs than to send elsewhere for iron products.

Gunpowder had assumed an important place among local manufactures by 1810, though the only Delaware powder manufacturer was an immigrant, Eleuthère Irénée du Pont, who had not come to America until 1800. He was the son of a distinguished French writer, political economist, and statesman, Pierre Samuel du Pont, who normally signed himself Du Pont de Nemours because he had represented the city of Nemours in the French assembly of 1789–91. A political liberal, the father had been downcast when his early hopes that the French Revolution would establish a constitutional government, responsive to the people, were blasted by the excesses of the Reign of Terror, leading eventually to a military autocracy under Napoleon. Seeing America as the hope of the future, he had come here with his two sons, of whom the elder, Victor, had previous experience in America in the French diplomatic service.

The du Ponts arrived in America on New Year's Day, 1800, with money to invest on their own behalf and for several European associates, but their first efforts were all failures. The salvation of the family's hopes came through the younger son, known as Irénée, who had once been secretary to the great chemist Lavoisier when he was superintendent of the French national gunpowder factory. Noting that American powder was of inferior quality, Irénée persuaded his father to back him in the establishment of a powder works in 1802 at a place he called the Eleutherian Mills on the Brandywine. He chose this site because (1) it had a constant, dependable flow of water to work the mills; (2) it was close to navigable rivers, which allowed importation of needed materials, like saltpeter and sulphur, and exportation of the finished product; and (3) it lay at a distance from a city, explosions being a constant threat in the powder business and capable of doing especially severe damage if the powder works were located where population was concentrated. Encouraged by his father's friendship with President Jefferson, E. I. du Pont, giving intelligent and unremitting attention to his enterprise, quickly became the leading manufacturer of a product that was in great need in a land with endless forests to be cleared, mines to be dug, and roads and canals to be built.

The site where E. I. du Pont built his first mill had previously been used by Jacob Broom for a textile mill. Broom's mill burned down in 1797, but by 1810 there were three cotton and two woollen mills, all in New Castle County, and their products ranked fourth in value among Delaware manufactures in 1810. Besides production in mills, much cloth was woven at home by housewives and then taken to fulling mills, scattered throughout the state, to be softened.

Paper ranked fifth among manufactures and was made in four mills, one at Newark on White Clay Creek and at least two on the Brandywine. The first and most famous was the mill of Joshua and Thomas Gilpin, erected in 1787 at Kentmere and employing the advanced techniques invented by the Gilpins or copied after English models. After several preliminary disasters, a great flood in 1838 completely destroyed the Gilpin mill, but others remained in production throughout the century.

The War of 1812 and the embargo acts that preceded it proved a great stimulus to manufacturing in Delaware. Old enterprises were enlarged and many new ones, particularly for textiles, were begun, in order to supply the domestic market when it was cut off from its normal supplies of European, especially English, goods. Delaware manufacturers were generally sympathetic to the Democratic-Republican party, partly because the Federalists in Delaware were dominated by downstate agricultural interests. The anti-French prejudices of the Federalists gave the du Ponts a special reason for supporting the party of Du Pont de Nemours's friend Jefferson; Victor du Pont ran successfully for the legislature and served several terms in both the lower house and the state senate as a Democratic-Republican.

When peace came, in 1815, British manufacturers sought to regain their American markets and flooded the country with their goods. Many of the new factories were forced to close, and all the manufacturers became anxious about their future. They began to lobby in Washington for protective tariffs and were enthusiastic supporters of the so-called American System of Henry Clay, for whom a mill village on the Brandywine was named.

The development of manufacturing and intensification of commercial life in Delaware had already led to the establishment of a number of banks. The first was the Bank of Delaware, chartered in 1796, but the next twenty years saw the establishment of many competitors in all parts of the state. The most important of the early banks was the Farmers Bank of the State of Delaware, founded in 1807 as the official state bank. It was modeled on the Bank of the United States, with one-fifth of the stock owned by the state and the remainder by private investors. Dover was the home of the main office of the Farmers Bank, but it had branches in Georgetown and New Castle, the other county seats. Before long, another branch was opened in Wilmington.

The Transportation Revolution

So many innovations occurred in modes of transportation in the first half of the nineteenth century that this period has been called the era of a transportation revolution. Among the first manifestations of these innovations in Delaware was the construction of new roads and bridges, both primarily built by private, limited-liability companies incorporated, like banks, by the General Assembly. The Brandywine Bridge Company, incorporated in 1806, constructed a new bridge across the Brandywine at the head of navigation without opposition, but bridges across the Christina at Wilmington and Newport were vigorously opposed by merchants upstream, who thought navigation would be hindered, and by other people who felt they would suffer by a diversion of traffic from its customary path.

Private companies at the same time began to build improved roads, called turnpikes because a toll was charged for their use and only on its payment was a bar (or pikestaff) across the road raised out of the way. Beginning in 1808, a number of turnpike companies were chartered, like the Gap and Newport Company, which constructed a road leading toward Lancaster, Pennsylvania. Only heavy use could repay investors; consequently, all of the Delaware turnpikes were in New Castle County, where improved land transportation was needed to aid traffic between farms in the interior and the ports of Wilmington and New Castle, or to assist in the passage of men and goods between the Delaware and the Chesapeake, as the New Castle and Frenchtown Turnpike did.

New Castle, despite transfer of the capital to Dover, had a kind of renascence after the Revolution. As maritime trade increased, its importance as a stopping place for ocean shipping bound to and from Philadelphia also grew, and so did its role in the north-south traffic between Philadelphia and Baltimore. The road from New Castle to Frenchtown, on the Elk River, was improved by a turnpike company in the second decade of the nineteenth century. At the same time, steamboats were employed in regular service from Philadelphia to New Castle and, at the other end of the turnpike, from Frenchtown to Baltimore.

The first steamboat making regular runs on the Delaware was built by John Fitch and put in service between Wilmington,

The New Castle waterfront, approximately 1825. The courthouse, the town hall, Immanuel Church spire, stage coaches, and a paddle- wheel steamboat are visible. Painting by Robert Shaw after an earlier work by an unknown artist. (Courtesy of the Historical So- ciety of Delaware.)

Philadelphia, and Burlington, New Jersey, in 1790, but it was not until over twenty years later that steamboats proved them- selves economically in the river trade. After the War of 1812, they gradually replaced sailboats on the river, and packet lines with fixed schedules connected the small towns downstate (and in New Jersey) with Philadelphia.

Parallel to the New Castle and Frenchtown Turnpike, but some miles to the south, a water route was built between the Delaware River and a branch of the Elk. This was the Chesa- peake and Delaware Canal, constructed in the years 1824–29, al- though an abortive beginning had been made earlier. As in the case of the turnpikes, the canal was the work of a private com- pany. Under its first president, Joseph Tatnall, the Brandywine miller, this company originally intended to connect the Elk River with the Christina River and in 1804 began construction of a feeder canal that would bring water from the upper Elk to the middle stretches of the main canal at Glasgow. In a year, how- ever, the company's funds were exhausted, and all construction stopped until 1824, when stock subscriptions by the states of Maryland, Delaware, and Pennsylvania and by the United States government allowed work to be resumed.

Henlopen Lighthouse and the Maritime Exchange signal station at Cape Henlopen, with the Delaware Breakwater in the background. From David B. Tyler, The Bay and River Delaware (Cambridge, Md., 1955). (Courtesy of John T. Purnell, Georgetown.)

The canal was eventually built on a different route from that originally planned. Its Delaware terminus was below New Castle, and in Maryland it entered Back Creek, a tributary of the Elk. New towns, Delaware City and Chesapeake City, for which great expectations were held, were constructed at the terminal locks on either side of the peninsula. The new route had been recommended by army engineers, who were influenced to avoid the Christina by the bridges built at Wilmington and Newport since the initial plans had been made. They were also choosing a more direct route to the Delaware and, perhaps incidentally, pleasing the principal sponsors of the canal, Philadelphia merchants who wished to use it as a way of diverting central Pennsylvania products floated down the Susquehanna River from going to Baltimore but had no desire to develop another rival port at Wilmington in the process. The Chesapeake and Delaware Canal continued to operate as a private corporation until 1919, when the federal government purchased it and moved the main terminus to Reedy Point, two miles south of Delaware City, while enlarging and deepening the canal and removing the locks to fit it for ocean shipping. Thereafter, its main importance was in giving Baltimore a shorter connection than before to Philadelphia and, via Delaware Bay, to New York and to ports in western Europe.

One of the most costly early federal public works projects authorized by Congress was the great stone breakwater constructed in 1829–35 in Delaware Bay off Lewes to provide ocean shipping a safe refuge from storms. Costing several million dol-

lars, the original breakwater, which was designed by William
Strickland, Philadelphia architect and engineer, served its purpose well for several decades until silting reduced the water
depth of the artificial harbor and necessitated construction of
an outer breakwater a mile and one-half long, forming a new
harbor of refuge.

The canal and the breakwater were of more importance to
neighboring states than to Delaware. Far more important to
Delaware were the railroads constructed in the mid-century, beginning with the New Castle and Frenchtown, which began
operations in 1831 and soon replaced the stage line on the turnpike between the same places. When opened, the New Castle
and Frenchtown Railroad used coaches pulled by horses, but
in 1832 a steam locomotive was imported from England in pieces,
and assembled at New Castle for use on the line.

A longer and more important railroad was constructed a few
years later, linking Wilmington with Philadelphia to the northeast and Baltimore to the southwest. Completed in 1838, this
railroad bypassed New Castle, which soon lost its importance as
a transit point. Wilmington, on the other hand, gained new advantages for manufacturing by the possibilities the railroad
opened for exporting its products and acquiring raw materials—
and fuel too—after railroad connections were developed in the
1840s to the coal mines of Maryland and Pennsylvania.

The railroad initiated the third phase—and third century—in
the history of Wilmington. In the first phase, from 1638 to the
1730s, it had been a tiny Swedish hamlet in the wilderness. In
the second phase, beginning in the 1730s, it became a busy port
and market town. In the third phase, Wilmington was gradually
transformed into a manufacturing city, as a row of factories appeared beside the new railroad tracks, especially where they lay
close to the Christina.

Another important railroad running the length of Delaware
was projected in the 1830s by the leading Delaware statesman
of the period, John M. Clayton, but a depression in 1839 inter-
fered with its construction, which was not undertaken until more
than a decade later.

The Foundation of Public Schools

Through these years of significant economic development,

there was another innovation in Delaware life that would be of great importance in the future. This was the establishment of a public school system, created by a statute of 1829. This first school law was very weak and quite inadequate in itself to insure schools for all children, but it was an important step in the direction of universal education.

There had previously been no public schools in Delaware. Traditionally, from Swedish times, the church bore a responsibility for education, but ministers seldom had time to provide even a basic education in reading and writing. The Friends, who had no clergy, felt it of basic importance that every member of their society should be able to read the Scriptures for himself; therefore, wherever their numbers warranted, they established an elementary school for both boys and girls. Only one of their schools in Delaware, the Wilmington Friends School, survives today, but, dating back at least to 1740, it is the oldest school in Delaware.

Before 1829 a large minority of Delawareans were illiterate. Most slaves received no schooling, and only in Wilmington, beginning. in approximately 1799, were there any schools for free blacks. Women were also likely to receive little or no education, though in some elementary schools girls were admitted on the same terms as boys.

Many early teachers were clergymen, who supplemented their meager salaries by teaching. Other, nonclerical teachers established schools by renting a room and seeking paying pupils. In the countryside a group of neighbors would sometimes join efforts in constructing a one-room schoolhouse in a convenient location and then hire a teacher whom they would in turn provide with board and room.

The best and most advanced schools in Delaware were the academies, generally incorporated and conducted by a hired staff supervised by a board of trustees. The two most distinguished of these institutions were the Newark Academy, incorporated in 1769 but founded in 1743 in New London, Pennsylvania, by Francis Alison, a Presbyterian minister, and the Wilmington Academy, built in 1765 and incorporated in 1773. An academy probably existed in Lewes at an even earlier date, and eventually academies were founded in most of the towns in Delaware.

Both the Wilmington and Newark academies had aspirations toward college status and made some tentative steps toward becoming colleges in fact or in name. Their development, however, was deterred by the obvious need for basic education for the majority. The constitution of 1792 recognized this need and provided for the legislature to establish schools "as soon as conveniently may be," but the Federalist assemblymen did not find a convenient time for many years. One step in this direction was taken in 1796 by a statute ordering the income from marriage and tavern licenses to be placed in a school fund; however, no educational appropriations were made from this fund until 1817, when a charitable grant of one thousand dollars was appropriated to each county to be distributed among the hundreds for the education of poor children. A further grant of up to twenty cents for each child taught was provided in 1821 to help support Sunday schools, which were not schools of religion then but schools that taught reading and writing to children who had to labor on the farm or elsewhere six days a week.

Octagonal Schoolhouse at Cowgill's Corner, near Leipsic. Built in 1836 as one of the first schools constructed under the 1829 School Law, it was reopened as a museum in 1971. (Courtesy of the Division of Historical and Cultural Affairs.)

This meager public aid was augmented by the School Law of 1829, written by Judge Willard Hall, a native of Massachusetts and graduate of Harvard who had come to Delaware in his youth to practice law. An active Democrat-Republican, he had served in Congress and been Delaware secretary of state before being awarded for his party loyalty and his ability by appointment as federal district judge in 1823. In the almost fifty years that remained of his long life, he utilized all his spare time on behalf of a number of public causes he championed, such as thrift, temperance, Sabbatarianism, and especially public education.

Hall's School Law of 1829 was by no means an ideal system. It divided Delaware into a large number of school districts and offered to match any sum up to three hundred dollars that a district might raise for public instruction. A district might raise —by tax or by gift—much more than three hundred dollars, or it might raise nothing at all. It could have a good school, a poor school, or no school, as it chose.

Weak as the law was, it was a beginning. The responsibility that the legislature recognized in 1829 led to increased provision for public education in the future. The octagonal school house at Cowgill's Corner, near Dover, built in 1836 and today maintained by the state as a museum, remains as an example of the many schools founded by local districts under the law of 1829.

Once a public school law had been passed, the General Assembly was receptive to the idea of turning Newark Academy into a college. Newark College received a charter in 1833 and opened the following year. A state lottery financed construction of the first building (Old College Hall) despite objections to this form of gambling voiced by the Rev. Eliphalet Wheeler Gilbert, a Presbyterian minister who was the first president of the new college. Although the name was changed to Delaware College in 1843, the school did not receive any regular state aid. Consequently, after flourishing for a brief period when it enjoyed the services of several remarkably good scholars on its small faculty, the college came upon hard times and was forced to close in 1859, its financial troubles magnified as a result of a murder during a student fracas in Old College Hall in 1858. The closing lasted for eleven years, until after friends of the college persuaded the legislature to name it as the state land-grant college and as the recipient of aid from the federal government in the form of warrants for public lands in the West.

The Whig Party and the Constitution of 1831

Judge Hall's success in getting a school law through the legislature in 1829 probably owed something to the reorganization of political parties that had occurred in the previous decade. While secretary of state to a Democratic-Republican governor in 1822, Hall had proposed establishment of a public school system, but he was then unable to get the necessary support either from his own party or from the Federalists. By 1829 political changes had occurred that left the Delaware legislature willing to adopt the educational proposal of an erstwhile Yankee lawyer.

These political changes had been slow in coming to Delaware because of the remarkable longevity of the Federalist party in this state. The election of John Quincy Adams to the presidency by the House of Representatives in 1825, when no candidate had a majority in the electoral college, precipitated a struggle to reverse this verdict by supporters of Andrew Jackson, who had led Adams in the electoral college vote. The inability of Delaware Federalists to agree which candidate to support divided them into a Jackson party and an Adams party in 1827, when a special congressional election was held. Leaders of the old Democratic-Republican opposition in Delaware also split on this issue and took sides with one or the other of the two new parties, which soon replaced the old party divisions.

One important figure in this political crisis was Louis McLane, a Federalist who had won an unprecedented (and still unequaled) record—for Delaware—of six straight elections to the House of Representatives, where, despite his party affiliation, he had become chairman of the important Ways and Means Committee before being elevated, in 1827, to the Senate. McLane led a group of Delaware Federalists into the new Jackson party and for his loyalty was appointed, successively, minister to Great Britain, secretary of the treasury, and secretary of state after Jackson became president in 1829. His former law clerk, James A. Bayard, the younger, followed McLane into the Jackson party, which soon became known as the Democratic party. So did Henry M. Ridgely, of Dover, a former congressman who was elected to the Senate with McLane in 1827.

Another wing of the Delaware Federalists supported the Adams Administration and opposed Jackson, both before and after his election. By 1834 these men became known as *Whigs,* a term that identified opponents of royal autocracy, in this case the "reign" of "King Andrew." Thomas Clayton (son of Governor Joshua Clayton) and his younger cousin, John Middleton Clayton, were leaders of this party. The names of two other prominent Whigs indicate how families were sometimes split by political sectionalism, for Richard H. Bayard, a brother of James A. Bayard, the younger, and John Jones Milligan, a brother-in-law of Louis McLane, both joined the anti-Jackson party.

This schism within the Federalist leadership may have been carried into the body of the party, but election results do not indicate that it was. On the contrary, elections in Delaware in the 1830s and 1840s very much paralleled those of earlier years. One party had solid control of Kent and Sussex and with its majorities in these two counties, controlled the General Assembly and, with a few rare exceptions, elected its candidates for governor, senator, and representative in Congress for two decades. The other party controlled New Castle County but seemed condemned to being in a perpetual minority in the state as a whole.

The Delaware Whigs, controlling both Kent and Sussex, and thereby the state, were the heirs of the Delaware Federalists, despite the loss of some of the old leaders. To counter this loss, the Whigs received an infusion of new strength, winning the support of most of the Brandywine manufacturers, including the du Ponts, by their advocacy of the policies of Henry Clay, the national Whig leader. Support of a protective tariff, of internal improvements (aid to roads, railroads, canals, and the improvement of rivers and harbors), and of a national bank (to help provide a stable currency) appealed to the descendants and successors of millers who had once (like Clay himself) been supporters of Thomas Jefferson.

The major figure in Delaware politics through these decades of the Whig supremacy was John M. Clayton, who was probably, in terms of party leadership, the most successful politician in Delaware history. Born in Dagsboro in 1796 and reared in Milford, he was graduated from Yale College with honors and then studied at the famous Litchfield, Connecticut, law school, where forty judges, ten governors, and fifteen United States senators were trained. While still in his twenties, he became Delaware secretary of state, and he was a United States senator when only thirty-three. Subsequently, he was elected three more times to the Senate, was chief justice of Delaware, and was secretary of state of the United States from 1849 to 1851. His home,

Buena Vista, is maintained by the state of Delaware, to which it was given by his collateral descendant, Governor (and Senator) Clayton Douglass Buck.

Clayton's ability at politics depended not only on his native intelligence and his education but also upon his intimate acquaintance with many Delawareans from all walks of life and all parts of the state, from his native Sussex, from Dover, where he lived in his middle years, and from New Castle County, where he resided near the end of his life. The untimely deaths of his wife and his two sons left him a lonely and somewhat broken man in his last years, though he still played an important role in Delaware politics. It was said that in his prime such were his friendships and such his courtesy in greeting people who approached him that it could take him an hour just to walk across Dover Green.

Clayton was the most influential member of a constitutional convention held in the fall of 1831, though a former governor, Charles Polk, was its president. The changes made in the constitution by this convention were relatively few except in the constitution of the law courts. Dissatisfaction with provisions for nine state judges had been a major reason for the calling of this convention. Complaining that it was impossible to find nine well-qualified judges, the New Castle delegates urged adoption of a three-judge system, with one resident judge in each county and no other judges of state courts. Sussex County was entirely satisfied with the existing nine-judge system, arguing that ordinary citizens were competent to serve as judges, even if they were not trained lawyers. The convention, however, adopted a compromise plan supported by Clayton, who was representing Kent County; his plan called for five judges, consisting of the chancellor, the chief justice, and three associate justices, each resident in a different county.

Another change provided by the constitution of 1831 was the substitution of biennial for annual elections, though the latter had been the rule since colonial days. Willingness to accept this change and to have the General Assembly meet only once in two years indicates a growing faith in the executive branch of the government, which was being trusted to govern for an increased period without legislative supervision.

The governor's term was extended to four years and so were the terms of state senators, while members of the lower house were henceforth to have two-year terms. Sheriffs and coroners had their terms shortened from four years to two and were to be directly elected, the double-nomination system being abandoned at last.

More important, the convention adopted a proposal of Clayton that made calling any subsequent constitutional convention very difficult, because a special election or referendum was required to be devoted to the single issue of calling a convention, and approval had to be given by a majority of the voters who had gone to the polls in the most popular of the three latest elections. The advantage of this provision to Clayton and others like him was that no new constitutional convention was likely to be called except in the case of an overwhelming public demand for it. Clayton felt that after three constitutional conventions in only fifty-five years, it was time to stop tinkering with the fundamental laws. Amendments were possible, but wholesale change through a convention was made very difficult.

Though the legislature that called the 1831 convention recommended submitting its results to the people's approval, this convention acted like its predecessors in 1776 and 1791–92. The new constitution, adopted unanimously by the convention, was simply declared to be the law of the state.

New Castle County had wanted more changes than the dominant downstate counties would permit, and it is likely that provisions making a new convention difficult were aimed at preventing New Castle from attempting to upset the status quo. The growth of Wilmington had occasioned some substantial amendments in its borough charter in 1809; twenty-three years later, in 1832, the legislature gave Wilmington a new charter as a city with a mayor and twelve councilmen in place of the old borough government. It is significant that the Wilmington council submitted the new charter to the voters, who signified their approval. In the first third of the nineteenth century, several other Delaware communities received charters from the legislature: Milford, in 1807; Smyrna, in 1817; Lewes, in 1818; Laurel, in 1827; and Dover, in 1829.

7

A Troubled Decade

Fall of the Whigs

The year 1850 marks the end of the period when the Whigs dominated Delaware politics. At the beginning of that year, the greatest of the Delaware Whigs, John M. Clayton, was a notable figure on the national scene as secretary of state under President Zachary Taylor. The congressional delegation from Delaware was solidly Whig, and the state legislature, as usual, was controlled by the Whigs of Kent and Sussex, despite the continued presence of a bloc of Democrats representing New Castle County.

The death of President Taylor in the summer of 1850 and the resultant dismissal of Clayton by Taylor's successor mark a reversal in Whig fortunes. The new president, Millard Fillmore, lacked the charismatic appeal of the old military hero, Taylor, or of the aged Whig favorite, Henry Clay. Nor was the veteran Clayton the vigorous, responsive leader he had been in the late 1820s, when he had seized control of the remnants of Delaware Federalism from the faction led by Louis McLane.

During Clayton's absence in Washington and his necessary preoccupation with national affairs, no new Whig leadership emerged in Delaware to keep the Whig political machine functioning successfully. There were movements afoot, such as abolitionism, temperance, and nativism, that were disruptive of old party ties, but in Delaware—and in the nation as a whole—the Democrats withstood these movements more successfully than did the Whigs.

Advocates of temperance in the use of alcoholic beverages accused both parties, with reason, of using the attraction of free liquor to gain an audience for their political rallies. As early as 1839 a Temperance party ran candidates in a Wilmington city

THREE U.S. SECRETARIES OF STATE FROM DELAWARE

Louis McLane (1784-1857), secretary of state under Jackson, 1833-34. Portrait attributed to John F. Francis but also to William E. West. Gift of Mrs. George F. Batchelder, Jr., to the University of Delaware. (Courtesy of the University of Delaware.)

John M. Clayton (1796–1856), secretary of state under Taylor, 1849–50. Engraving, approximately 1849. (Courtesy of the Historical Society of Delaware.)

Thomas F. Bayard (1828–1898), secretary of state under Cleveland, 1885–89. (Courtesy of the Historical Society of Delaware.)

election, and in 1850 a state Temperance party ran candidates'
for the governorship, for Congress, and for the legislature, and
apparently, they took more votes from the Whigs than from the
Democrats.

Abolitionists were also making themselves heard. In 1847 an
abolition bill barely failed to be adopted in the legislature, being
rejected only by the casting vote of the speaker in the Senate
after passing the lower house. Unfortunately, however, the near
success of this abolition bill may have set up a backlash against
its advocates as disturbers of the status quo. Some feelings of
this sort seem to have arisen against the Northern Whigs who
supported provisions that were a part of the Compromise of 1850
to limit the extension of slavery into western territories.

In general, Delawareans, being strongly unionist, favored
compromise measures, but on this occasion the Democrats seem
to have been able to make a virtue of their opposition to compromise, and in the election of 1850 they swept to unprecedented
successes in Delaware, winning control of the legislature and
the one seat in Congress, as well as retaining the governorship,
which they had carried in 1846.

Their success allowed the Democrats to send James A. Bayard,
the younger, to the United States Senate, where he was soon to
become one of the leading members, as his father, the distinguished Federalist, had been in the early years of the century.
Success also allowed the Democrats to gratify a popular movement
for a constitutional convention, as they promised to do in their
1850 election slogan of "Ross, Riddle, and Reform," William
Ross and James Riddle being the Democratic candidates for
governor and congressman, and "Reform" meaning constitutional revision.

The Constitutional Convention of 1852–53

The movement for constitutional revision that led to the
election of a convention in 1852 was rooted in the democratic
ferment of the Jacksonian period. Delaware reformers called
for the abandonment of such aristocratic elements in political
life as life tenure for judges and property requirements both for
voting and for membership in the state senate. There was also
demand for a gubernatorial veto (Democrats being supporters of
Jackson's use of the presidential veto), for the election of all

public officials, and for single legislative districts to replace the countywide tickets that had usually permitted the Whigs (and the Federalists before them) to choose two-thirds of both houses of the assembly by their pluralities in Kent and Sussex. New Castle County, the Democratic stronghold, having grown rapidly in the last two decades, was also agitating for increased representation in the legislature.

In setting in motion machinery for constitutional reform, the Delaware Democrats of the early 1850s probably exhibited the last signs of whatever reforming spirit had motivated them in the days of Andrew Jackson. The progress of reform, however, was greatly hampered by the constitutional provision adopted in 1831 recommending that a call for a constitutional convention be supported by a majority of all qualified voters at a special election in May (when no other issues, like elections for vacant offices, might help draw voters to the polls). The Democrats refused to be hamstrung by this requirement. They argued that the people had an inalienable right to a government of their own choosing and that the constitution, in its own words, merely prescribed "an unexceptionable mode" of ascertaining the popular will. Therefore they set not a time in May but a date in November 1851 for a referendum on calling a convention.

The result of this referendum was a decisive majority for a convention, in the state as a whole and in each county. Disregarding Whig complaints that the majority for the convention was far from a majority of the qualified voters, as demonstrated by the vote in recent general elections, the Democratic legislature pressed on to provide for the election of convention delegates in November 1852. In doing so, they disregarded another provision of the 1831 constitution, for instead of calling for the election of delegates in the same manner—that is, by a countywide ticket —in which legislators were elected, the Democrats provided for the election of delegates by hundreds. Ten delegates were to represent each county, which was easy to arrange in New Castle and Sussex because they each had ten hundreds, but in Kent, which had only six hundreds, four of them were allowed to elect two delegates apiece.

Accustomed to being the minority party in Delaware, the Democrats doubted their ability to repeat their 1850 victory and thought election by hundreds would give them some downstate delegates and break up the Whig machine in Kent and Sussex that usually had produced a solid majority of Whig representatives. But the election turned out otherwise. Hundred representation destroyed the solid Whig blocs from Kent and Sussex, but it also broke the Democratic control of New Castle, where the Whigs carried seven of the ten hundreds. In all, the Whigs won eighteen convention seats, easily a majority of the total of thirty.

When the convention met in December 1852, it did so in strange circumstances, with a party opposed to its ever being called in control. Three Whig delegates from New Castle County announced their refusal to participate in a convention they regarded as unconstitutional, but the majority, adjourning to March 1853, refused to be deterred from drafting a new constitution. In the proceedings, sectional loyalties were more important than party affiliations, but it was clear from the first that the delegates could not expect the easy public acquiescence in their conclusions that had followed the drafting of the constitutions of 1776, 1792, and 1831, all accepted without submission to popular vote—and without significant opposition.

To add to other difficulties that the new constitution would face, bitter feeling grew out of the efforts of Senator James Bayard, a resident of Wilmington, to reallocate representation so as to recognize the growth his city had experienced since 1830, as well as to provide for future reallocation of seats in single-member districts that would change their boundaries after every census in order to preserve a rough equality in numbers.

Bayard's proposal frightened rural Delawareans, who recognized that the population of Wilmington had grown by 67 percent (from 8,367 to 13,979) between 1840 and 1850, while the state outside Wilmington had grown in population by only 11 percent (from 69,718 to 77,553). If this trend continued and Bayard's proposal was adopted to adjust the allocation of legislative seats to fit a new distribution of population, the locus of political power in Delaware was likely to shift radically, to the advantage of the Wilmington Democrats.

But Bayard's proposal was not adopted. Nor was a proposal to divide New Castle County in two. Instead, the convention adopted a compromise, retaining equal representation in the state senate for each county and establishing a modest proportional representation in the house, with ten representatives allocated to New Castle County, nine to Sussex, and eight to Kent. No provision was made for reallocation to meet population changes in the future.

Since New Castle County had, by the 1850 census, almost 47 percent of the population of Delaware, this allocation did not satisfy Senator Bayard. (He could not know that it was, nevertheless, more nearly proportional than any apportionment in Delaware would be for the next hundred years.) Consequently, Bayard turned against the new constitution and urged its defeat in October 1853, when it was presented to the people in an unprecedented public referendum.

While Bayard and the Wilmington Democrats complained that the new constitution accomplished too little, specifically in not realizing their expectation of a more democratic apportionment, John M. Clayton and many of his Whig supporters protested that it did too much—and was unconstitutional besides. No wonder, then, with their ablest leaders in opposition, that the people of Delaware decisively rejected the proposed constitution (4,876 to 2,717), with every county (though not every hundred) voting against it.

The democratic features of the new constitution—the more nearly proportional allocation of seats, the election of many officials previously appointed, including judges, the abolition of life tenures, the easing of the method of amendment and of calling a convention, the abolition of property qualifications for voting and for holding office—did not suffice to rally support and may even have produced a strengthened conservative opposition. It is interesting to note that James Bayard, leader of the Democrats, who called for the representation in the legislature of men, rather than land, sought constitutional provisions forbidding the abolition of slavery and the immigration of free blacks. He was accused of seeking friends in Sussex County for his reapportionment program, but his provisions regarding slavery and black immigration were rejected, primarily through the opposition of two Whigs, Daniel Corbit, an Odessa Quaker, and Truston P. McColley, a Milford merchant who was a Methodist local preacher.

The American Party

Even Senator Bayard, while seeking to prevent any future legislature from passing an abolition bill, conceded that slavery could not be expected to last long in Delaware. The number of slaves had fallen to 2,290 in 1850 and, through voluntary emancipation, was falling still further, as the 1860 census, revealing a remnant of only 1,798 slaves, demonstrated. But Bayard was worried by the number of free blacks in Delaware (19,829 by 1860, which was 18 percent of the total population), the largest percentage of free blacks, it was said, in any state. He hoped to reduce this number gradually by voluntary colonization of blacks, in Africa or elsewhere.

Though there was little outright abolition sentiment in either of the old Delaware political parties, the Whigs were more disturbed by the slavery issue than were the Democrats. There was, however, another issue raised in the 1850s that the Whigs embraced with real fervor. This was nativism, a movement to exalt the native-born American, along with his attitudes and beliefs, and to view with alarm the great number of European immigrants who had been entering the United States in the last two decades. A great many of these immigrants were Catholics, and the nativist frenzy of the 1840s and 1850s was essentially an anti-Catholic movement, directed against Catholic Irish and German immigrants in particular.

The Whigs of Delaware, rooted in the rural areas, where there were few immigrant Irish or Germans to consider, entered the new movement with fervor. At its heart was a secret lodge, the Patriotic Order of the Star-Spangled Banner, whose members were called Know-Nothings because of the negative response they gave to inquiries about their organization. The wider impact of the movement was made through its political arm, the American party, to which the Whigs gave way in the Delaware election of 1854, a year in which it seemed likely that the Americans, or Know-Nothings, would soon replace the Whigs as the chief national opposition to the Democrats.

Nativism had considerable popularity in Delaware. Probably the growth of Wilmington and Senator Bayard's efforts in 1853 to recognize this growth by a redress of the political balance in the legislature raised a specter of growing immigrant power to frighten Delawareans of native birth and ancestry. Much of Wilmington's growth consisted of Irish laborers, come to take any jobs available in the shipyards and mills along the banks of the Christina River and beside the tracks of the Philadelphia, Wilmington, and Baltimore Railroad. But Irish immigrants were not confined to Wilmington. They had been a significant part of the labor employed in digging the Chesapeake and Delaware Canal in the 1820s and in clearing the roadbed and laying the tracks of the P.W. & B. in the 1830s. When these construction projects were completed, they settled in the vicinity wherever they could find employment, at the Du Pont mills or others on the Brandywine and in the tiny mill villages that began to proliferate in otherwise rural areas of New Castle County. And where they settled, churches soon appeared.

The American party in 1854 promised to oppose foreign influence at home and abroad, to extend the five-year period required for naturalization, to deny aliens the right to vote or hold office, to prevent the immigration of paupers or criminals, to oppose "homestead" bills offering free lands in the west, and, in a plank intended to refer to Roman Catholics, "to trust no sect with a public office which recognizes the power of a foreign potentate as superior to our own laws." Most of the old Whigs of Delaware rallied to the American party because its campaign against foreign influence offered them a national, rather than a sectional, issue. Preservation of the Union was an important issue to Delawareans, who were eager to ignore divisive sectionalism.

The Democrats, smarting from the wounds they suffered in their unsuccessful quest for constitutional reform in 1853, were demoralized at the next election, all the more so because there was no presidential contest to give them a national candidate to rally around. As a consequence, the Americans swept Delaware in 1854, carrying all three counties and electing both a congressman and a governor.

In only two years, however, the American party had moved from triumph to disaster. One reason for the quick decline of the Know-Nothings was their identification with an unpopular prohibition law that they passed in 1855. This attempt to enforce total abstinence upon Delawareans was particularly unpopular because anyone who could afford it was able to buy all the liquor he wanted by crossing the state line. Moreover, the fear of immigrant power, particularly insofar as it was spurred by lurid tales of imagined Catholic conspiracies, proved difficult to maintain, at least at the pitch of excitement needed to support the pretensions of the American party. At the next election the Democrats charged back, aided by the appeal of a presidential candidate, James Buchanan, from neighboring Lancaster County, Pennsylvania. The brief flirtation of Delaware with political nativism ended as abruptly as it had begun; the Democrats in 1856 captured every hundred in New Castle County and all but a few hundreds, where the Americans inherited basic Whig strength, in Kent and Sussex.

After this defeat, the opposition party changed its name once again. Now no longer willing to be known as Know-Nothings, they reorganized under the name of the People's party, winning some dissatisfied Democrats to their ranks. They still had a nativist tinge, but in this regard their emphasis now was on preventing the immigration of criminals and paupers. Their true reason for existence was to furnish an opposition to the Democrats, but their chief theme was devotion to the Union, a cause that had had a demonstrated appeal to Delawareans since the days of Washington. They straddled the issue of slavery extension in the West by supporting popular sovereignty in the territories. To Delawareans this position was more popular than the adamant opposition to expansion of slavery espoused by another new party, the Republicans, who were nevertheless allied to the People's party by their advocacy of protective tariffs.

In 1858 the People's party showed strength but lost the election—by only 203 votes in the gubernatorial race. In 1860, however, national developments gave the new party a unique opportunity in the Delaware state elections.

The Northern Connection

The approach of the presidential election of 1860 and the increasing emotionalism of a sectional crisis found Delaware indelibly welded to the Union. There was genuine sympathy for the South in this state that shared its longest boundaries with rural Maryland, which, like the South, had a basically agricultural society and tolerated at least the remnant of slavery. But there was also strong and growing socioeconomic connection to the North, which provided a realistic base to the sentimental attachment of the First State to the Union.

In the decade before 1860, the population of Delaware grew considerably, and the growth was such as to emphasize the Northern connection. The total population growth of 22.6 percent was higher than recorded in any other decade before or since until the 1950s. The most rapid growth by far was exhibited by the city of Wilmington, where the population increased by more than 52 percent between 1850 and 1860. By the latter year Wilmington's population was 21,258, a figure that just twenty years earlier would have been comparable to the population of one of the counties. Nineteen percent of the people of Wilmington were foreign-born, a majority of them Irish, with Germans and English trailing in that order. Though this is not as high a percentage of immigrants as in Philadelphia (where 29 percent were foreign-born) or New York (where the proportion of foreign-born was 48 percent), Wilmington was no longer of importance as a port of entry and had to draw its immigrant population away from the major ports.

The rapidity of the growth in the immigrant population of Delaware, an increase of 87 percent since 1850, is more surprising than the absolute numbers, though they do mean that one in every five persons in Wilmington was an immigrant, and one in every eight was born in Ireland. In view of the latter ratio, it is not surprising that this period saw the flourishing of the first Catholic school in Delaware. The founder was Father Patrick Reilly, assistant rector of St. Peter's, Wilmington. In about 1837 he began to conduct a school for boys, which was so successful that in 1847 he enlarged his ambitions for the school and secured a charter for it as St. Mary's College. Apparently only one college class, that of 1850, was graduated with degrees, but the school continued to function successfully, despite anti-Catholic pressure on the legislature to cancel the charter. Father Reilly's chief interest was the education of boys of about eight to fourteen years of age, though his school, housed in a new four-story building with facilities for two hundred boarders, attracted some older students. Though the school was an advantage to Wilmingtonians, the boys came from many states, with always a sizable Latin-American (chiefly Cuban) contingent. After 1859, when Father Reilly was required to start a church, also called St. Mary's (dedicated by the Bishop of Philadelphia, canonized in 1977 as St. John Neumann), on the east side of Wilmington, where the Irish were settling, he had too little time for his school, which closed in 1866. For a few years the Visitation nuns conducted a girls school in the building.

Though the growth in the percentage of the foreign-born in Wilmington and indeed in the whole of New Castle County is statistically impressive, there were other elements in the growth of population in Delaware that may have been more significant. One of these elements was the reversal of the long-term movement of Delawareans out of the state. Though the population had been increasing almost constantly throughout the nineteenth century, this was due to the excess of births over deaths, for more people had been leaving to make their fortunes elsewhere than had been entering Delaware. In the 1840s this trend was reversed, and more migrants came to Delaware than left. Since no other factors are known to account for this trend, it seems likely that economic opportunities in Delaware were more attractive in the 1850s than they had been in past decades.

According to the 1860 census, the larger part of the people who had come from elsewhere to settle in Delaware were not foreign immigrants, but native Americans, born in other states. The largest single group of these, the natives of Pennsylvania, outnumbered the Irish-born Delawareans of 1860 by 7,852 to 5,832. Natives of Maryland, 5,110, were close behind. But in view of the comparatively great length of the Delaware-Maryland boundaries and the long tradition of an exodus into Delaware from the Eastern Shore, it is surprising that the migration from Pennsylvania was larger than that from Maryland. It is also worth noting that more Delawareans came from other Northern states, such as New Jersey (1,877), New York (456), and Massachusetts (216), than from Virginia (171) or other Southern states. These statistics refer to the state of birth, and since many of the foreign immigrants may have worked in the neighborhood of Philadelphia or New York, where they landed, before coming to Delaware, it seems evident that the connection of Delaware to the Northern states was being strengthened by a human factor.

Wilmington, only twenty-seven miles from Philadelphia, always had a Northern orientation, and since colonial times the Delaware River had served to connect much of Delaware to Philadelphia. In the 1850s, however, another connective to Philadelphia was being supplied in the shape of the Delaware Railroad, built southward from Wilmington and New Castle through Dover and Seaford to the southern boundary with Maryland, which it reached at Delmar in 1859. Avoiding the coastal marshes, the railroad kept inland and, by its course, opened up a part of the state that had been hitherto sparsely settled or, as in the case of Seaford and Laurel, that had hitherto found it easier to send produce to the Chesapeake Bay, by streams like the Nanticoke, than to the Delaware.

The railroad, pointing directly toward Philadelphia and, beyond it, New York, offered Delaware farmers new opportunities to send their produce to the growing markets of these cities, just as the Baltimore and Ohio Railroad, which had reached Cumberland in 1846 and Wheeling in 1852, gave a similar opportunity to reach a Baltimore market to the farmers, and the miners, of western Maryland and western Virginia. Along the tracks of the Delaware Railroad appeared such new communities as Clayton, Wyoming, Felton, and Harrington.

Everywhere the increased access to market brought new vigor to agricultural life. Lands in the backwoods were cleared that had not been farmed before. Farmers, especially in northern Delaware, found it profitable to increase the productivity of their fields by careful systems of rotating crops and by the liberal use of fertilizers and chemicals, like lime, to enrich the soil. New crops were introduced that had an especial value in city markets, the chief of these being peaches. Peach culture had become a major agricultural enterprise in Delaware, beginning in about 1840, soon after Isaac Reeves introduced the artificially "budded" tree in Red Lion Hundred. Maj. Philip Reybold, of near Delaware City, was the acknowledged "peach king" at his death in 1854, when the progress of the Delaware Railroad southward made it possible for Delaware peaches to reach city markets more quickly by rail than by steamboats from Delaware City.

As peaches and other truck crops for the city markets were encouraged by the extension of the railroad downstate, the mills and factories along the Christina River and the Philadelphia, Wilmington, and Baltimore Railroad tracks in the Wilmington area were also growing. Industry settled especially on the tier of land in southern and eastern Wilmington between the river and the railroad tracks—shipyards, rolling mills, machine and car wheel shops. There were 7,284 farmers and 4,122 farm laborers in Delaware in 1860, according to the census, but there were also 550 factory hands, 229 machinists, 124 moulders and iron workers, and 210 ship carpenters, as well as 208 wheelwrights, 124 morocco dressers, and 90 powder makers. River and rail furnished an easy connection between this industrial society and nearby mass markets, just as they performed the same service for the agricultural society that still constituted the major part of the Delaware population.

8

The Civil War

The Election of 1860

The 1860 elections posed special problems for Delaware voters because of schisms in both of the old parties. Nationally, the American party had failed in its efforts to pose as the legitimate successor to the Whigs in a two-party system, and no one party had taken its place. The Republican party had absorbed much of the old Whig—and Know-Nothing—strength in the North, but in the border states many Whig and Know-Nothing sympathizers preferred the new Constitutional Union party, which nominated John Bell, of Tennessee, for president.

A group of delegates that consisted mainly of Southerners, but which included many conservative leaders of Congress from both sections, had attempted to block the Democrats from nominating the vigorous Senator Stephen Douglas of Illinois, by walking out of the Democratic convention. Senator James Bayard and Congressman William Whiteley of Delaware participated in this movement, but their withdrawal led only to the creation of two Democratic tickets, Douglas being the nominee of a reconstituted convention and Vice-President John Breckinridge of Kentucky the candidate of the bolters.

Emotional defenders of the slave system objected to Douglas because he insisted that settlers in the West could block the extension of slavery if they wished, despite a Supreme Court decision (in the *Dred Scott* case) to the effect that slave owners had a constitutional right to take their slaves into the Western territories. This was not an issue that would move many Delawareans, but there was also opposition to Douglas on the grounds that he was an inordinately ambitious man, who had previously antagonized party leaders by pushing himself forward, in party conventions as well as in the Senate. He had only reluctantly taken a back seat to the elderly Buchanan in 1856, and his ambition had raised resentment among some Democrats.

Senator Bayard was one of the congressional leaders determined to block Douglas, and despite an effort of some Democrats, including a so-called faction of the three brothers (meaning Senator Willard Saulsbury, Eli Saulsbury, and Dr. Gove Saulsbury), to leave the Delaware Democrats uncommitted between Breckinridge and Douglas, Bayard had his way and brought the majority of the party with him into the Breckinridge ranks. A small minority, however, led by a political maverick, Samuel Townsend, defied Bayard and supported Stephen Douglas. This defection did not hurt Breckinridge, for he carried Delaware easily, but the insistence of the dissidents on backing their own candidate for Congress led to the defeat of Benjamin Biggs, who ran for Congress on the Breckinridge ticket against the united opposition of the anti-Democratic parties.

The popular vote in Delaware in the eventful 1860 presidential contest was as follows:

Breckinridge (Democrat)	7,323
Bell (Constitutional Union)	3,833
Lincoln (Republican)	3,811
Douglas (Democrat)	1,001

In giving its electoral votes to the candidate of the Southern Democrats, Delaware was not manifesting its clear support for Southern political attitudes. What the election shows about Delaware is that its Democrats stuck together in support of their leaders, who were resolved to block Douglas even if it ruined their party. The election also demonstrates that the opposition party in Delaware was almost evenly divided as to the presidential candidate.

In the Congressional race, however, the People's party united the Republican and Constitutional Union elements, nominating and electing George P. Fisher, a Dover lawyer. The People's party also carried the state house of representatives by a narrow margin (eleven to ten) and came within an equally narrow margin (four to five) of controlling the state senate.

The strength of the People's party was in three coastal hundreds of Sussex County (Indian River, Baltimore, and Cedar Creek), in the southern and northern hundreds of Kent (Milford and Duck Creek), and in northern New Castle. The notable development is that the Democrats, as they strengthened their position in Delaware, were becoming the party of rural Delaware, of the mainly agricultural counties, while their opponents were retaining strength in some coastal areas downstate—perhaps because of a strong influence from upstate and Philadelphia by maritime trade—and gaining strength in northern Delaware, possibly with the aid of opposition to the low-tariff and proslave attitudes of the Democrats.

It is interesting to note that Lincoln outpolled Bell in New Castle and Kent and that in four hundreds he also outpolled the Democrats: Brandywine and Christiana in New Castle, Milford in Kent, and the adjoining Cedar Creek Hundred in Sussex. The only two hundreds won by Bell were Baltimore and Indian River in Sussex.

Attitudes toward Secession

Apparently, Milford was a center of Republican strength, but the governor of Delaware in 1860, the elderly Dr. William Burton, came from Milford and was a Democrat. Elected in 1858, he had some sympathy for the Southern states that began to secede after the outcome of the 1860 election became clear, and he was sympathetic to the idea that a special convention should be chosen in Delaware to determine the course this state should follow. The new legislature, however, did not agree with him, and though the members agreed to hear an envoy from Mississippi, Henry Dickinson, who addressed them in January 1861, attempting to justify secession, they adopted a resolution by a decisive vote (unanimous in the lower house, 5 to 3 in the state senate) disapproving of secession as a remedy for grievances. Alabama and Georgia also sent representatives to influence opinion in Delaware, but to no avail.

These Southern representatives did conclude, however, that the people of Delaware were sympathetic to secession, though unwilling to consider it for themselves unless Virginia (which had not yet acted) and Maryland voted to secede. Probably, these Southerners deluded themselves, but it was true that an astonishing proportion of the most prominent Delawareans in the early months of 1861 were sympathetic to the South—including Governor Burton, Secretary of State Edward Ridgely, and the whole congressional delegation—Senators James Bayard and Willard Saulsbury and Congressman William Whiteley.

But the legislature was probably more truly representative of the feelings of the average Delawarean. None of the politicians just named had been elected within the past year. The two senators were not chosen by the people at all but by the legislators, Bayard in 1851 and again in 1857; Saulsbury in 1859. Secretary of State Ridgely was appointed by Governor Burton, who had himself been popularly elected back in 1858. Congressman Whiteley was also popularly elected, but in 1856 and 1858; he had not sought reelection in 1860, when his party's choice to succeed him had been rejected at the polls. In the early months of 1861 Whiteley was a "lame duck" congressman.

Insofar as the legislature represented the opinion of the average Delaware voter, it seems likely that he disapproved of secession, for his own state or any others, and that he remained strongly Unionist, as his ancestors had been in 1787. At the same time that he rejected the idea of secession, he also rejected militant abolitionism. He wanted to find some compromise that would patch up the Union and avert a resort to force. If the South persisted in leaving the Union, he would be sorry but would let the seceding states depart in peace.

There were extremists, of course. Those who were most ardent for the Southern cause, however, were circumvented by the course of events. Since Maryland did not secede, secession was not a course for the Delawarean to consider. No resolution advocating secession was ever introduced into the Delaware legislature, and though Governor Burton suggested calling a convention to consider the course for this state, his suggestion was ignored.

Senator Saulsbury, in December 1860, suggested that the central states, slaveholding and nonslaveholding, should form a confederation of their own, separate from both South Carolina and New England, but his colleague Senator Bayard thought this was a foolish idea. The governor of Maryland made a similar suggestion to Governor Burton, and a Kent County state senator proposed a Philadelphia convention of the central states, but Burton was noncommittal and the Senate rejected the proposal.

On the other hand, both houses of the General Assembly enthusiastically supported suggestions to compromise sectional differences so as to leave the Union intact. By overwhelming votes, they supported amendments to the Constitution proposed as a compromise by Senator John J. Crittenden, of Kentucky, and they appointed a delegation of five men, representing both parties, to a peace convention held in Washington at the call of the Virginia legislature.

Compromises that might have appealed to the South were rejected by the new Republican administration of Abraham Lincoln, and the inevitability of war became clear with the attack on Fort Sumter in April 1861. As rallies began to be held in Delaware to urge support for President Lincoln, a former Democratic congressman, John W. Houston, voiced what may have been the creed of the average Delawarean: "Stay at home in the Union until the crack of doom, or until it goes to pieces, . . . and we are left standing solitary and alone with our feet planted firmly on the rock of the Constitution . . . as the last survivors of the federation of the American States."

Southern Sympathies

Governor Burton's reaction to the fall of Fort Sumter and to President Lincoln's appeal for troops was to recommend formation of volunteer companies of Home Guards throughout Delaware, which had no statewide militia organization. Some of the volunteer companies entered the Union army, but others had no intention of doing so and were even suspected of sympathizing with the Confederacy. The governor took an important step toward support of the Union cause in May 1861 by appointing Henry du Pont, a graduate of West Point, to command all of the military companies in Delaware. Du Pont, who had abandoned his military career many years earlier to help run the powder mills his father had founded, was a strong Unionist, and his responsibility for military affairs in the state reassured Northern sympathizers.

Such reassurance seemed needed on June 27, when a large "peace convention" met on Dover Green. With former governor William Temple presiding, the convention was clearly in opposition to the Lincoln administration. Former Congressman William Whiteley, Secretary of State Edward Ridgely, and Thomas F. Bayard, gifted son of the senior senator from Delaware, made speeches generally interpreted as pro-Confederate. They did not advocate secession as a practical course for Delaware, but they urged that the Southern states be allowed to go their way in peace, and they called for an end to what they deemed an unconstitutional, as well as fratricidal, war.

Both Delaware senators, though bitter rivals for control of the Democratic party, were sympathetic to the South. Senator Bayard had traveled through the Southern states, visiting many political leaders, in April 1861. Though his business on the trip was apparently purely personal, all sorts of rumors circulated, and when he took the train to Philadelphia, soon after his return, authorities made him leave his coach several blocks before the depot in order to avoid a mob waiting to tar and feather him. Senator Saulsbury, as late as December 1861, urged the establishment of a commission to make peace. Throughout the conflict he assailed Lincoln and his administration in public speeches and in private, though his effectiveness was reduced by overindulgence in intoxicating liquors.

Some young Delawareans, perhaps numbering into the hundreds, were such ardent supporters of the right to secede that they fled South and offered their services to the Confederacy. Among them were sons of former Governors William H. Ross and William B. Cooper, both of Sussex County, and two sons of the Presbyterian minister in Newark, James Vallandigham, who was a brother of the noted copperhead congressman from Ohio, Clement Vallandigham. Southern sympathizers surreptitiously opened a route to the South for both men and supplies, frequently utilizing the Delaware Railroad to Seaford and then the Nanticoke River to the Chesapeake Bay. Some refugees reached the bay farther south, but in any case, the critical problem was crossing to the western shore, for the part of Virginia that was on the Delmarva Peninsula, the eastern shore, was sucessfully invaded and occupied early in the war by Union troops commanded by a Delawarean, Henry H. Lockwood. Later in the war, in July 1863, four residents of Seaford were arrested for smuggling supplies across the Chesapeake. As punishment, they were exiled to the Confederacy, sent through the lines under a flag of truce.

Some of the Delaware volunteer militia companies were of such doubtful loyalty to the Union that on two occasions, first in October 1861 and then again in March 1862, Federal troops were ordered into Delaware to seize their arms and, in some cases, their commanding officers. At election time in November 1862, and also in 1863, when a special election was held, Federal troops returned to Delaware at the request of supporters of the Lincoln

THE ROSS MANSION, NEAR SEAFORD. THE HOME OF GOVERNOR WIL-
LIAM H. ROSS (1814–1887), THE MOST PROMINENT SUPPORTER OF THE
CONFEDERACY IN DELAWARE.

As it appeared in the nineteenth century.

As it looked in 1977. (Both views courtesy of the Division of Historical and Cultural Affairs.)

administration, who feared that the Democrats would steal the election by keeping their opponents from voting unless the polls were carefully policed. Democrats, of course, protested that the shoe was on the other foot, that the soldiers were being used to overawe any expression of opposition to the Republican government of the nation.

Service to the Union

While a few Delawareans were fleeing to the South, thousands were joining the armed forces of the Union. The First Delaware Regiment entered Federal service in May 1861, under Colonel Lockwood. Its soldiers had volunteered for only three months; reorganized under Col. John W. Andrews, this regiment was mustered into the service again in October and served through the war, though suffering the loss of almost one-third of its seven hundred men by death or injury at the battle of Antietam alone.

Three other Delaware infantry regiments served for long periods, as did one regiment of cavalry and an independent artillery company. Other military units were called up for special duty—for example, to guard railroad bridges or factories when Confederate raids seemed likely. At first, all the soldiers were volunteers, with bounties offered to aid recruiting, but later, men were drafted by lottery, though draftees were permitted to offer substitutes if they could find them.

A good many of the recruits in the Delaware regiments were Irish immigrants, to whom army service, including the bounty for enlisting, had an economic appeal. One extraordinary Irish immigrant, Thomas A. Smyth, raised his own volunteer company at the beginning of the war and by his valor and ability rose gradually to the rank of brigadier general until he was killed on April 7, 1865. Smyth's troops were then in pursuit of Lee, who was fleeing toward Appomattox, and Smyth was the last general officer killed in the war. A. T. A. Torbert, of Milford, who was a West Point graduate, also rose to the rank of brigadier general, as did Henry Lockwood, who, though an army officer, had taught at the Naval Academy before the war.

The most distinguished naval officer from Delaware was Samuel F. Du Pont, first cousin of General Henry du Pont. (The cousins disagreed on the use of capital letters in the family name.) At the beginning of the war, Samuel Du Pont had charge of the Philadelphia Navy Yard, and he played an important role in devising the decisive naval strategy of the war, the blockading of Southern ports. He commanded a successful amphibious invasion of the Sea Islands of South Carolina in the fall of 1861, but he failed to capture Charleston in 1863 after launching a naval attack on orders from Washington and against his own judgment.

Besides the military service of its sons, Delaware aided the Northern war effort by the produce of its industries. From one-third to one-half of the gunpowder production of the North came from Du Pont mills in Delaware or elsewhere. Numerous leather and textile factories in New Castle County were busy with government contracts, as were the wagon makers and the railroad car and wheel shops. Shipbuilders turned out naval vessels, including iron monitors. The industrial productivity of the Wilmington area, especially the importance of the Du Pont powder mills, occasioned nervousness in the area whenever the Southern armies seemed capable of taking the offensive.

The chief fortification in the area was Fort Delaware, which guarded access to the ports and shipyards of Wilmington and Philadelphia by its location on Pea Patch Island in the Delaware River off Delaware City. Since the Confederate navy was too weak to pose a serious threat, the fort was converted, early in the war, into a camp for prisoners of war and for some residents of Delaware and nearby states who were arrested and held without trial under suspicion of giving aid to the South after President Lincoln suspended use of the writ of habeas corpus. Some prisoners were held in dungeons within the walls of the fort, but most were housed in wooden barracks quickly constructed on the marshy island. Primitive sanitary facilities and the general unhealthiness of the small island, especially when crowded by as many as 12,500 prisoners after the Battle of Gettysburg, gave it a deserved notoriety. Over 2,400 prisoners died there. Occasional exchanges, along with daring escapes, provided some turnover in the prison population.

A Compensated Emancipation Plan and the Democratic Reaction

In the fall of 1861 President Lincoln proposed to Congressman Fisher, his only supporter in the Delaware congressional

FORT DELAWARE, ON PEA PATCH ISLAND.

A photograph taken in the summer of 1862. (Courtesy of W. Emerson Wilson.)

A sketch by Max Neugas, November 1, 1864, showing the fort with outbuildings erected on the island for use of the prisoner-of-war camp. (Courtesy of the Historical Society of Delaware.)

delegation, that Delaware should free its remaining slaves with compensation to the owners from a fund provided by the federal government. Lincoln felt that if compensated emancipation were tried in Delaware, it could soon be extended to the other loyal slave states and then, as soon as the rebellion could be ended, to the states that had left the Union. As long as slavery remained, according to Lincoln, it would be a divisive and provocative issue. "This is the cheapest and most humane way," he told Fisher, "of ending this war and saving lives."

Returning to Dover, Fisher and another Republican lawyer, Nathaniel B. Smithers, prepared a bill providing for abolition of slavery in Delaware, with compensation to slave owners according to a value set for each slave by a local board of assessors. The average payment was to be five hundred dollars, and therefore Congress was to provide nine hundred thousand dollars to cover the emancipation of the 1800 Delaware slaves.

Unfortunately, Fisher and Smithers ran into trouble when they canvassed the legislators to assess support for their bill. While they had the votes they needed in the Democrat-controlled Senate, where two delegates elected as Democrats, Wilson Cannon and Jacob Moore, joined the opposition in support of the bill, they could not persuade a majority in the lower house to favor it.

The opposition to Lincoln's proposal of compensated emancipation was partly a question of party politics, for most Delaware Democrats looked at it as a Republican measure. Some Delawareans viewed the proposal as an instance of federal interference with state's rights, including the state's right to end slavery when it chose. Others said the proposal was financially unrealistic and oppressive, as well as unfair. Many Delawareans who had previously freed slaves had done so without compensation, whereas now every taxpayer would bear the burden of compensating those who had perpetuated slavery. Though Fisher argued that nine hundred thousand dollars was but the cost of one-half day of the war, the sum needed to free slaves in all the states seemed astronomical to his contemporaries.

So the compensated emancipation bill was given up. Delaware, despite the small number of its slaves, remained a slave state until after the war ended and Lincoln was dead. Finally, adoption of the Thirteenth Amendment, in December 1865, ended slavery everywhere; by that time, it still persisted only in Kentucky, the Indian Territory of Oklahoma, and Delaware.

With the failure of his plans for emancipation in Delaware, Lincoln bided his time before undertaking another step toward ridding the country of slavery. After the battle of Antietam, or Sharpsburg, in Maryland, in September 1862, a significant Union victory in which Lee's first effort to invade the North was repulsed, Lincoln thought the time was ripe for an Emancipation Proclamation. He announced that on January 1, 1863, he would declare all slaves free who resided in states or parts of states that were then in rebellion against the United States government. This proclamation obviously did not affect the status of the remaining slaves in Delaware. Its legality depended on Lincoln's war powers against rebels; he had no constitutional authority to end slavery in the loyal states.

Fisher's support of Lincoln and of emancipation was of little help to him in the election of November 1862; quite the reverse. The Democrats made a great point of stigmatizing the Republicans as an abolition party that sought Negro equality. Despite the presence of troops at the polls and Lincoln's agreement (at Fisher's request) to leave some newly mustered Delaware soldiers in the state long enough to allow them to vote, Fisher lost his bid for reelection to the Democratic candidate, William Temple, a former governor. The margin was close, thirty-seven votes, and the supporters of the Lincoln administration, who called themselves the Union party, did succeed in electing their candidate for governor, William Cannon, a prosperous Sussex County merchant-farmer and a former Democrat. Cannon probably succeeded in winning downstate votes, particularly in Sussex, from his Democratic opponent, Samuel Jefferson, who came from New Castle County. New Castle was the only county the Union party carried, but Cannon lost Sussex by only six votes, and his plurality in New Castle won him victory despite a decided defeat in Kent. Though losing the governorship, the Democrats picked up enough assembly seats to control both houses of the legislature for the balance of the war.

William Temple died in May 1863, before he had ever attended a session of Congress. In special elections in the fall, the Republicans ran Nathaniel Smithers for the seat and elected him almost without opposition because of a strategic decision of the Democrats. Faced once again with the appearance of soldiers at the polls—some of them Delaware troops assigned home obviously so they could vote—the Democrats decided to boycott the election. They could do this with little loss because no offices except the seat in Congress were being filled in this off year, and the loss of one place in the congressional minority did little damage to the Delaware Democrats, particularly since they held both seats in the Senate.

Only thirteen Democratic votes were cast in opposition to Smithers. Possibly Democrats hoped the House of Representatives would declare the election null and void, but Smithers was seated without difficulty. In future Delaware elections, however, the Democrats made political capital out of the events of 1863, repeatedly castigating President Lincoln, Governor Cannon, and Republicans in general for the use of federal troops at the Delaware polls.

In 1864, at the request of Governor Cannon, troops were again sent to watch the Delaware polls, but this time the Democrats felt there was too much at stake to permit a boycott. Instead, they waged a very vigorous campaign, proclaiming themselves the "White Man's party" and the peace party, advocating an immediate suspension of war. "No more drafts, no more taxes, no negro equality" was their slogan, and they rolled up pluralities in Kent and Sussex counties large enough to carry the state, though they again lost New Castle County. Their victory meant that Delaware was one of only three states to prefer Gen. George McClellan to Lincoln in the presidential race. It also meant continued Democratic control of the assembly and a solid Democratic delegation in Congress, since Nathaniel Smithers was defeated by his Democratic opponent, John Nicholson.

The death of Governor Cannon, March 1, 1865, turned the executive branch of the state government over to the Democrats, the constitutional successor to the office being the president of the state senate, who was a Democrat, Dr. Gove Saulsbury, brother of Senator Willard Saulsbury. The replacement of a chief executive who had advocated passage of an abolition law by one who would rebuke Congress for interfering with slavery was more important than a mere change in party or in personnel in the governorship.

Despite their opposition to many of the policies of the Lincoln government, Delawareans regarded themselves as loyal to the Union. They disagreed among themselves regarding the powers and policies of the Union government. Majority opinion was decidedly for peace rather than for war, and yet Delawareans supported the Union war effort in terms of both men and supplies. The number of men recruited into the army in Delaware is said to have been larger, in proportion to population, than in any other Northern state. Many of the recruits may have been immigrants, but the bounties offered in Delaware encouraged their enlistment in this state.

Lee's surrender set off wild celebrations in Wilmington and other parts of the state, but a few days later news of Lincoln's assassination plunged Delaware into gloom. Every newspaper, even those that had been vigorously anti-Republican, deplored this murder, which a leading Democrat, Thomas F. Bayard, called "disgraceful, . . . horrible, . . . insane."

9

Dynastic Politics
of the Reconstruction Period

Postbellum Sentiments

The most significant and lasting event in Delaware in the postbellum years, the progress of industrialization and urbanization in Wilmington and its environs, was not primarily a result of the war. This change was underway before the war began, as table 2 suggests:

TABLE 2

GROWTH OF WILMINGTON, 1850–1920

Census Year	Population of Wilmington	Population of Delaware	Percent Increase in Delaware Population	Percentage of Delaware Population in Wilmington	Percent Increase in Wilmington Population
1840	8,367	78,085	1.7	10.7	. . . .
1850	13,979	91,532	17.2	15.3	67.1
1860	21,258	112,216	22.6	18.9	52.1
1870	30,841	125,015	11.4	24.7	45.1
1880	42,478	146,608	17.3	29.0	37.7
1890	61,431	168,493	14.9	36.5	44.6
1900	76,508	184,735	9.6	41.4	24.5
1910	87,411	202,322	9.5	43.2	14.3
1920*	110,168	223,003	10.2	49.4	26.0

* The population of Wilmington declined in the 1930 census, recovered in 1940, but then entered a period of rapid decline.
SOURCE: U.S. Census

Until the 1880 census, incidentally, no community in Delaware except Wilmington had as many as twenty-five hundred residents. There were no figures for Wilmington in the decennial censuses prior to 1840; so the comparison of the growth of the state and the city cannot be begun earlier with statistical assurance. The great difference between the situation in postbellum and antebellum years is not in the fact that Wilmington was growing faster than the state, for the differential in their rate of growth was decreasing, but in the increased importance the city gained in comparison with the rest of the state.

For a quarter century after the Civil War, however, this major long-term development took place in a political and social environment that was largely established by the Civil War. While the war lasted, the critical situation of the Union stimulated support for Lincoln and his government, but once the war had ended, all sorts of festering resentments surfaced and were strengthened by opposition to federal policies regarding the conquered Southern states and the black population.

Federal policies for blacks included the Thirteenth, Fourteenth, and Fifteenth Amendments, adopted in 1865, 1868, and 1870, respectively, and offering freedom, civil rights, and voting privileges, in that order. All three of these amendments were rejected by the Delaware legislature. Federal policy toward the conquered states involved the establishment of military rule in most of them, with the result that an occupying army was kept in some parts of the South until 1877. Delawareans who, despite their own loyalty to the Union, felt that there had been at least a good legal case for the right to secede, resented the Reconstruction policy adopted by Republican-controlled Congresses and sent a succession of Democrats to Washington who pleaded the cause of the defeated states with such consistency that Delaware came to be regarded, in political terms, as part of what eventually was known as the *Solid South*.

To preserve their popular support, successful Democratic candidates in Delaware effectively used campaign appeals almost precisely the opposite of those employed with success by Republican candidates in Pennsylvania and in other states to the North. In Pennsylvania Republican candidates argued that theirs was the "Grand Old Party" that had saved the Union, while the Democratic party was the party of rebellion. In Delaware, Democratic strategists emphasized their devotion to the Constitution and declared that the Republicans played fast and loose with the laws of the land, both during the war and after.

Several events during the war had aroused ill feeling against the federal government—for example, invasion of Delaware by soldiers sent to disarm militia companies of doubtful loyalty and to guard the polls during wartime elections. Another federal measure that aroused great resentment in Delaware was the suspension of the use of the writ of habeas corpus. By this action, Delawareans could be jailed without trial on mere suspicion of wrongdoing. The fact that the prison to which some suspects were sent was Fort Delaware, with its notorious reputation for overcrowding and unsanitary conditions, made the resentment this policy aroused all the greater. Stories regarding the use or abuse of Fort Delaware's facilities in restricting civil rights were grist for the Democrats' campaign mill. They would tell, for example, of twenty-five residents of New Castle who were arrested and jailed because they organized a picnic to raise funds for green vegetables that would augment the inadequate diet of prisoners. They would note the imprisonment of William Hitch, a state senator from Laurel, for his Southern sympathies. Or they could refer to the story of the Reverend Dr. Isaac W. K. Handy, a Presbyterian minister at Portsmouth, Virginia (and formerly in Delaware), who received a military pass permitting him to bring his wife, a native of Delaware, to visit her relatives at Port Penn and Bridgeville but was arrested and sent to Fort Delaware on the mere suspicion, which was false, that he had been a chaplain in the Confederate army. Handy printed his prison journal in 1874 under the title *United States Bonds; or, Duress by Federal Authority: A Journal of Current Events during an Imprisonment of Fifteen Months, at Fort Delaware,* keeping alive memories the Democrats found of political value.

In 1864 Senator James A. Bayard, recently reelected to his third term, grew angry at Senate passage of a resolution requiring all members to take a so-called ironclad oath of loyalty to the Lincoln administration. He regarded the resolution as specifically aimed at him because he had challenged the constitutionality of this 1862 oath and was the only senator who had not yet signed it. To establish his loyalty and show up his enemies, he did sign the oath in February 1864 but immediately resigned rather than serve in a Senate imposing such a requirement. "I have lived," he complained in his farewell speech, "to see the elective franchise trodden under foot in my native State by the iron heel of the soldier. . . . I have lived to see her citizens torn from their homes and separated from their families . . . without any charge expressed . . . and without any known accuser."

The Delaware legislature promptly filled Bayard's place with another Democrat of similar opinions, George Read Riddle, a former congressman, but when Riddle died suddenly in March 1867, James Bayard returned to Washington to complete his term and carry on his fight against Republican policies. Bayard was seventy in 1869, the year his term expired, and to mark its complete support of his views, the Delaware legislature chose his son Thomas F. Bayard to be his successor.

White Supremacy Politics

The popular support Democrats won in Delaware by dwelling upon resentment of Republican actions during the Civil War was strengthened by resentment of Reconstruction policies. At the highest level, Delaware Democrats complained that the Republicans were changing the nature of the Union, adopting paternalistic policies—like the protective tariff and railroad land grants, which used federal powers to aid special interest groups—and running roughshod over states' rights, as in demands made of the Southern states, which were required to approve amendments to the Constitution (amendments that might otherwise have failed of approval) before being readmitted to the Union and freed of occupation by federal soldiers. To the extent that they pressed these arguments, Democratic senators, like Willard Saulsbury and his brother Eli, who succeeded him in the Senate in 1871, and James and Thomas Bayard, could claim to be in the tradition of Jacksonian Democracy, in opposition to special interests (to the railroads and the manufacturers, as Jacksonians had opposed the United States Bank) and in favor of a federal government pursuing laissez-faire policies.

But on a lower level, the appeal of the Democrats was flagrantly racist. "The immutable laws of God," declared a Democratic legislature, "have affixed upon the brow of the white races the ineffaceable stamp of superiority, and . . . all attempt to elevate the negro to a social or political equality . . . is futile and subversive." When Delaware College reopened in 1870 with the assistance of federal funds appropriated under the terms of the Morrill Land-Grant College Act, it instituted a brief (1872–86) experiment in the education of white women but had no place whatever for blacks of either sex. In 1890 Congress, in renewing its financial assistance to land-grant colleges, demanded that a fair proportion of the new appropriation should be used in each state for black students; under this stimulus Delaware belatedly chartered the State College for Colored Students in 1891.

The Democrats, who had won complete control of the state in March 1865 upon the death of Governor William Cannon, retained control by election victories in 1866, 1868, and 1870. There were areas of Republican strength, notably in northern New Castle County. The city of Wilmington voted Republican in every election to 1878, as did neighboring Christiana Hundred, while two other northern hundreds, Brandywine and Mill Creek, were very frequently Republican.

Downstate there were also pockets of Republican strength. In Kent County, Milford Hundred usually voted Republican, as did East Dover Hundred after 1872 and North Murderkill after 1880. In Sussex County Republicans were strong in the three coastal hundreds (former Whig strongholds) of Cedar Creek, Indian River, and Baltimore, as well as in North West Fork Hundred. These hundreds voted Republican whenever the party presented a ticket, and even in 1886, when it did not, Baltimore Hundred and North West Fork supported the Temperance Reform party rather than the Democrats. Dagsboro Hundred was frequently Rpeublican after 1872 and Nanticoke Hundred after 1886. Still, neither Kent County nor Sussex County as a whole voted Republican until 1888.

Continued Democratic successes rested partly on preventing the black element in the population, which amounted to about 18 percent of the total in the 1860s, from voting. Under Delaware laws, only white males were eligible to vote. In 1867 an integrated meeting at Wilmington protested the situation and asked Congress to investigate whether Delaware had a republican form of government. It did not, was the conclusion of a congressional committee that heard evidence on Delaware politics, but the matter died there as more urgent matters claimed the attention of the Radical Republicans who controlled the postwar Congress.

Several cases are known of abuse of blacks in Delaware just after the Civil War. In Sussex several Negro church meetings were broken up, and Negro veterans were arrested for possessing firearms even though these weapons had been given to them upon their discharge from the Union army. In December 1866 a group that included the Episcopal bishop, Alfred Lee; a Methodist minister, Levi Scott; a Dover physician, Dr. Isaac Jump; and a prominent lawyer, Samuel M. Harrington, Jr., met in

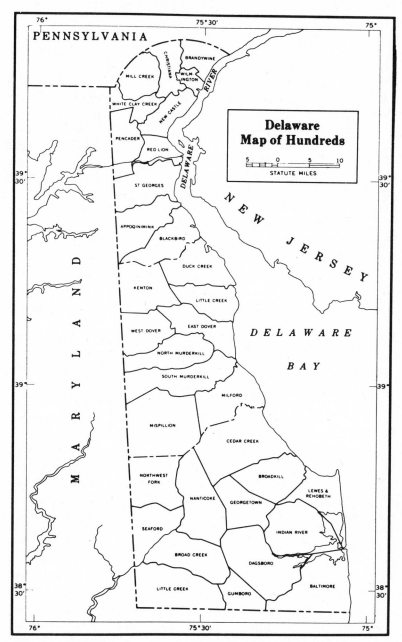

Map of Delaware as divided into hundreds. The hundred is an ancient English territorial unit, of undetermined origin, used until recently for some functions of local government. Preserved almost nowhere else on earth, the hundred corresponds to the township in Pennsylvania and New Jersey and to the town in New England. From Delaware Place Names, U.S. Department of the Interior Geological Survey Bulletin 1245 (1966).

Wilmington to organize the Delaware Association for the Moral Improvement and Education of the Colored People. Thomas Kimber, a Quaker who was a railroad executive, became president of the association, which performed significant service in stimulating the growth in the number of schools for blacks from a mere seven in 1867 to thirty-nine in 1876. Although the teachers, white and black, provided by the association were sometimes harassed and a schoolhouse in Slaughter Neck was burned, the association persisted, aided by funds provided by local people, including blacks, by philanthropic groups in Northern states and in England, and by an agency of the federal government called the Freedmen's Bureau, which opened a Wilmington office in 1867. Howard High School in Wilmington, founded as a normal school for blacks, was named after Gen. Oliver O. Howard, head of the Freedmen's Bureau, in appreciation of his interest.

Ratification of the Fifteenth Amendment in March 1870 raised Republican hopes of winning the elections in the fall of that year, since there was now a potential black vote of forty-five hundred added to the electorate. But the Democrats closed ranks under the banner of the white man's party and utilized their control of political offices to keep blacks from voting, despite the presence of federal marshals at the polls. Marshals were deputized in numbers for poll duty at every congressional election in postbellum Delaware as long as Republicans controlled the presidency, in an attempt by the Republican federal bureaucracy to counteract the Democratic bureaucracy in Delaware. But in 1870, as in most elections, local officials had the upper hand, and the marshals, who were actually driven from the polls in Smyrna and Odessa, were powerless to stop the Democratic political machine.

At this election James Ponder, brother-in-law of Senator Willard Saulsbury, was elected governor. When the legislature met, it refused to reelect Senator Saulsbury, probably because of his notorious alcoholism, but replaced him with his brother Eli, whom it preferred by a narrow margin to ex-Governor Gove Saulsbury. In two years Governor Ponder appointed Willard Saulsbury chancellor, after the latter presumably made a pledge, which he kept, to give up drinking.

Inasmuch as Thomas Bayard had succeeded his father in the other Delaware senatorial seat two years earlier, it is easy to understand why Delaware was referred to as a "pocket borough" of the Bayards and the Saulsburys.

The Assessment and Collection Laws of 1873

The frustrated Republicans, convinced they were being cheated in the elections, bided their time until March 1872, when District Attorney Anthony Higgins brought charges against the members of the New Castle County levy court and several collectors of county taxes for violation of a federal law that forbade discrimination on the basis of race or color in the application of state voting laws. Delaware laws required that a voter pay a county tax, which could be either a property tax or a capitation (poll) tax. Higgins charged Delaware officials with failing to collect taxes from blacks and removing their names from the lists of voters, often by erroneously claiming them to be deceased or out of state.

The only one of these cases actually to come to trial was that of a tax collector named Archibald Given, who was found guilty in the federal circuit court of submitting false returns. The Democratic state legislature almost passed a bill to pay Given's fine for him; possibly the legislators were dissuaded by the argument of Senator Bayard, who had been one of Given's lawyers and now warned that if this were done, the next similar case would probably result in a jail sentence. Instead of a state appropriation, Bayard suggested that a private subscription should be taken up to help Given.

In view of the rough treatment federal marshals had received at some Delaware polls in 1870, troops were sent into the state by the Grant administration in 1872. The election that year resulted in the first Republican victories since the Civil War, but it is unlikely that either the presence of soldiers or the Given trial, which had been heard in October 1872, was the main cause of the unusual election result. The national Democratic party in 1872 adopted the presidential candidate of the Liberal Republicans, Horace Greeley, hoping to profit from a Republican schism. But Greeley, a veteran New York editor, had expressed opinions over the years that were anathema to Delaware Democrats, who nominally accepted their party's choice but were unwilling to do much to help him. The Republican candidate, President Grant, who was seeking reelection, was, on the other hand, extraordinarily popular, and though linked to the Radical Republicans, he had an independent stature as a candidate that arose from his military reputation rather than from his politics.

While voting for the first time for a Republican presidential candidate, Delaware also chose a Republican congressman, James

R. Lofland, of Milford, and New Castle County chose a Republican delegation to the legislature for the first time since the war. Whether it was the weakness and apathy of the Democrats or the new strength of the Republicans that accomplished these results, the legislature, still heavily Democratic, took steps to make the Fifteenth Amendment ineffective in Delaware.

The new strategy of the Democratic legislators was embodied in two laws, called the Assessment and Collection Laws, enacted in 1873. Put simply, these laws made it the responsibility of a Delaware resident to see that his name was on the assessment lists for the county tax and, likewise, to see that his tax was paid. Only by paying the tax could he qualify himself as a voter, and before he could pay his tax he had to be assessed. A special, and important, provision of both laws was that if a man were delinquent in paying his tax, his name would be removed from the tax list for one year by the levy court. In the case of Republicans, and especially in the case of blacks, it was possible for Democratic officials to time the removal of names so that a man whose name was removed from the assessment lists would be unable to qualify himself as a voter for a period of almost two years.

For fifteen years the Assessment and Collection Laws were important props to the maintenance of Democratic hegemony in Delaware. They were not, it should be noted, absolute bars to voting by blacks. The use of these laws depended on the local officials, the assessors, collectors, and levy court commissioners. Therefore, when a county went Republican, as New Castle County did in 1872, the local officials would be more apt to seek out than to exclude black voters.

Nor did the lack of money for taxes necessarily keep poor men from voting. In the Federalist period, candidates had found ample supplies of rum more attractive to some voters than a candidate's opinion on the issues of the day. By the Reconstruction period, a five-dollar bill had become a more attractive inducement to a voter than rum, though a free drink of liquor was often used to seal the bargain made in bank notes.

Republicans in Delaware were not, as a party or as individuals, notably poorer than the Democrats. In fact, the reverse was probably true. The strength of the Republicans was concentrated in the most prosperous and growing parts of the state. Increasingly, the Republican party was becoming the party of the larger merchants and manufacturers. Without question, the Republicans could raise money to pay the tax bills of delinquent voters.

But for many years the Democrats, retaining control of the election machinery, made it very difficult for delinquents, especially black delinquents, to qualify as voters.

A Republican journalist called this period the medieval period in Delaware politics. In a sense, it was, with the Democratic politicians—the Bayards, the Saulsburys, and others—acting like feudal lords of this little principality, resolved to keep the peasants—if they were black—in their place and to prevent them from being made use of by the nouveau riche Republican merchants and manufacturers of the cities.

The Weakening of Dynastic Politics

Although the economic and demographic changes—the growth of manufacturing and of the urban population—occurring in Delaware in the Reconstruction years would eventually undermine the rule of the feudal Democratic lords, like the Bayards and the Saulsburys, there was one element in the new order that struck up a natural alliance with the Democratic old guard. This was the immigrant laboring population, especially Irish workers that economic opportunity was luring to Delaware. The Catholic Irish had been coming to New Castle County for several decades, helping to dig canals and build railroads, and then settling down as mill hands on the Brandywine or on the Red Clay or near the new factories in Wilmington.

The 1870 and 1880 censuses demonstrate that Delaware was losing natives to other states, native whites and blacks both, faster than it was able to attract native Americans. But the loss was more than made up by the natural growth of the population (the excess of births over deaths) and by immigration from overseas. Proportionally, the immigrants were a smaller element in the population in 1870 than before the Civil War, but they were still a substantial number and were still concentrated in Wilmington, where the Irish comprised 11 percent of the population of Wilmington in 1870.

Their natural affinity was with the Democrats, partly for historical reasons. The Democrats had sought the immigrant vote from the beginnings of party politics, whereas the Republicans were to some degree heirs to the Know-Nothings, the particular enemies of the Irish. By reason of their lowly economic situation, the Irish also may have felt some rivalry with the blacks. At any rate, the Irish population of Wilmington was just large enough to cancel any advantage the Republicans could derive from a black urban vote, because blacks comprised only 10 percent of the Wilmington population in 1870.

The existence of a phalanx of Irish Democrats in Wilmington, a citadel of Republican strength, helps explain the success of the Democrats in 1874 and 1876, when they won the elections for all state offices and for the assembly in all three counties. In 1878 the Republicans were so discouraged that they did not even nominate a ticket, leaving Delaware a one-party state except for such opposition as the feeble Greenback Labor party could supply.

In 1880, a presidential election year, the Republicans displayed renewed vigor. Amid charges of taxpaying and outright vote-buying by both parties, a heavy turnout of 76 percent of the eligible voters was secured, but the result was the same as in the past—a Democratic triumph—though the Republicans did win control of New Castle County. In the next two elections, the Republicans did not do even that well, and in 1886, as in 1878, they decided not to present a ticket.

Yet, just at this time, when the Democrats were riding high, the fortunes of the two parties began to change. There are two explanations to be offered, a short-term explanation of Republican success in 1888 and a long-term explanation of the forces that converted Delaware from a Democratic stronghold in Reconstruction years to a bulwark of Republicanism in the early twentieth century.

For the short-term change in 1888, the explanation is to be found in the recent successes of the Democrats, which set this party up to destroy itself. For three decades the Democrats had been led by Bayards and Saulsburys in uneasy alliance. When their interests seemed to clash, they had generally succeeded in compromising their differences and dividing the loaves and fishes of office among their followers.

In 1885 the new Democratic president, Grover Cleveland, chose Thomas Bayard to be at the head of his cabinet as secretary of state, a natural appointment in view of the very high standing Bayard's ability had won for him in the Senate and in the Democratic party, where in three successive national conventions he had been runner-up for the Democratic presidential nomination.

When Bayard left the Senate, he was able to secure his seat for a political ally from New Castle County, George Gray. But in 1888, when Eli Saulsbury was nearing the end of his third senatorial term, a service unprecedented in Delaware history, he was unwilling to step aside for a successor even though he was seventy-one years old. The chief Democratic rival for his place was James L. Wolcott, who was twenty-four years younger than Saulsbury and who had read law in his office. Choice of a senator rested, of course, with the legislature, and Wolcott and Saulsbury forces battled so furiously over the legislative seats from Kent and Sussex that the Republicans won both counties and found themselves controlling the legislature for the first time in history.

Given their first opportunity to elect a United States senator, the Republican legislators decided upon Anthony Higgins, the former district attorney, who had attended Delaware College and Yale, as well as Harvard Law School. His most famous case was *Delaware* v. *Neal* in 1880, in which he defended a black man accused falsely of rape. A first trial in Delaware led to a verdict of guilty and a sentence of hanging, but Higgins successfully appealed the case to the Supreme Court of the United States on the basis that Neal had been denied a trial by his peers because no blacks had been called for jury duty. A retrial led to Neal's acquittal.

The Republicans owed some of their success downstate in 1888 to the vigorous campaign conducted by their candidate for the national House of Representatives, Charles H. Treat, a Georgetown manufacturer who originally came from New York. Treat himself was defeated, but his efforts, and probably his money, foreshadowed Republican successes in future years, when an alliance of the Republican party and the manufacturers, cemented by their common devotion to the protective tariff, would overcome the rule of the Democratic establishment of lawyers and the landed gentry, the old Bourbon aristocracy of Delaware.

10

Change and Resistance to Change: The 1897 Constitution

Industrialization

It is a peculiar fact in the history of Delaware that the parties of Alexander Hamilton and Henry Clay, the Federalist party and the Whig party, theoretically the proponents of American manufactures and of a nationalist, protected economy, had their greatest support in this state in its most agricultural areas, the downstate counties of Kent and Sussex; whereas the agrarian parties of Jefferson and Jackson were popular in Wilmington, a center of trade and of such manufacturing as Delaware possessed. The Civil War and the Jackson party's increasing conservatism changed all this, and by the Reconstruction period, the Democratic party was decidedly the agrarian party of Delaware. Wilmington and neighboring hundreds along the industrialized Brandywine and Red Clay Creek were now the citadels of the new Republicans, and from this basis they set out to reconquer a state that had been a bastion of Clay's "American System" in the days of John M. Clayton.

The progress of manufacturing in the Wilmington area in the Reconstruction period was notable. Whereas in 1860 about $5.5 million was invested in manufacturing enterprises, in 1900 their capital had risen to $41 million. The number of wage earners had grown in the same period to 22,203 from 6,421—and from 3,888, in 1850, for, as demonstrated earlier, this growth began before the Civil War.

The industrialization of the Wilmington area involved not only changes in magnitude but also changes in quality. In the mid-century, flour, carriages, and textiles were the leading local products. As the century continued, their relative importance decreased. The large flour mills of William Lea and Son continued to operate through this period, but the center for flour milling had long ago moved westward. The carriage-making industry, a major enterprise in Wilmington in the 1850s, also suffered from Western competition, though the related field of railroad-car building and repair continued to flourish. One factory that prospered throughout this period was the cotton textile finishing mill of Joseph Bancroft and Sons, founded by a Manchester-born English immigrant, who died in 1874.

Some industries of importance in the period had a short life span in Delaware. For example, another English immigrant, Henry Courtney, invented and manufactured the so-called parlor match, but after his company had become part of the Diamond Match Company, it moved out of Wilmington in 1890. Rolling mills of the Diamond State Iron Company furnished employment to a large number of men, in shifts working twenty-four hours a day, until the company ran into financial problems and closed in 1904.

The major characteristic of Wilmington manufacturing in these years was its diversity. Wilmington profited from having a variety of industrial enterprises, rather than just one specialty, though there were some industries for which Wilmington was a notable center. The leather industry, for example, was represented by many factories in Wilmington, particularly those engaged in production of leather from imported goatskins, often called morocco or kid. The product was shipped away, often to be used in the manufacture of shoes.

Vulcanized fiber was another local specialty. To a degree, it is an outgrowth of the paper industry since the fiber is a product of chemically treated paper that is jelled, laminated to the thickness desired, and then dried and pressed. The inventor was an Englishman, who took out his patent in 1859, but the Vulcanized Fibre Company of Wilmington, founded in 1875, may have made the first commercial use of the patent. Fiber found diverse uses, such as horse shoes and carriage-wheel washers, but its greatest growth was as electrical insulation and therefore waited on the development of the electric industry. There were at least five fiber companies in Delaware in 1900 producing a substantial amount of the nation's fiber product.

At the same date, there were six paper companies operating

eight paper mills in Delaware. These mills were relatively small, however, some specializing in paper of the finest grade, and their future was limited because of their distance from abundant supplies of wood pulp. Their existence helped stimulate the growth of another Delaware industry—the manufacture of paper-making machinery. There were a number of small machine shops in Wilmington, but the largest employers were the foundries manufacturing heavy machinery. Some of the foundries were operated in conjunction with shipyards, but the cyclical nature of the shipbuilding industry, which had recurrent periods of boom and bust, was in contrast to the steadier employment offered by many Wilmington industries. The local shops of the Pennsylvania Railroad, of the Pullman Company, and of Jackson and Sharp, another manufacturer of railroad cars, also employed a significant part of the Wilmington laboring force.

The most famous of the local manufacturing specialties of the Wilmington area, though in 1900 it was not the largest either in value of product or in number of employees, was the gunpowder industry. It was remarkable, however, that this enterprise, founded in 1802 by a French immigrant, acquired and retained a substantial national reputation while remaining under local Delaware ownership and management. Though the value of this industry was especially evident in wartime, the growth of the company depended more upon the commercial uses of powder in mining and in the construction industry, especially the construction of roads and canals.

Throughout the nineteenth century the company was operated as a family partnership, completely dominated for many years by Gen. Henry du Pont, a son of the founder. Through the Gunpowder Trade Association, organized in 1872, the E. I. du Pont de Nemours Company, with a few associated companies, controlled black powder prices and production throughout the United States. There were several subsidiaries of the Delaware company, like the Du Pont Company of Pennsylvania, at Scranton, and Du Pont had become a substantial stockholder in still other companies, thus gaining access to company records and improving coordination of price and production policies.

On Henry du Pont's death in 1889, he was succeeded as company president by his nephew Eugene du Pont. Under Eugene du Pont's presidency, the company continued its development as before, remaining one of the two dominant manufacturers in a middle-sized industry. Black powder continued to be produced

Three Cousins, Members of the Fourth Generation of the Family in the Du Pont Company, Who Took Over Direction of the Company in 1902.

T. Coleman du Pont (1863–1930), who became president of the Du Pont Company in 1902.

Alfred I. du Pont (1864–1935), who became vice-president of the company in 1902.

Pierre S. du Pont (1870–1954), who became treasurer in 1902 and president of the company in 1915. (All three photographs courtesy of the Eleutherian Mills Historical Library.)

on the Brandywine, but newer explosives, such as dynamite and smokeless powder, were made out of state, some at plants across the Delaware River at Gibbstown and Carney's Point, New Jersey. Not until 1899, when Delaware adopted a new general incorporation law, was the old Du Pont partnership turned into a corporation.

In the late nineteenth century, business consolidation was a major economic trend, and in this period, especially after the depression of 1893, many Delaware enterprises were sold by their local owners. The American Car and Foundry Company, for example, bought Jackson and Sharp, and Harlan & Hollingsworth was also sold to a large out-of-state corporation, the Bethlehem Steel Company.

The Du Pont Company narrowly escaped a similar fate. When Eugene du Pont died in 1902, the senior directors planned to sell the company to its chief competitors until a junior director, Alfred I. du Pont, who was then only thirty-eight, protested. Given an opportunity to purchase the company, Alfred I. associated himself with two young cousins, T. Coleman du Pont, then thirty-nine, who had wide managerial experience but had never worked for the powder company, and Pierre S. du Pont, thirty-two, who had left the company in 1899, discouraged about his prospects for advancement. T. Coleman du Pont became the new Du Pont Company president, Alfred I., vice-president and works manager, and Pierre S., treasurer. Together the three gifted young cousins set the old family company on the path to becoming one of America's largest industrial enterprises.

The Dominant Role of the Pennsylvania Railroad

Consolidation was as evident in the field of transportation as in manufacturing. The Delaware Railroad, completed to Delmar in 1859, was controlled from the beginning by the Philadelphia, Wilmington, and Baltimore Railroad. The latter railroad was never owned by Delaware interests but was an independent line that became a pawn in the rivalry of the great trans-Appalachian railroads of Baltimore and Philadelphia, between which it furnished the shortest and most convenient connection. In 1881 the president of the Baltimore and Ohio Railroad thought he had succeeded in buying the P.W. & B. and rashly ordered the Pennsylvania Railroad to give up its customary use of this line. At the last minute, however, the B & O was frustrated when the Pennsylvania bought a majority of the stock of the P.W. & B. out from under the B & O.

Rather than risk losing its entry to Philadelphia and New York, the B & O set about building its own line parallel to the P.W. & B. When the new tracks were completed in 1886, the industrial value of New Castle County land was augmented by the availability of a second major transportation route through the county from Newark to Wilmington and on to Chester and Philadelphia, where use of the Philadelphia and Reading and the Central of New Jersey tracks gave the B & O the access to New York it wanted.

Other railroads also were constructed north and west from Wilmington. Some were mere spurs of the two main lines. The Wilmington and Western hoped to develop into a new major railway, but its growth was limited, and it became only a branch of the B & O serving the industrial Red Clay Creek Valley. The Wilmington and Northern was a longer road that led through the Brandywine Valley to Birdsboro, Pennsylvania, south of Reading. It had intended to penetrate the Pennsylvania coal fields but stopped short of its destination, and eventually, it became a branch of the Philadelphia and Reading Railroad, which gained access by this route to the harbor of Wilmington.

The most important effect of railroad expansion and consolidation in Delaware in the late nineteenth century was the dominant position accorded the Pennsylvania Railroad in the local economy by virtue of its acquisition of the P.W. & B. and of the network of railroads that served the Delmarva Peninsula, radiating like branches east and west from the main trunk of the Delaware Railroad line. From junction points such as Townsend, Clayton, Harrington, and Seaford, these branches led off right and left to various towns of the peninsula, including Centerville, Chestertown, Easton, and Cambridge on the Eastern Shore of Maryland, as well as Milford, Lewes, and Rehoboth, in Delaware.

The Junction and Breakwater Railroad, which ran eastward from Harrington to Milford, Georgetown, and Lewes in 1869, was extended south from Georgetown through Selbyville into Worcester County, Maryland. Two other rail lines crossed the Delaware Railroad: one ran from Delaware City through Newark to Pomeroy, Pennsylvania, west of Coatesville; the Queen Anne's Railroad, later called the Maryland, Delaware, and Virginia, was completed in 1898 from Lewes through Milton and Greenwood to Love Point, on Kent Island, Maryland, terminus of a twenty-seven-mile Chesapeake Bay ferry service from Baltimore.

As a result of this network of rail lines, the Pennsylvania Railroad, with its subsidiaries, became the largest property owner and the largest taxpayer in Delaware. To look after its interests at the General Assembly, the railroad company is said to have established the largest, or at least the best financed, lobby in Dover. As a means of winning the friendship of assemblymen, judges, and other leading state officials, the company gave them free passes on what Delawareans called "the cars."

Railroads were not the only means of transportation. On the Delaware and some smaller rivers, regular steamboat service was available and cheap, both for passengers and for freight. There were scheduled daily trips between Wilmington and Philadelphia, and, somewhat less frequently, steamboats connected these ports with downstate Delaware towns, including Milford, Lebanon, Odessa, and Frederica. In the summer, steamers ran from Wilmington and New Castle to a pier on the bay shore near Cape May, New Jersey, one of the earliest fashionable ocean resorts. A motley collection of river craft moved farm produce toward Wilmington and Philadelphia from lower Delaware and also from south Jersey.

The street railway systems of Wilmington, electrified after 1887, permitted urban workers to live at a distance from their shops or factories and encouraged the development of the first suburbs. By 1900 electric trolley cars were running from Wilmington to New Castle and Delaware City to the south, to Elsmere and Brandywine Springs to the west, and to Chester and Darby (where there was a connection to Philadelphia) to the north. The only trolley line constructed below Delaware City was one connecting Middletown with Odessa.

It was the railroad, however, with its capacity for rapid long-distance carriage of both people and freight, that had the greatest impact on Delaware life at the end of the nineteenth century Besides being much faster than other available means of transportation, the railroad offered service to areas of Delaware that had no ready access to river shipping. The peach orchards that had become profitable around Delaware City in the 1830s spread downstate in the wake of the railroad and brought new prosperity to many areas. In 1875, for instance, 5 million baskets of peaches, amounting to over nine hundred thousand carloads, were loaded at stations on the Delaware Railroad.

Transportation by rail. Loading watermelons on the Delaware Railroad at Laurel, 1925. (Courtesy of the Division of Historical and Cultural Affairs.)

Transportation by water. The O. H. Vessels *(built at Cambridge, Maryland) unloads a cargo of tomatoes from Leipsic at a cannery landing in about 1910.* (Courtesy of Henry P. Marshall, Lewes.) *Both photographs appeared in Harold B. Hancock,* The History of Sussex County, Delaware *(1976).*

After 1890 the acreage devoted to peaches was gradually reduced because of a blight called the "yellows" that damaged the crop, but other "truck crops" (crops farmers sold to housekeepers in market, such as vegetables and fruit) remained popular. Corn and wheat still were important, but the availability of rail transport to the growing metropolitan markets encouraged attention to garden crops, such as strawberries, beans, peas, and melons. Canneries, including the important Richardson and Robbins plant at Dover, were opened in most Delaware towns from Newark southward to take advantage of the bounty of Delaware farms.

Although the railroad was a boon to the Delaware farmer, it also gave him cause for complaint. If he lived inconveniently distant from a river port like Milford, a rise in railroad rates could wipe out his profit. Complaints arose that the railroad took advantage of its monopolistic position in charging more for short hauls from Delaware farms than for longer hauls from areas where it had competition from other railroads or from steamboats. It was said, for instance, that before the B & O Railroad came to Newark, the railroad fare from there to Wilmington was higher than from Wilmington to Philadelphia, a route where river shipping offered competition. Downstate farmers were particularly annoyed that the railroads of the Delmarva Peninsula offered lower rates for northward-bound goods originating at Norfolk, Virginia (where ocean carriers offered competition), than from intermediate points on the peninsula.

The cause of the farmers against the railroad was taken up in Delaware as elsewhere by a farmers' organization, the Patrons of Husbandry, which had organized a Delaware branch in 1875. In 1887 this branch, the Delaware State Grange, instituted a suit before the Interstate Commerce Commission against the Pennsylvania Railroad and its major subsidiaries on the peninsula, accusing them of unjust and unreasonable charges, especially for perishable fruit, of preferential rebates to favored shippers, and of lower rates and more rapid service for some localities than for others that lay closer to the markets. Despite charges that such discrimination might destroy the production of fruit and vegetables in Delaware, four years and more of effort secured only a 10 percent reduction of freight rates from Seaford north. Some downstate farmers hoped their freight charges might be reduced by construction of a competitive railroad line through eastern Kent County from Milford to Delaware City, but it never materialized. Only the advent of the automobile trucking industry in the 1920s destroyed the predominant position of the Pennsylvania Railroad in Delaware transportation.

Farmers' complaints about the railroad monopoly are evidence of a spreading malaise among rural Delawareans in the late nineteenth century. Although some farmers found profit in new crops, agriculture was obviously no longer king in Delaware. The census of 1900 reveals that more individuals and vastly more wealth were employed in manufacturing than in agriculture. Delawareans resented the new situation, this topsy-turvy exchange of importance between agriculture and manufacturing, between the farm and the city, even more than they might have otherwise because they saw that control of much of Delaware manufacturing, as of almost all transportation, lay outside the state in Philadelphia or beyond.

There never developed in Delaware any such intense populist distrust of metropolitan bankers and manufacturers as swept the Western states in the 1890s. Philadelphia (more immediately the personification of the big city than New York) was too close and too intimately connected with Delaware life for that. The Delaware farmer might well have a son or a brother in a factory office or a bank in Philadelphia.

Nevertheless, at the end of the nineteenth century, rural Delaware was on the defensive. In its despair, it wrote guaranties into a new constitution, guaranties that gave some protection to rural, traditional Delaware against urban wealth and ambition.

The Constitutional Reform, I

At various times, New Castle County politicians talked of changing the state constitution to allow increased representation of the growing population of Wilmington, but failure to adopt the proposed constitution of 1853 indicated just how difficult constitutional change could be. In 1881 Wilmington was made the county seat of New Castle County after the inconvenience of going to New Castle for all official business involving courts or county records had long been evident. In 1883 the General Assembly approved a constitutional amendment that would have allowed Wilmington additional representation in the lower house, along with making some other alterations in the government, but the next General Assembly, in 1885, withheld the assent necessary for final ratification.

In 1887 the legislature approved Governor Benjamin Biggs's call for a referendum on the possibility of holding a constitutional convention. The referendum disclosed sentiment overwhelmingly in favor of a constitution, the vote being 14,205 to 431, but still it was a failure because the supporters of the referendum cast a thousand votes less than necessary according to the constitutional provision requiring a majority of the votes cast at the largest of the last three general elections.

To solve the old difficulty of getting voters to go to the polls at a special referendum, when no offices were being filled, in anything like the numbers that turned out at a general election, advocates of reform decided they must first amend the constitution so as to allow the referendum to take place at the same time as a general election. This was accomplished by 1893, and in 1894 the necessary majority was at last secured (by a vote of 22,842 to 2,364) in a referendum on holding a convention. The next assembly session passed legislation providing for the convention, which was elected at the general election in the fall of 1896.

By the enabling legislation, each county was allotted ten delegates to the convention, and before the election it was widely urged that bipartisan delegations should be chosen. In Sussex County these suggestions were followed; the Sussex Democrats nominated only five candidates, who were elected with five Republican colleagues. New Castle and Kent Democrats, on the other hand, insisted on naming complete tickets, and vigorous contests resulted. Two factions of Republicans presented tickets in New Castle, four names appearing on both tickets. These four Republicans were elected, along with six Democrats.

In Kent County both Republicans and Democrats claimed victory, with the sheriff certifying the election of ten Democratic candidates and a board of canvass certifying the Republican slate. The Sussex and New Castle delegates to the convention, consisting of eleven Democrats and nine Republicans, set up a credentials committee with a three-to-two Democratic majority. It adopted a compromise, seating five Kent Democrats and five Republicans. By so doing, however, it preserved the Democratic majority of two votes in the convention, which now had sixteen Democrats and fourteen Republicans.

When the convention met, in December 1896, a Democrat from New Castle County, John Biggs, son of former Governor Benjamin Biggs, was elected its president. Before it adjourned, on June 4, 1897, the convention wrote an extraordinarily lengthy, detailed constitution that was destined to remain in effect much longer than any of the three Delaware state constitutions that preceded it. Despite a legislative recommendation that the new constitution be submitted to the people for approval in a referendum, the convention decided to declare its handiwork in effect merely by promulgation, as had been done in the case of all previous constitutions except the one that had been rejected in 1853. Six delegates were opposed to this course; all were Democrats, but their reasons for desiring a referendum may have varied greatly. One was from Sussex, one from Kent, and four, including the president of the convention, were from New Castle County.

Perhaps the assembly was conscious of the fact that it was disregarding another recommendation of the legislature—that it should provide representation proportionate to the distribution of population, which it did not do. What it did do was to allocate representation to single-member constituencies, both in the senate and in the house, in place of the former countywide constituencies. Furthermore, additional representation was awarded to New Castle County, which was allotted seven senators and fifteen representatives, as compared with five senators and ten representatives awarded to Kent and Sussex. This was not exactly proportional, because New Castle County had over half the population of Delaware.

But it was the city of Wilmington, rather than the county, that was treated badly. The 1890 population figures were as follows: New Castle County, 97,182 (of which number 61,431 lived in Wilmington) ; Kent County, 32,664; Sussex County, 38,647. Obviously, proportionate representation would have provided Wilmington more legislators than Kent or Sussex. Yet only two senators were to be chosen in Wilmington and only five representatives, as against five senators and ten representatives each from Kent, Sussex, and rural New Castle County, each area inferior to Wilmington in population.

Under the old constitution, Wilmington had no special allocation, but since the New Castle County delegates were elected at large, Wilmingtonians participated in the choice of one-third of the members of each house. Since Wilmington had more voters than the rest of the county, Wilmingtonians to that degree controlled the choice of one-third of the legislators. The new constitution, written after decades of complaining about the lack of proportionate representation, actually reduced the influence of Wilmington in the legislature. By its terms Wilmingtonians voted for only one-seventh (five out of thirty-five) of the members of the house and two-seventeenths of the members of the senate. And since amendments to the constitution were to be made only by a two-thirds vote in each house in two successive assemblies, it was impossible for Wilmingtonians ever to correct this mal-apportionment unless they won the alliance of a good majority of the rural assemblymen.

In refusing to submit their completed constitution to a popular vote, the members of the convention deprived the voters of Wilmington of any chance of using the ballot to protest against the inequitable apportionment of seats. Since Wilmington was generally Republican, it could hardly expect much sympathy from downstate Democrats, but in general, the convention seems not to have been divided by the party affiliations of the members. Most committees, for example, were evenly balanced by party and also by county. More important was the fear in rural Delaware, including part of rural New Castle County, of the growing population and wealth of Wilmington. One delegate compared Wilmington to an octopus, getting its wishes whenever it chose by stretching out tentacles and drawing people into its grasp. Several delegates noted that Wilmington residents had not the same stake in the welfare of Delaware that farmers had. City people were said to be a floating population who would and could leave Delaware very easily if better jobs opened up somewhere else. Besides, one delegate protested, thousands of them could not speak English. (Almost 14 percent of Wilmingtonians, by the census of 1900, were foreign-born, but over half of this foreign-born element came from English-speaking countries, and others had come as children.)

The apportionment provisions of the 1897 constitution were a defensive bulwark thrown up by old, rural, agrarian Delaware against the new, urban, industrial elements in the state, a defense of the few against the many, of the poor against the rich, of the traditional against the innovative. They could be looked upon as a limitation established by a minority upon the otherwise overwhelming power of a majority. Rural overrepresentation in the legislature did not function as a positive bar to changes demanded by the industrial elements, both of capital and of labor, for the weight of their numbers and wealth was very great, and there were more affiliations than antagonisms between rural and urban

Delaware, more understandings than misunderstandings. But the
apportionment of 1897 did serve for over fifty years as a mild
brake upon reform, a defense against sudden change.

The Constitutional Reform, II

Generally, the innovations provided by the new Delaware
constitution were directed toward the enlargement of democratic
controls over government and toward recognition of needs that
had become manifest since the 1831 constitutional convention.
A notable change was in the basis for the franchise, which became a literacy requirement (the ability to write one's name
and to read the constitution in English) instead of the payment
of a county tax. Payment of a registration fee of one dollar was
still required, but the old need of being first assessed was dropped
and, with it, all possible use of assessment methods as a device to
keep citizens from voting. The registration fee itself was abandoned by constitutional amendment in 1907; the ready availability of money at Delaware elections had made it meaningless.

The governor, whose role had been weak since independence,
was at last given the right to veto legislation, including items
in appropriation bills, though the legislature could enact bills
over his veto by a three-fifths vote in each house. He was also,
for the first time, permitted to serve a second term, consecutive
or otherwise, though this was the limit. His appointments to
office, however, were now required to be confirmed by the senate,
and the governor lost his previous right to approve constitutional
amendments.

The process of amending was eased. An amendment needed
only a two-thirds vote in each house of two successive legislatures,
with a general election intervening. No referendum was provided, but the amendment had to be published three months
before the general election, thus presumably allowing voters to
influence candidates.

The office of lieutenant governor was established, its occu-
pant to be chosen at the same election as the governor, whom he
was to succeed in case of death or resignation; meanwhile, he
would serve as president of the senate with the right to vote
there to break a tie. Obviously, the office was modeled on that
of the vice-president of the United States.

A number of other offices were made elective: the attorney

general, insurance commissioner, treasurer, and auditor at the state level; and the prothonotary, clerk of the peace, register of wills, recorder of deeds, and register in chancery at the county level. It was intended to make these officials, who had four-year terms—except for the treasurer and auditor, who served two years—directly dependent on the voters. However, the result was to present the voter with a very long ballot, which also could include the names of presidential electors, congressman, assemblymen, governor, levy court commissioner, sheriff, coroner, and county treasurer and comptroller. In many cases, the voter was overwhelmed by the number of choices before him and apt to take advice from a friendly party worker.

There was talk at the convention of making judges elective, but, instead, their terms were reduced from life (that is, during good behavior) to twelve years. Apparently, there was concern over the idea of allowing the New Castle County majority to dominate the election of state judges. Even the terms of justices of the peace were reduced. It was also provided that not more than a bare majority of the five Superior Court judges might be of the same political party. These judges also served on the Orphans' Court (abolished in 1970) and, with the addition of the chancellor, made up the Supreme Court. In the case of an appeal to the Supreme Court, only those judges sat who had not heard the case in the lower courts; therefore, the Supreme Court became known as "the court of left-over judges." A half-century passed before a separate and independent Supreme Court was created by constitutional amendment in 1951.

The convention made a serious effort to reduce the likelihood of bribery or unfair pressures in elections and in legislative procedures. Besides the changes in franchise requirements (accompanied by deletion of the former landholding requirement for senators), provisions were made for the trial of bribery cases without a jury. Divorces and incorporations (with some exceptions, including the incorporation of banks and municipalities) were no longer to be subjects for legislative action. Divorces were to be handled in the courts; incorporations under provisions of a general incorporation law. Previously, both subjects had frequently taken legislative time from other business. In divorce cases, there was too much opportunity for favoritism, as there was also in bills for incorporation, where one company might seek an advantage over others.

Nineteenth-century concerns were demonstrated by provisions

for a State Board of Health and a State Board of Agriculture. Gambling, including the once common use of lotteries for public purposes, was forbidden. Prohibitionists succeeded in winning provisions for local option, to be determined by referenda in each of the counties and in Wilmington. Rejected, however, was an appeal by Wilmington labor unions (led by the cigar-makers union, a notably intellectual group) for a wider use of the referendum, plus a popular initiative of laws by petition.

In making provision for free public schools, the convention required annual appropriations to school districts exclusively for the payment of teachers' salaries and for free textbooks. Racially segregated schools were required, but no distinction was to be made on the basis of race or color in appropriations. The appeal of one white schoolmaster, who argued that whether schools were segregated or integrated racially should be left to the local district, was disregarded.

So were appeals from two reform groups who testified before the convention. The Single Tax Association, composed of followers of Henry George, argued that only land, as the common inheritance of mankind, should be taxed, leaving to each man's initiative the use he would put it to since he would be regarded as a renter or leaseholder, rather than as a landowner. Disregarding this proposal as a radical idea, the convention specifically insisted that property taxes be assessed on both the land and improvements. In the 1896 election the Single Taxers had sought to spread their ideas in Delaware, which they chose because of its small size, but they had little success. A few years later, however, backed by Joseph Fels, a Philadelphia soap manufacturer and philanthropist, a group of Single Taxers led by Frank Stephens and Will Ross founded a community that they called Arden, near Grubb's Corner in Brandywine Hundred. Instead of selling individual tracts of land outright, the founders distributed the land by long-term leases and based the rent on the value of the land itself, not the improvements made on it. Arden prospered and eventually became the center of a group of three single-tax communities.

The 1897 convention also heard and rejected a proposal to extend the right to vote to women, the one notably excluded group, now that black men had been admitted to the franchise. A group of Delawareans had been seeking women's suffrage at least since 1869, encouraged by the abolitionist Thomas Garrett and led by Mary Ann Sorden Stuart, of Greenwood. Their efforts secured the introduction of a women's suffrage amendment in the legislature in 1881, but it was rejected. Through these years, however, beginning with the Married Woman's Rights Law of 1865, the legislature did enact a number of statutes relieving married women of the injustices they suffered under the common law in relation to the control of property, which had once belonged exclusively to husbands.

In 1888 the Women's Christian Temperance Union organized a franchise department, directed for many years by Martha Cranston, of Newport, and in 1895 a Wilmington Equal Suffrage Club was formed that became the basis for a state Equal Suffrage Association. This association prepared a petition to the constitutional convention that was signed by 1,592 men and 1,228 women. When a hearing was arranged for January 13, the association brought its distinguished national leader, Carrie Chapman Catt, to Dover to address the convention. Emalea Pusey Warner, Margaret W. Houston, and Emma Worrell were among the local women who also spoke, but in vain, for on February 16 the convention rejected women's suffrage by a vote of seventeen to seven.

All seven of the votes cast in favor of women's suffrage came from downstate Republicans, four from Sussex, two from Kent, and one from St. George's Hundred in lower New Castle County. It is interesting to note that the two most vocal Republicans in the convention, William Spruance, a graduate of Princeton College and of Harvard Law School, and Edward Bradford, a Yale graduate who had married the daughter of Alexis I. du Pont, were both opposed to women's suffrage. Spruance argued that few women property owners exercised the right of suffrage that had been given them in school board elections. The majority of Delaware women, he declared, and particularly the majority of the most intelligent and most highly cultivated women, did not want the franchise; if women were given the right to vote, the ones who would exercise it would be those least qualified to do so. The solid opposition of Democratic delegates to women's suffrage suggests that they may have shared Spruance's apprehensions. Still priding themselves on being a "lily white" party, the Democrats could only view with alarm the possibility of a considerable enlargement of the solidly Republican black vote.

11

Addicks and Du Pont

Corruption of Elections

The unspoken fear that aligned even the most liberal Democrats against women's suffrage in 1897 was the specter of a doubling of the number of votes available for purchase. Since the purchase of votes was illegal, the men who engaged in this activity did so as secretly as possible; consequently, detailed information is scanty. There was general agreement, however, that by 1897 it was an important factor in Delaware politics.

The origins of the election corruption prevalent in 1897 can be traced to the practices of early nineteenth-century politicians who roused their followers to partisan enthusiasm with plentiful and free liquid refreshments. "Rum is their Federalism, and rum is their Democracy," wrote one bitter commentator.

Since the voter had to be a taxpayer, the candidate who had money was tempted to help a poor but faithful supporter by paying his tax bill. He might go a bit further, by giving him a drink of liquor and perhaps two dollars. Sometimes a hat, a coat, or a pair of boots would do as a gift, or a dress for a man's wife. There were many poor men who eked out a precarious living, doing chores, fishing, and picking berries in season. Even if a man had no property, he was still assessed a capitation tax and could vote if it were paid. Before 1897 there was no requirement that a voter be able to read and write.

Upon passage of the Fifteenth Amendment, the number of poor electors was considerably increased in Delaware by the addition of poor blacks to poor whites. The Democrats sought to limit the effect of this addition by the Assessment and Collection Laws of 1873. These laws worked only as long as the Democrats controlled the pertinent local officials—that is, the county as-

173

sessors and tax collectors. After the Republican victory in 1888, Democratic control of the assessment and collection rolls was uncertain, and it became increasingly easy for black men to vote.

Before very long, Republicans were not only welcoming the black vote but actively, and often illegally, soliciting it, just as the vote of poor white men had been actively, and often illegally, solicited by both Republicans and Democrats for many years. The period immediately before and after the constitutional convention of 1896–97 witnessed a struggle for control of the Republican party that led to far more lavish campaign expenditures than had ever been known in Delaware before.

Of course, many campaign expenditures were perfectly legitimate. Halls were rented and bands provided for election rallies. Printing bills had to be paid, and so did party workers on election day. Some of the latter watched the polls, while others sought out lazy or forgetful voters. In 1891 a Voters' Assistant Law was passed at the same time that provision was made for use of the secret, Australian ballot. Each party was to provide a voters' assistant at every polling place to help any voter who requested assistance in marking his ballot.

Though the original intention was to offer legitimate help to a voter who might well be illiterate or otherwise handicapped, the Voters' Assistant Law contributed to the corruption of the franchise. The voter who wanted to sell his vote would request assistance in marking his ballot. When he had properly marked and deposited his ballot, he would be given some token as a sort of receipt for his vote, along with instructions as to where to find the party treasurer, who would exchange an agreed sum for the token. In one case that became notorious because it was described in a court of law, the payoff token was a salted chestnut, handed at the polls to a voter who then would exchange it for his payoff—usually five or ten dollars—at a nearby livery stable.

Repealed in 1897, the Voters' Assistant Law was reenacted in 1901 and remained an instrument of corruption until its final repeal in 1913. Its advantage to the vote-buyer was very great. This law, according to one frank state senator, insured that a bought vote stayed bought. "It insures delivery of the goods," he said; "when I buy a horse, I want my horse."

Even after the repeal of the Voters' Assistant Law, what was called the *loose ballot system* encouraged voting irregularities. Many more ballots were printed than were needed so as to permit their distribution to voters at home. This system permitted every voter to become familiar with the names of all the candidates, but it also opened the way to some skulduggery. It was perfectly legal to vote a ballot marked at home with the help of a party worker, though at the polling place the voter was first required to enter a booth, where he had privacy and could mark a fresh ballot if he chose to. If his vote was purchased, however, he was expected to come out of the booth quickly to avoid suspicion of changing his ballot.

It should be noted that there is some question whether many votes were available to the highest bidder. Probably, a majority of the Delaware voters who took money for voting could not easily be persuaded to shift from one party to another. The black voter, for instance, would not in these years vote for a Democrat. White voters were likely to be aligned with one party or another. Where vote-buying was most effective was in resolving factional disputes within a party, as in the case of a terrific schism that rent the Republican party from 1895 to 1906, or in getting out the maximum vote a party could hope for in a close election.

A voter accustomed to receiving money for his vote was not so likely to shift parties as he was to stay home on election day if no payment was offered by his party. Some voters came to think that a ten-dollar bill was as much as their right on election day as early nineteenth-century voters had thought themselves entitled to a free drink at the expense of the candidate of their choice—or as a voter a few years later might demand that his party give him an automobile ride to the polls if it cared about his vote. Perhaps the difference between a drink and a ride, on the one hand, and a ten-dollar bill, on the other hand, is only a difference in degree. The drink or the ride, however, was a small matter, a gift that many candidates could afford. The purchase of votes with a gift of money opened a Pandora's box of troubles, threatening to turn elections into auctions that could be won by the highest bidder.

The Addicks Phrenzy

The highest bidder at Delaware elections in the late 1890s was John Edward Addicks. A Philadelphian by birth and rearing, son of a Republican politician who held a modest public post, Addicks, though aided initially by marriage to the daughter of a wealthy pork packer, was a self-made millionaire. His first fortune, built on grain speculation, was wiped out in the depression of 1873, but he started quickly to accumulate another, mainly by organizing and manipulating gas companies. His success won him the sobriquet *Gas Addicks*.

Though his business enterprises, which often involved negotiations with municipal politicians, took him to many cities, he moved his official residence in 1877, when he was thirty-six years old, to Claymont, Delaware, a railroad stop for suburban trains to Philadelphia. He admitted later that he lived in Claymont for two months before realizing it was not in Delaware County, Pennsylvania. Delaware politics gradually became of consuming interest to him, for two reasons. First, he sought from the Delaware legislature, successfully, a charter for his Bay State Gas Company, which operated in Massachusetts. Second, he sought from the same legislature, unsuccessfully, election to the Senate of the United States.

The idea of running for senator came to him, he said, when he read of the Republican victory in 1888. Whether true or not, there would previously have been no chance for a Republican in Delaware to hope for a Senate seat. Between 1888 and 1894 Addicks spent a large sum of money helping the Republicans accomplish what they called "redeeming the state" from the Democrats. The great national issue was the tariff, and to Republican manufacturers, including those in Philadelphia, the citadel of high-tariff protectionism, it was important to stop Delaware from sending low-tariff Democrats to Washington.

Perhaps Delaware manufacturers were willing to help—for example, Charles Treat, a Georgetown manufacturer had run for Congress in 1888—but Addicks surpassed them all in his liberality. According to an active Republican, Addicks contributed enough money to keep almost two thousand Republican voters on the election lists in Kent in 1893, after the party had appealed for financial support in vain to Senator Anthony Higgins; to Gen. James H. Wilson, leader of the Wilmington Republicans; to the Richardsons, Dover canners; and to George V. Massey, attorney for the Pennsylvania Railroad. Despite Addicks's efforts, Kent County remained Democratic in 1894, but otherwise the election was a Republican triumph such as had never been known before. Joshua Marvil was elected as the first Republican governor since the Civil War, and victories in New Castle and

Sussex gave Republicans control of the legislature, which was due to elect a senator.

The general expectation was that Republican Senator Anthony Higgins would be reelected to a second term, particularly as he was the first-ballot choice of a majority of Republican legislators. But Addicks's ambition stood in Higgins's way. Two days after the election, Addicks declared that he had spent $140,000. "I've bought it," he is reported to have said; "I've paid for it; and I'm going to have it."

What he was intent on having was the senatorship, and the slogan of his supporters, "Addicks or nobody," became clear soon after the legislature met. Six Addicks supporters refused to join the other Republicans in caucus. Through 177 ballots, from January 15, 1895, to May 9, Addicks was able to prevent the election of a senator. The Democrats, a minority of eleven against nineteen Republicans, watched the Republican schism gleefully; they regarded Addicks as a carpetbagger, but, to them, all Republicans were anathema. Higgins gave up when he saw that his reelection was impossible, and the Republicans tried various other candidates in an attempt to persuade some of Addicks's men to compromise. Two of Addicks's band of six did desert, and the Republicans were able to cast 15 votes on May 9 for Col. Henry Algernon du Pont, a West Point graduate and a partner in the company of which his father, Gen. Henry du Pont, had long been president.

This should have been a majority, because the death of Governor Marvil in April had made the Democratic Senate president, William T. Watson, acting governor. But on May 9, Watson, possibly encouraged by friends of Addicks as well as by his Democratic colleagues, reappeared in the Senate and insisted that though acting governor, he still had a vote as an elected senator. Counting Watson, there were thirty legislators, and therefore fifteen was not a majority.

Enraged, the Republican majority declared du Pont elected, and the contest moved on to the United States Senate when du Pont presented his credentials there. To his misfortune, the Senate was so evenly balanced between Republicans and Democrats that control was in the hands of a few western Populists, who were unfriendly to Colonel du Pont on several grounds, seeing him as an Eastern manufacturer who would favor policies they opposed, notably a gold standard and a protective tariff. On May 15, 1896, du Pont's credentials were rejected, and Ad-

dicks's ambition had been responsible for a vacancy in one of
Delaware's two Senate seats.

In the next ten years, the same or a similar drama was re-
played several times. In 1896 angry Republicans tried to expel
Addicks's supporters for what was regarded as treachery to the
party, but the Addicks men formed their own Union Republican
party, with a star as its symbol, and in a relatively short time
demonstrated that they and not their opponents were the majority Republican faction in an election. The Union Republicans had their greatest strength in Kent and Sussex; the Regular
Republicans, who were now also spending money liberally to
fight back, retained control of New Castle County.

Strong pressure from the national Republican party forced
the Delaware factions to unite on one slate of presidential electors in 1896, 1900, and 1904. Sometimes they also compromised
on a state ticket. But when the election was over and the legislature began to vote for a senator, the division between the two
factions was wide and deep. In 1896, aided by some skulduggery
on the part of the board of canvass in Kent County, the Democrats carried the legislature and chose a senator. But thereafter
the Republicans were in a majority. For seven years, from 1899
to 1906, no Delaware seat in the United States Senate was ever
filled on time, and only once, in 1903, was there any election
at all.

Addicks remained determined through these years that his
very considerable contributions to the Republican party in Delaware—perhaps amounting in all to $3 million—should be re-
warded by a senate seat, and, except in 1903, he refused to permit
his followers to support anyone else unless he was elected first.
His opponents, some actuated by idealism and some by a species
of class snobbery (the feeling that Addicks was an outsider and
not a gentleman), could never get over the fact that Addicks's
selfishness had blocked the majority of the party from making a
choice in 1895. Though only a minority in their party thereafter,
they refused to surrender, walking out of a party convention that
Addicks controlled in 1896 and using their best efforts in national
party circles to blacken Addicks's name and keep him from
getting control of the federal patronage.

Both factions tried at various times to win the Democrats to
an alliance, but the latter insisted on a Senate seat as their price,
and the national Republican party was furious at such an idea.
One additional Democratic senator in Washington could be a

Howard Pyle (1853–1911), illustrator and author, in his studio.
(Courtesy of the Delaware Art Museum, Wilmington.)

threat to confirmation of treaties, which needed a two-thirds vote. There is no evidence, incidentally, that the adoption of new franchise requirements and the abolition of the need for jury trial in cases of bribery, changes instituted by the 1897 constitution, caused any decline whatever through these years in election corruption.

In 1899 Addicks received twenty-one of the twenty-seven votes necessary to a senatorial election; in 1901 he received twenty-two votes. In neither case was anyone elected, though in 1901 there were two seats to be filled. In 1903, after Delaware had been wholly unrepresented in the Senate for two years, pressure from national leaders, possibly augmented by talk of the Democrats helping to elect two Regular Republicans, led Addicks to agree to a compromise, the election of his lieutenant, J. Frank Allee, a Dover jeweler, to one seat and of Dr. L. Heisler Ball, a Regular Republican who had just completed a term in the House of Representatives, to the other.

In 1905 Ball's term ended, for this Senate term had been unfilled for four of the six years. In this year, once again, Addicks was able to block an election until the legislature adjourned. This legislature, however, was different from those just preceding it in that Addicks's supporters began to desert. In January, when balloting began, Addicks had twenty-two votes; at adjournment in March he had only fifteen.

Rumors had begun to circulate that Addicks was embarrassed financially at the same time that he faced domestic troubles, for the Bay State Gas Company was near receivership and his third wife was suing him for divorce. "If business misfortunes were to strip Addicks of his money," Senator Higgins had predicted, "he would not remain longer a factor in our politics." A sign of Addicks's fall and of the truth of Higgins's prediction was given in September 1905 when Senator Allee, whom Addicks had made an officer of the Bay State Gas Company, announced he could no longer support Addicks. At a special session of the legislature in 1906, a united Republican party elected its caucus nominee, Col. Henry A. du Pont, to a seat in the Senate, the body that had rejected him in 1895. It was a strange end to a story that had covered eleven years and had begun when Addicks caused a minority of Republican legislators to turn down their caucus choice to further his own ambitions. To Addicks's enemies 1906 marked the end of the carpetbagger era in Delaware politics.

Du Ponts in Politics and Delaware at War

From another point of view, however, the Addicks era could be viewed as a decisive turning point in the history of Delaware politics. In Republican terms, the state had been redeemed from fealty to a feudal backward-looking reign of Democratic barons, like the Saulsburys and Bayards, to whom Delaware was a pocket borough. The new era had arrived. Blacks not only could vote, but were urged to vote. The manufacturing elements had attained political as well as economic primacy; in 1907 a Dover canner, Harry Richardson, joined Colonel du Pont in the United States Senate, and the governor was Preston Lea, a Brandywine flour miller.

These are the elements that brought Delaware out of the Reconstruction era and into the twentieth century: an alliance of high-tariff, sound-money manufacturers with downstate businessmen and politicians, bulwarked by the solid support of the black population everywhere, who knew very clearly that the Democrats did not want them. The effect of Addicks's large expenditures was felt long after he passed from the Delaware scene, even after his obscure death in a New York sanitarium in 1919. The newspapers that had been purchased in the factional fight remained, if they were at all viable, in Republican hands. The political machine—the workers, the techniques, honest and dishonest, of turning out the vote—remained at the service of a united party when Addicks was gone.

Addicks bragged that he had made Delaware Republican. His enemies within the party refuted the claim. Probably the truth is that he accelerated a process that was occurring before he entered the scene. The old-line Democratic leaders were not adjusting to the times. They could not forever deny blacks the right to vote. They could not forever deny the richest, most populous part of the state a leading role in political councils. When the new industrial aristocracy of the Wilmington area refused to accept Addicks's aggressive self-aggrandizement, it was forced to become more political than ever before, to look to Dover sometimes instead of to Philadelphia and New York, to seek downstate allies instead of out-of-state partners. Addicks developed his strength in Kent and Sussex; when he collapsed, the materials for a successful, lasting combination were easily joined together.

The new Republican regime did have the support of a majority of the people. Women were excluded from the franchise until 1920, but their vote, when it was given, did not upset the governing combination. It did not seem to matter at all that Wilmington was sadly underrepresented in the legislature, because the Republican machine was very sensitive to the political needs of the ruling elements in Wilmington. The economic power of Wilmington and the political power of rural Delaware ruled the state in more or less happy unison for thirty years.

Despite the almost continuous Republican control of Delaware through the first third of the twentieth century, despite the fact that in all this period the Democrats were unable to elect even one governor, Delaware was not a one-party state. The Democrats were never so weak as the Delaware Republicans had been in the Reconstruction era. Frequently, as Democratic politicians liked to comment, it was only the black vote, solidly Republican, that made a difference between the two parties. The Democrats early regained control of Kent County from Addicks's old allies, and through these years Kent was the center of their strength downstate, while some urban minority groups of industrial workers, like the Irish and the Poles, gave them strength, though not control, in Wilmington.

Occasionally, the Democrats profited from quarrels among the Republicans. In 1912, when the third-party campaign of Theodore Roosevelt divided the Republicans, Delaware voted for a Democratic presidential candidate (Wilson) for the first time since 1892. The Republicans had united on a gubernatorial candidate in the face of a Democratic candidate abhorrent to some voters because he was an Irish Catholic, but Republican division permitted the Democrats to win a majority in the legislature and to elect Willard Saulsbury, Jr., to the Senate seat his father had vacated forty years earlier.

By 1916 the Republican division was still not healed, though once again there was unity behind the gubernatorial candidate, this time John G. Townsend, Jr., a Sussex Countian of modest background (in terms of wealth and education) who eventually made himself a leader in banking and agriculturally oriented business. Remnants of the 1912 schism were encouraged by Alfred I. du Pont, who had fallen out with several of his cousins and determined to defeat the reelection efforts of Senator Henry A. du Pont, who was now seventy-eight, from enmity for both the Senator and for T. Coleman du Pont, who had served as the senator's political manager for more than a decade.

The 1916 election, the first popular election of a senator in Delaware, consequently resulted in the choice of a Democrat, Josiah Wolcott, whose father's feud with the Saulsburys over the senatorship had caused the defeat of the Delaware Democrats in 1888. The old agrarian aristocracy might have been thought to be restored if Alfred I. du Pont's agency in the campaign was forgotten and if the fact that Willard Saulsbury, Jr., had married a du Pont was ignored.

T. Coleman du Pont, who had proved himself an adept political manager, seemed to have turned the tables on his cousin Alfred in 1921 by his appointment to the Senate when Wolcott resigned to accept, from a new Republican governor, an appointment to the most respected judicial post in Delaware, the chancellorship, a position his father had held and that he was known to desire. Charges of a "deal," however, as well as support given the Democrats by Alfred I. du Pont, helped defeat Coleman's bid for election to a full Senate term in 1922. The victor in this contest was another representative of the old Democratic political aristocracy, Thomas F. Bayard, Jr., who, like Willard Saulsbury, Jr., had married a du Pont.

T. Coleman du Pont, however, was not a man to be thwarted easily. When the other Senate seat (in which Republican Dr. Ball had replaced Saulsbury in 1919) fell vacant, Coleman received the nomination and this time (in 1924) won the election. Cancer of the larynx forced him to retire in 1928, shortly before his death, but his son Francis V. du Pont succeeded him in the leadership of the Delaware Republican party and a son-in-law, C. Douglass Buck (who was a collateral descendant of John M. Clayton), became governor of Delaware for two terms beginning in 1929 and later senator for a term beginning in 1943. By this time, however, the Great Depression had occurred, and in its wake, significant political changes took place in Delaware.

The effect of the First World War on Delaware politics, on the other hand, had been indirect and subtle. The United States was a participant in this war for only eighteen months. About ten thousand Delawareans entered the armed forces, but many of them were called up too late to participate in the fighting.

As would be true in the Second World War, a part of the National Guard was called out a year before the United States declared war. In this case it was trouble on the Mexican border that led President Wilson to federalize two battalions of Delaware troops in June 1916 and order them to Deming, New Mexico. These troops returned to Delaware and were mustered out of the service in February 1917, but a month later one battalion was recalled to guard bridges, particularly those on the main railroad lines across the Brandywine and the Christina, where it was feared German saboteurs might strike. Eventually, Delaware troops constituted the major part of the 59th Pioneer Infantry, which sailed to France at the end of August 1918 and was rushed into the front lines the next month. Several of the officers who led Delaware National Guard outfits in the Second World War

John G. Townsend, Jr. (1871–1964), governor and senator.

Townsend's, Inc., plant near Millsboro. A modern agribusiness founded by Governor Townsend. (Both photographs courtesy of Preston Townsend.)

gained their first combat experience with the 59th Infantry in France at this time.

The Townsend administration, inaugurated in January 1917, as the war approached, proved to be a particularly active one in terms of its legislative accomplishments, aided not only by the especial ability of Governor Townsend and his secretary of state, Everett C. Johnson, but also by the spirit of service and the economic prosperity that were both generated by the war. A workmen's compensation law, an income tax, a pension for needy mothers of young children, a home for the feebleminded, provision for vocational education and for an Americanization program for immigrants, a budget system for appropriations, and a state highway department were among the creations of this active administration. It is a measure of its reforming zeal that the administration secured ratification of the Eighteenth Amendment, backed by the so-called Klair Law, banning the sale or use of alcoholic liquor in Delaware, and that it sought, unsuccessfully, ratification of the Nineteenth Amendment. Perhaps its greatest achievement was its encouragement of educational reform, though the new school code of 1919 was extensively revised two years later.

The most important immediate effects of the First World War on Delaware were economic. Though the period of American military participation in the war was relatively short, the war itself lasted for more than four years, and war orders stimulated the Delaware economy for some time before the United States entered the war. The shipyards on the Christina and the powder mills on the Brandywine were quickly pushed to capacity production. Some new industries appeared, like the Pyrites Company, a British firm that in 1917 moved its American plant to Wilmington from Roanoke, Virginia, to utilize the harbor. Most sensational was the effect of the war on three Wilmington-based powder companies, Du Pont, Hercules, and Atlas.

The mounting profits of Wilmington investors offered a new tax source at a time when costs of government seemed to be mounting rapidly. Assemblymen, largely representing rural constituencies, decided to tap the profits of Wilmington businessmen in 1917 by an income tax of 1 percent on gross incomes of over one thousand dollars, with many exceptions, including agricultural profits and real estate rents. The need to finance an improved school system led to modification of this tax in 1921, with rates graduated so that a 2 percent tax was paid on incomes between three thousand dollars and ten thousand dollars and 3 percent on incomes over ten thousand dollars. Every adult was required to file a return and to pay a filing fee of three dollars, a fee that proved unpopular and was abandoned in 1927. The exemption of agricultural and real estate profits was also abandoned, as was a state property tax on real estate that had been employed from 1921 to 1929.

Although the income tax gradually became the principal source of state revenue, it was rivaled by taxes on businesses, largely from out of state, that incorporated in Delaware. As a source of revenue, the General Incorporation Law of 1899 has proved to be a gold mine. Lenient requirements, low fees, proximity to financial centers, stable political institutions, and, in time, a bench and bar experienced and competent in corporate litigation gave Delaware an advantage over other states that sometimes sought to capture this business; a mere modification of laws or reduction of fees did not equal the combination of advantages possessed by Delaware. In 1900, the first year of operation of the new law, 193 companies were incorporated in Delaware; in the next year, 1,407 companies; and by 1919, the number of new incorporations had risen to 4,776. (The number continued to rise; there were almost 80,000 Delaware corporations in 1975.)

The Company

The first third of the twentieth century, the years of the Republican domination of Delaware in which individual du Ponts played a large role, were also remarkable years in the history of the Du Pont Company. The three du Pont cousins, Coleman, Alfred, and Pierre, who took over management of the company in 1902, proved to be, each in his own way, men of remarkable ability. Within a week after assuming management of the family company, they began considering the purchase of its chief, but friendly, rival, Laflin and Rand. Consummation of this purchase, as well as other mergers and consolidations that followed, gave the du Ponts control of the greater part of the powder manufacture in the United States.

In consequence of the dominant position of the du Ponts, the United States government instituted a suit in 1907 charging them with monopolistic practices forbidden by the Sherman Anti-Trust Act. In 1912 final decision of the suit required that two new companies should be established to take over part of Du Pont operations, except for the manufacture of military smokeless powder, which was allowed to remain a Du Pont monopoly for reasons of national security.

The new companies, the Hercules Powder Company and the Atlas Powder Company, set up their headquarters in Wilmington, perhaps because they were given access to certain Du Pont facilities, such as research and engineering, until they could establish similar departments of their own. The stock of the new companies was distributed to Du Pont stockholders, so that, initially, the ownership was the same, but from the beginning the management was different, and in a relatively short time the normal activity of the stock market, stimulated by the First World War and the prosperity of the 1920s, led to such buying and selling that the ownership became quite distinct too.

The antitrust suit that broke up the Du Pont Company in 1912 changed the direction of the company's growth but by no means stopped it. Realizing that there were legal limits upon their growth in the explosives industry, the du Ponts began channeling their profits into such fields as lacquers, enamels, paints, dyes, and automobiles, the last through an investment in the infant General Motors Corporation. In the years of the First World War, Du Pont profits were very great, for even though the company management was cautious in its expansion up to the time the United States entered the war, Du Pont was a major supplier of the Allies, and it has been estimated that 40 percent of the powder fired by Allied artillery was supplied by this company.

In the first year of the war, a crisis in company management precipitated a serious family quarrel that had repercussions, already mentioned, in Delaware politics. In December 1914 Coleman du Pont, a restless, expansive man, reared in Kentucky and, having less attachment than his cousins to the powder business or to the Brandywine Valley, offered to sell the company a portion of his stock. For some years he had been investing heavily in office buildings, hotels, and an insurance company in New York, where he was spending much of his time.

Alfred I. du Pont, who was notably headstrong, had for years been on poor personal terms with some of his cousins because of their open disapproval of circumstances surrounding his divorce of his first wife, and the relationship had been further strained by a company reorganization arranged by Pierre in 1911

under which Alfred ceased being general manager of powder production, a position he prized, though he remained vice-president.
Old grudges such as these may have led him to object to the
price Coleman wanted for his shares, but Alfred became bitterly
angry when Pierre organized a syndicate, later the Christiana
Securities Company, which bought all of Coleman's Du Pont
Company stock.

After a long court battle, arraying du Ponts against du Ponts,
the purchase was approved. Thereafter, though Alfred I. du Pont
retained his own large financial interest in the company, he gave
his attention to other enterprises, including the Delaware Trust
Company, which built an office building that housed the home
offices of Hercules and Atlas and was higher than the Du Pont
Building. Eventually, he developed large commercial holdings
in Florida that included the Florida National Bank of Jackson-
ville and vast tracts of timber in northwestern Florida, the basis
of the St. Joe Paper Company, founded in 1936, a year after Alfred's death.

Meanwhile, Pierre, in especially close association with his
brothers Irénée and Lammot, who each in turn succeeded him as
company president, and with his former secretary and confidante,
John J. Raskob, moved from one industrial and financial success
to another. Not the least of these successes was the transformation
of the Du Pont Company after the First World War from an
explosives company, as it had been almost exclusively for a century, into the largest American company in a far larger industry,
the chemical business. Explosives became a very small part of
the Du Pont Company's total interest (2 percent in 1924 and
1939, for example). Many businesses were acquired by purchase,
like the Grasselli Chemical Company, of Cleveland, and the
Krebs Pigment and Chemical Company. The latter company was
founded in Delaware by a Danish immigrant, Henrik J. Krebs.
Its factories at Newport and Edge Moor are now (1978) the
only Du Pont manufacturing facilities in northern Delaware, the
Brandywine powder yards having been closed in 1921.

Du Pont expansion also took place by acquisition of foreign
patents and processes for such products as dyes, rayon, Dacron,
Lucite, and cellophane. Other new products were developed by
research studies undertaken at the Du Pont Experimental Station
on the Brandywine, among them neoprene (a synthetic rubber)
and nylon.

For production of nylon, a new Du Pont plant was built at

Seaford in 1939. In Delaware, however, Du Pont expansion generally took the form of construction for management, service, and research departments, rather than new factories. In 1902 the company offices were moved to central Wilmington, and in 1907 they were installed in the first section of the new Du Pont Building, at Tenth and Market Streets. This building was enlarged several times over the following decades, as was the Experimental Station on the Brandywine. Various other Du Pont facilities in northern Delaware range from the company machine shop on Maryland Avenue, in Wilmington, to the instrumentation laboratory near Glasgow and the veterinary chemical and toxicological laboratories near Newark on the Maryland state line. Notable installations are the Louviers Building, at Milford Cross Roads, to which the engineering department was moved in 1952, and the Chestnut Run laboratories, just west of Wilmington.

The most remarkable single step taken by the Du Pont Company in its expansion, its investment in General Motors, had only indirect effects on Delaware. Pierre du Pont and John Raskob had begun to invest in this company on their individual accounts in 1914, before the beginning of the First World War, and in 1915 Pierre became chairman of the General Motors board of directors. In 1917 the Du Pont Company itself made a large investment in General Motors, amounting to over one-fourth of the General Motors common stock. To protect this investment, Pierre du Pont assumed the presidency of the large automobile company in 1920.

Though Pierre left the presidency of General Motors in 1923 and the chairmanship of its board in 1928, the Du Pont interest in General Motors remained very great for three more decades. Eventually, the United States government forced the Du Pont Company to relinquish its control of General Motors, when a court decision in 1957 condemned the combination on the grounds that trade was restrained by this alliance between what had become the largest American chemical and automobile companies. Through the years from 1917 to 1957 there were frequent rumors that General Motors might move its headquarters to Delaware, but the only visible presence of this company was the opening in 1948 of an assembly plant at Woodcrest, where the annual meeting of General Motors stockholders was held from 1948 to 1964.

12

A Social Conscience

The Social Conscience of the Manufacturers

Besides the significant role he played in the development of the largest industrial company in Delaware, Pierre S. du Pont is a figure of great importance in the history of Delaware education and of Delaware fiscal policy. More than any other single person he was the founder of the modern Delaware public school system, and as state tax commissioner from 1925 to 1937 and again from 1944 to 1949 he saw to it that the schools had adequate financial support, providing part of the cost of an expanded, efficient tax department from his own pocket.

To some degree, Pierre du Pont's interest in public education stemmed from his strong family consciousness and highly developed sense of responsibility. He was well aware of the interest of the ancestor for whom he was named, Pierre Samuel du Pont de Nemours, in public education; he encouraged publication by the University of Delaware Press of a treatise *On National Education in the United States of America* that Du Pont de Nemours had written for Thomas Jefferson. As the recognized head of the Du Pont family, Pierre had inherited a tradition of responsibility not only for blood relatives but for the larger community of Du Pont employees in the Brandywine Valley. And as the company had grown in his lifetime, the removal of its offices to Wilmington being symbolic of this growth, Pierre's feeling of responsibility grew to encompass the people of Wilmington and of all Delaware.

But besides the peculiarities of Pierre du Pont's inherited paternalism, his interest in civic improvement had additional sources. He had worked, as a young man, in the Ohio enterprises of Tom L. Johnson, an industrialist who became famous as the reform mayor of Cleveland. And in the Wilmington area, where

Pierre du Pont was born and reared, the manufacturing class had a tradition of concern for civic improvements.

Indeed, the Wilmington manufacturers had shown interest in social concerns of the community long before they sought a leading role in politics. In the Reconstruction period, when Delaware politics was controlled by reactionary Democrats, the manufacturers, outvoted, left the field to the lawyers and the agricultural classes. Wilmington politics, in which the manufacturers customarily played a part, was a petty business under the city charter of 1832 because there was no centralized authority. Gradually, the dominant figures in the economic and social life of Wilmington dropped out of politics, leaving the field to the shopkeepers and the artisans.

The Wilmington manufacturers found more satisfaction and more chance of achievement in terms of civic improvements from service on special boards or from commissions, which the legislature was happy to establish, particularly since they did not increase the power or patronage of the Republican city government. Prominent among these agencies were the Board of Water Commissioners, the Street and Sewer Commission, and the Board of Park Commissioners, all created by the legislature in the expectation of enlisting the efforts of community leaders to accomplish tasks not to be entrusted to the mayor and council. Another useful agency, the Board of Trade, was a voluntary society, a promotional group that later termed itself a chamber of commerce.

The Board of Park Commissioners was created because of the offer of William P. Bancroft, a Quaker textile manufacturer descended from William Shipley, the first chief burgess of Wilmington, to give the city a valuable tract of land along the Brandywine. Bancroft was also responsible for the Woodlawn development, where several hundred houses for working-class families were built in a parklike setting and rented for nominal sums. His gift to the Wilmington Institute transformed this private library and cultural center into a free library in 1894. Supervised by a private board but receiving annual appropriations from the city thereafter, the Wilmington Institute Free Library was for many years the only large, comprehensive library in Delaware and the nucleus of a county library system.

Samuel Bancroft, Jr., younger brother of William, though also a Quaker and a textile manufacturer, was in many ways a maverick among Wilmington manufacturers. Where William

Bancroft's interest was in practical measures to improve the lot of the working man, Samuel Bancroft's hobby was the collection of English Pre-Raphaelite paintings (by such artists as Dante Gabriel Rossetti, Henry Burne-Jones, and William Leigh Hunt), a collection that was given by his heirs to the Wilmington Society of the Fine Arts. The Pre-Raphaelites were a group of English artists of the mid-Victorian period who, repelled by the materialism and social oppression of their day, celebrated virtues of the past. It seems likely that the same motivations that led Samuel Bancroft to collect paintings of this sentimental, neo-medieval school, led him to break with the Republican party of his youth and his class and to join the Delaware Democrats, on whose ticket he ran, unsuccessfully, as a candidate for Congress in 1894. As owner of a Wilmington paper, the *Every Evening*, he provided the Democrats with an urban outlet for their opposition to the dominant Republicans in the period of the Addicks and du Pont political ascendancy.

J. Taylor Gause and George G. Lobdell fit more neatly than Samuel Bancroft into the mold of the Wilmington manufacturer. Lobdell, president of a company that made wheels for railroad cars and iron rolls for paper mills, bequeathed his estate at Minquadale as a home for the aged. As president of the Delaware Masonic lodges, he encouraged construction in 1871 of a grand iron-fronted Masonic Hall in Wilmington containing an opera house that for many years was the largest and most magnificent theater in Delaware.

J. Taylor Gause, the president of Harlan and Hollingsworth, railroad car builders, may have been propelled by his wife, Martha, into a leading role in many social welfare programs in Wilmington. Martha Gause was founder of a home for destitute children and, with her husband, of the Homeopathic Hospital (later the Memorial Hospital). At its foundation in 1888, it was the first hospital in Delaware not privately run by a physician or established for a temporary need, like the Tilton Hospital for soldiers in the Civil War. In just one year, however, a second Wilmington hospital, the Delaware, was opened with a board of directors that had a second car builder, Job H. Jackson (president of Jackson and Sharp), as its president. Job Jackson and J. Taylor Gause together were largely responsible for the construction of Wilmington's Methodist "cathedral," Grace Church, which they meant not only as a thank-offering for their worldly

BROTHERS AND PHILANTHROPISTS

William Poole Bancroft (1835–1923), founder of the New Castle County park system. (Courtesy of the Historical Society of Delaware.)

Samuel Bancroft, Jr. (1840–1915), art patron and collector. (Courtesy of the Delaware Art Museum.)

blessings but also as a center for citywide missions to the unfortunate.

Emalea Pusey Warner (1853–1948), the daughter of a manufacturer, was one of the most notable of social and educational reformers in Delaware history. Married at twenty to a successful businessman, she was able to provide leadership to a number of movements over a very long life. One of her most notable successes was the organization in 1884 of the Associated Charities of Wilmington, later called the Family Society. Modeled on societies in Buffalo and Philadelphia, the Associated Charities sought to supplement and coordinate all activities aimed at giving aid to the poor and reducing poverty. Supported by the business community, it used women visitors, supervised by a professional social worker, to investigate applicants for aid. It provided work relief through a sewing room and a wood pile, instituted a visiting nurse service, established a day nursery, encouraged instruction in cooking and sewing, and provided vacations in the country for the urban poor. It was also effectual in replacing the old jail at New Castle with a county workhouse at Greenbank, equipped with work rooms permitting prisoners to be gainfully employed and, hopefully, taught a trade.

Emalea Warner also employed her talents for leadership effectively through the Wilmington New Century Club, founded in 1889, and, after its union in 1898 with similar clubs in Newark, Middletown, Dover, Georgetown, and other communities, through the Delaware State Federation of Women's Clubs, of which she was the first president. Often working in close collaboration with the Associated Charities on social welfare projects, the club women also took a deep interest in enlarging educational opportunities for Delawareans. They were instrumental in persuading the legislature to charter a Women's College. Opened in 1914, on a campus in Newark adjacent to Delaware College, to which it was linked administratively (they officially became the University of Delaware in 1921), the Women's College, under the inspired leadership of Dr. Winifred J. Robinson, a botanist from Vassar, provided the first opportunity for white women to take a college degree in Delaware since William H. Purnell's program of coeducation had been abandoned by Delaware College in 1886. (Delaware State College, then limited to black students, had been coeducational from its opening in 1892.)

Members of the Federation of Women's Clubs were not united on the issue of votes for women. The one existing organiza-

CIVIC LEADERS

Martha Gause (Mrs. J. Taylor Gause) (1828–1890), leader of the group that founded the first hospital. (Courtesy of the Historical Society of Delaware.)

Emalea Pusey Warner (1853–1948), with Winifred Robinson, first dean of the Women's College, on the campus of the University of Delaware. (Courtesy of the University of Delaware Archives.)

tion for women that strongly supported women's suffrage, besides, of course, the ad hoc Equal Suffrage Association, was the Women's Christian Temperance Union. Despite frequent appeals to the legislature for constitutional amendments, the women of Delaware were still denied the franchise at the end of the First World War, when the United States Congress passed the Nineteenth Amendment and submitted it to the states.

In the spring of 1920, encouraged by the support of Governor John G. Townsend, Jr., and Secretary of State Everett C. Johnson, who, as a legislator, had played a key role in the establishment of the Women's College, the Delaware suffragists saw a possibility of having Delaware cast the thirty-sixth and decisive vote to ratify this amendment. Governor Townsend called a special session of the legislature for the purpose and had the support of many influential citizens—including the three cousins Coleman, Alfred, and Pierre du Pont. There was surprising antisuffrage sentiment, however, and exciting days followed in Dover that were called the war of the roses, because the two sides chose contrasting colors, the antisuffragists wearing red roses and the suffragists wearing yellow. Despite appeals from such prestigious figures as President Wilson, most of the Democrats in the legislature followed the leadership of Senator Wolcott and former Senator Saulsbury in opposing women's suffrage, apparently primarily because it would mean doubling the number of blacks who could vote. Republicans alone could have carried the measure, but they did not, partly because of the activity of Governor Townsend's rivals in his native Sussex and partly because of an active opposition among wealthy Wilmington Republicans, including old Gen. James H. Wilson and his daughter, Mary Wilson Thompson, wife of a manufacturer and the acknowledged leader of Wilmington society. A band of Wilmington society matrons led to Dover by Mary Thompson rejoiced in thwarting the suffragists, who numbered among their leaders the equally blue-blooded Florence Bayard Hilles, daughter of a United States secretary of state and descendant of three other senators.

Three years after the honor of the decisive ratification went to another state, the Delaware legislature, in 1923, went through the meaningless ceremony of ratification. The whole incident is reminiscent of the refusal of Delaware to ratify the Fifteenth Amendment until 1901. In both cases the state declined to encourage extension of the franchise. In both cases—relatively quickly in the case of women's suffrage—the state did eventually approve of the extension. There was a notable difference, however. Both parties quickly accepted women's suffrage, but in the case of voting by blacks, one political party, the Democrats, had still not relented in the 1920s, over half a century after emancipation.

Pierre du Pont as Social Reformer

Though there are implications in the word *progressive* that may make it seem improper to use in connection with the greatest of the Wilmington manufacturers, the shy, but strong-minded, Pierre du Pont, administrative architect of both the Du Pont Company and General Motors, it was he, more than anyone else, who helped Delaware rise out of the torpid frame of mind, the intellectual backwater, that made it slow to extend the franchise to blacks and women and to accept many other innovations, some good and some bad, of the twentieth century.

Some of Pierre du Pont's earliest contributions to education were made to the University of Delaware. Between 1914 and 1920 he gave the University over a million dollars, mainly to enlarge the campus, to erect two new buildings, and to reconstruct Old College Hall. His friendship to the students and faculty was demonstrated in many ways—for example, by his treating them to a night at the theater in Wilmington, and sending them there on a private train; by entertaining the entire summer school at dinner at the botanical conservatory he developed beside his country home at Longwood, Pennsylvania; by providing cultural events, especially concerts, on campus; and by underwriting the original Junior Year Abroad Program in France, the creation of a young professor named Raymond Kirkbride. In his benefactions to the University of Delaware, Pierre du Pont was often joined by others, as when his brothers Irénée and Lammot shared in providing sixty scholarships for the training of teachers soon after the opening of the Women's College. Eventually, several relatives and associates, notably his brother-in-law H. Rodney Sharp, an alumnus, exceeded Pierre in their gifts to the university.

But in terms of his contributions to the total educational program in Delaware, Pierre S. du Pont stands alone. It is not merely that he made large gifts of money, some through endowments that perpetuated his giving after his death in 1954. He provided the same background of rational, orderly management to the improvement of education in Delaware that he applied to the reorganization of the Du Pont Company and of General Motors. He brought experts to the state to make studies. He encouraged the hiring of able administrators to carry out the results of these studies. He helped provide facilities needed for the success of the best efforts of good men. He sought to provide a sound, lasting fiscal basis for the continued effective operation of the new schools. And, finally, he was willing to take personal responsibility for his work by accepting public office.

His initial contribution to the reformation of state government was made through an organization called Service Citizens of Delaware, which came into being as a result of the effort being made by Governor Townsend and Secretary of State Johnson to arouse public spirit for volunteer state service to meet the challenges imposed by the entrance of the United States into the First World War. Pierre du Pont became president of the Service Citizens and provided funds with which this group hired the New York Bureau of Municipal Research to survey governmental organization in Delaware and to prepare a plan for reorganization of the numerous agencies and bureaus through which state administration was conducted. Besides this survey of state administration, the Service Citizens sponsored surveys of public health programs and Americanization procedures before turning their major attention to education.

After his retirement from the presidency of the Du Pont Company in 1918, when he was forty-eight, Pierre du Pont accepted appointment to the state board of education, where he served as vice-president until 1921, when he resigned because a crisis in General Motors had forced him to assume the presidency of that company for a three-year period, 1920–23. The major problem in Delaware education at that time was with the rural schools, outside of Wilmington, which were largely subject to local control and funding.

Progress had been made, but it had been woefully slow. Only in 1861 had the local districts been required to raise money and to provide schools—and then only for white students. In 1870 one-sixth of the residents of Delaware were illiterate. The United States commissioner of education declared in his annual report that year, in reference to Delaware: "There is no State supervision, no provision for training teachers, no school law adequate for keeping schools open. . . . The schools in the state generally are of an inferior class, and, so far as organized under the school law of the state, provide only for the education of the whites."

In the years from 1870 to 1917 some progress occurred. The illiteracy rate for residents ten years old or older was reduced from 17 percent to 8 percent, and for youths between ten and twenty from 16 percent to 3 percent. In 1881 the state had begun to support schools for blacks. In 1891 the state assumed the responsibility of providing free textbooks. In 1907 a compulsory-attendance law was passed. In 1875 the office of state superintendent of education was created to provide leadership, but this reform lasted only until 1887, when the office was abolished and localism again prevailed.

In 1913 a reorganized state school board proposed a revamping of school laws, but little had been accomplished other than the establishment of a state education commissioner when the Service Citizens began their work. The great problem was the decentralization of educational leadership and financial support, with about 425 local school districts electing school committees, hiring teachers, and raising most of their funds. With no required certification standards for teachers or buildings, with over half of the schools open for less than seven months a year, it is not strange that Delaware ranked thirty-eighth among the states in 1918 according to a highly regarded rating system. In school attendance, Delaware rated even lower, thirty-ninth. And besides having segregated schools for blacks, Delaware, alone among the states, required that local taxes for these schools should be levied only on the property of black citizens.

In a few places, notably Wilmington, which was growing and prosperous, and probably also New Castle, where the income from the Town Common was used for education, the schools were relatively good. Wilmington had even developed its own teacher-training school, which was abandoned a few years after the Women's College opened. Besides the public schools, there were also a few private schools of varied quality, like the Friends School and the Ursuline Academy in Wilmington, the Methodist Wilmington Conference Academy (the predecessor of Wesley College) in Dover, and Catholic parochial schools. But, in general, the private academies that had once existed in almost every Delaware town had found it impossible to survive against the competition of the free public schools, however inadequate the latter were.

Such was the situation uncovered when a commission set up

by the legislature in 1917 enlisted the General Education Board, a Rockefeller foundation, to make a survey of Delaware schools outside of Wilmington. "Delaware," the survey concluded, "buys a low and cheap brand of education. Probably not more than seven other states spend so little. It is, however, still true that Delaware pays high for what it gets."

Pierre S. du Pont and the Service Citizens soon went to work to improve the situation. A new school code was written and adopted in 1919 that changed the organization of the public schools so drastically in favor of centralized control that a reaction set in and it had to be revised in 1921. The Wilmington schools and the school districts in the other major communities, such as Newark, New Castle, Dover, Milford, and Georgetown, were given a large measure of autonomy, but the rural schools, though retaining their local boards of education, were placed under the supervision of a state department of public instruction, directed by a superintendent. Teacher certification, attendance rules, and salary schedules were established on a state basis. The financing of the schools was also to be the primary responsibility of the state, though provision was made for a local district to raise additional funds on the basis of real estate and capitation taxes if it chose to do so. A portion of the cost of new buildings would be borne locally if the residents approved. In most districts, the decision in these matters was left to a referendum; in Wilmington, where the school district and the city had the same boundaries, the decision was left to city council, although, within certain limits, council was required to provide supplementary school funds to meet requests of the school board.

The state department was permitted to merge one-room-school districts when the attendance fell below a stated minimum, but larger districts were also encouraged to merge in order to provide improved facilities. Free transportation was offered to consolidated schools, but each merger had to be approved by a referendum in the districts concerned. Racial segregation continued, for it was required by the 1897 constitution, but schools for blacks and whites were put on the same legal basis in such details as teachers' salary scales, attendance rules, and state support per student.

Realizing that voters might be slow to approve funds for new schools for blacks, Pierre du Pont personally remedied the situation by providing funds through the Delaware School Auxiliary Association to replace the generally miserable existing schools throughout the state. The construction of new black schools in every community made the white residents, who had initially resisted the idea of new schools, even as a partial gift from Pierre du Pont, eager to have them and willing to support a share of the cost.

At Pierre du Pont's expense, three Columbia University professors had prepared standards and plans for new buildings. He visited many of the buildings personally and provided small improvements quietly, without fuss. Through the Delaware School Auxiliary he established trust funds for school construction, including money for supervision of new buildings to see that contractors met their responsibilities by, for example, using specified materials. Every school district in Delaware profited by being relieved of such supervisory duties, which they were usually ill-equipped to perform. It has been estimated that from 1920 to 1935 Pierre du Pont spent $6 million on new school buildings in Delaware—30 percent of the total expenditures on buildings.

Besides raising funds for buildings, he subsidized agents who toured the state organizing residents into parent-teacher associations that would support and stimulate measures to improve the schools. Libraries were set up in country schoolhouses. In only six years, from 1918 to 1924, the average attendance at school was raised from 90 to 148 days a year, an improvement that raised Delaware's standing in this respect from thirty-ninth to seventh among the states. The Ayers index, which had rated the Delaware school system thirty-eighth among the states in 1918, ranked Delaware tenth in 1930.

If the improvements being made with the stimulation of gifts were to be permanent, it was important that careful supervision and adequate funding should be supplied. The great difference in resources between different school districts indicated that support of education should be based on a larger unit, which the availability of income and corporation tax revenues suggested should be the state government. When problems arose about the efficient collection of taxes, Pierre du Pont accepted appointment as state tax commissioner, creating an unusual situation where the most prominent rich man (and possibly the largest taxpayer) was also the tax collector. Quite late in his life, Pierre du Pont once again demonstrated his zeal for the public schools when in 1947 he instituted, and won, a taxpayer's suit against the Wilmington city council for not setting a real estate tax rate high enough to meet the request of the city board of education.

In this period of his civic service, Pierre du Pont also gave a valuable site for a new building to the Wilmington Institute Free Library and financed a new public highway on the route of the Wilmington and Kennett Turnpike, a private toll road that he purchased. This road, the Kennett Pike, led to his country estate at Longwood, which he opened to the public. He was also active in the Association against the Eighteenth Amendment, because he felt the attempt to prohibit the use of alcoholic beverages was a failure that led to corruption and to disregard of law. He served as chairman of the executive committee of this national organization until the prohibition law was repealed; thereafter, he accepted appointment as Delaware State liquor commissioner in order to establish a new system of dispensing liquor that would be free of the worst abuses of the old system.

Highways and Transportation

Although the total of Pierre du Pont's contributions to Delaware, through gifts and through personal services, exceeded that of any of his contemporaries, his interest in improving conditions of life in Delaware was shared by a number of his relatives, some of whom even preceded him in their gifts to Delaware. T. Coleman du Pont, as one prominent example, made a major contribution to the economy of Delaware by constructing a north-south highway from Wilmington to the southern boundary below Selbyville, thus building, as he is reported to have said, a monument one hundred miles high and laying it down the length of the state.

Since Coleman, who was far more outgoing and ebullient than Pierre, did have political ambitions, as Pierre emphatically did not, there may have been some basis for the suspicion with which his desire to build the world's best road was looked upon in 1911, when he set up his own company, the Coleman du Pont Road, Incorporated, to build a highway with a right-of-way of two hundred feet. Though Coleman's ideas regarding access roads and services were in advance of his times, some standpat Delawareans greeted his plans as grudgingly as they had greeted Pierre's plans to improve schools that had been, they said, good enough for them.

Objectors so delayed road construction that it was not until 1917 that the first section of the road, which was in Sussex County, was completed and presented to the state. In this same year, under the progressive Townsend administration, which also enacted the new school law, the State Highway Department was established and took over the work of construction, though Coleman du Pont continued to pay the bill, which had amounted to just under $4 million by the time the road was completed in 1924.

Coleman du Pont's interest in highways did not die with him but was carried on by others in his immediate family. His son-in-law Clayton Douglass Buck was chief engineer for the State Highway Department from 1921 to 1929, when he began the first of his two terms as governor. Coleman's son, Francis V. du Pont, succeeded his father as a member of the highway commission in 1921. In his long service of about three decades on this commission, Francis V. du Pont continued and expanded upon his father's work. He was a principal sponsor of the construction of the first Delaware Memorial Bridge, which in 1951 linked the road system of Delaware to that of New Jersey and allowed motor traffic from the South to reach New York without passing through Philadelphia.

The new highway system was the most important factor in the economic development of rural southern Delaware since construction of the Delaware Railroad. A major development of the twentieth century was the great increase in population in the metropolitan areas of the east coast, which, linked by railroads and highways, came to form almost one extended urban area, a megalopolis, as it has been called, from Boston to Washington. The highway system gave the farms of Delaware even easier access to the markets of this urban area than the more restricted railroad afforded. In doing so, it led Delaware farmers to adjust their products to suit new marketing possibilities, to produce young chickens, called broilers, for instance, and to emphasize liquid milk production in Kent County because the milk could be rushed to metropolitan markets in refrigerated tank trucks.

The Du Pont Highway and the network of roads that led into it confirmed the ancient transportation pattern in Delaware that was established by the geography of the Delmarva Peninsula. Just as had been the case with river shipping and with the Delaware Railroad, the highway directed traffic (until the opening of the Memorial Bridge) toward Philadelphia. The economic connection made by transportation facilities remained a social and intellectual connection as well.

From Dover southward the main state highway soon developed a second stem, westward of the original Du Pont Highway and leading past Camden, Seaford, and Laurel on a course parallel to the tracks of the Delaware Railroad. The new highway network gradually caused a readjustment of the location of residential housing and of business construction. New building foiled efforts to avoid traffic congestion by roads around established communities. Where once towns clustered around railroad depots, now the most valuable land was that with access to the highway. Suburbs grew along all the roads leading out of Wilmington, and developments downstate stretched communities out into the countryside.

One notable development of the highway age was the increasing popularity of the beaches along the Delaware ocean shore. Rehoboth Beach, originally a Methodist camp meeting site, had grown into a small resort town after being reached by an extension of the Junction and Breakwater Railroad, and it also had the advantage of the Lewes and Rehoboth Canal, which connected Rehoboth Bay to the sheltered harbors behind the breakwaters in Delaware Bay. Bethany Beach, south of Rehoboth. was founded as an ocean resort and meeting site for members of the Disciples of Christ, or Christian Church, from the Pittsburgh area. No railroad reached Bethany, but a steamboat on Indian River Bay brought vacationers from the railroad to the shore early in the twentieth century. These two resorts were eventually linked to each other by an oceanside road and a bridge across the Indian River Inlet, and south of Bethany the road went on to Fenwick Island and to Ocean City, Maryland. The more important highway developments, however, were those connecting these beaches to inland metropolitan centers, to Baltimore and Washington (after completion of the Chesapeake Bay Bridge in 1952) as well as to Wilmington and Philadelphia. Rehoboth, developing primarily as a cottage resort in the mid-twentieth century, became so popular with well-to-do Washingtonians from political and diplomatic circles that it bragged of being the nation's summer capital.

By this time, motor traffic had largely replaced railroads in Delaware, as railroads in the nineteenth century had replaced river shipping. Yet old methods of transportation were not immediately abandoned upon the appearance of new methods. River boats continued to run from Philadelphia to ports in Delaware well into the twentieth century. The boat to Frederica, for example, operated until 1929, while the Wilson Line provided passenger and freight service between Wilmington and Philadelphia for two decades longer.

The great depression of the 1930s saw the beginning of a gradual reduction in railroad service. Many tracks, like those to Rehoboth, were abandoned completely. On others, all passenger service was discontinued, until by 1975 the only passenger trains left were those running on the tracks of what had been the Pennsylvania Railroad, later the Penn Central, as they crossed northern Delaware between Baltimore and Philadelphia.

With this exception, motor coaches furnished all the public mass transportation that was available within Delaware at the beginning of the last quarter of the twentieth century. Electric city railways (trolley cars) had by this time long been replaced. A ferry ran between Lewes and Cape May; though fees were charged for its use, its effective support in most years came from tolls charged on the Delaware River bridges by the Delaware River and Bay Authority, an interstate organization. Use of the Nanticoke River, in southwestern Delaware, by Chesapeake Bay steamers carrying passengers had long been abandoned, but some freight, especially petroleum, was still carried on the Nanticoke to Seaford. A few commuter airlines, as well as charter air services, used Delaware airports.

Alfred I. du Pont and the Needy

The third of the three Du Pont cousins who had taken over management of the family company in 1902 also made his distinct contribution to social welfare in Delaware. Alfred I. du Pont's early charitable impulses were largely directed to the powder workers on the Brandywine, among whom he spent the early years of his working career. He spent much more time than Coleman or Pierre in active participation in manufacturing processes, and as general manager in charge of production, he developed a sympathy for ordinary workingmen and their families that was genuine and deep. His earliest charitable donations, though numerous, were unorganized and largely unrecorded, consisting of help to needy people of the area whose wants were made known to him.

In 1916, angry about the sale of T. Coleman du Pont's stock, Alfred I. du Pont allied himself with old elements of the Bull

Moose, or Progressive Republican, faction in Delaware in order to stifle the political ambitions of his cousins T. Coleman and the elderly Senator Henry A. du Pont. Alfred I. himself refused to run for public office, but his participation in politics led him to sponsor a number of reforms through newspapers he purchased or subsidized and through an organization called the Voters' Non-Partisan League. The latter group, which may have helped stimulate Pierre du Pont's interest in the Service Citizens, issued a call for reform in the late fall of 1916 that was largely written by Alfred du Pont and included demands for revision of antiquated revenue and taxation laws (by adoption of a graduated inheritance tax and taxation of interest-bearing securities at the same rate as real estate), for an improved school system, for good roads, for a tuberculosis sanatorium, and for better care of the deaf, dumb, and blind.

Variations in his own personal fortunes made it necessary for Alfred I. du Pont to give up this politically motivated program, but in 1929 he proved his concern for the needy by sponsoring an old-age pension bill, providing a stipend for all elderly residents who were in need. Since 1791 Delaware had cared for the poor mainly in almshouses, principally because this type of indoor relief seemed more efficient and economical than the older colonial system of outdoor relief—that is, helping the poor in their own homes.

By 1929, however, old-age pensions had been adopted by many European countries, and Alfred I. du Pont hoped to see Delaware become the first American state, after Montana, to adopt such a program. Bitterly disappointed when the legislature rejected his bill, he decided to institute a state pension system himself. Consequently, he hired a staff that compiled a list of names of old people needing assistance, and on November 1, 1929, he inaugurated a private, statewide old-age pension by sending out eight hundred checks. The amount of each check varied from five dollars to twenty-five dollars, according to the degree of the recipient's dependency, but the average at the first mailing was sixteen dollars.

Governor Buck, son-in-law of T. Coleman du Pont, the old antagonist of Alfred I., supported the latter's aims by appointing him, even though Alfred was by this time officially a resident of Florida, chairman of an Old Age Commission instructed to draw up a permanent policy of old-age relief. By the time the General Assembly met again, the Great Depression was upon the country, and several states had adopted or were considering similar programs. Consequently, an old-age pension bill drafted under Alfred I. du Pont's personal supervision was easily enacted in 1931.

On July 1, 1931, Alfred I. du Pont sent out his last batch of personal pension checks to a list now grown to sixteen hundred recipients. By this time, he had distributed $320,000 in this program. Alfred I. du Pont's list and his staff were taken over by the state, though he continued to send pensions to a few people whom the state removed from the list as not meeting its criteria of need. Alfred I. also succeeded, through the Old Age Commission and with the governor's aid, in persuading the legislature to agree to build a state home and hospital for the indigent. The State Welfare Home, opened at Smyrna in 1933, in conjunction with the pension program, replaced the nineteenth-century system of county poorhouses.

It was at Alfred I. du Pont's death, however, that his largest benefaction was discovered, for his will provided that after his widow's death the bulk of his wealth was to be used to create and maintain on his three-hundred-acre estate outside Wilmington a charitable institution for the care and treatment of crippled children (but not incurables) or the care of old men and women, especially old couples. In either case, first consideration was to go to residents of Delaware. "It has been my firm conviction throughout life," Alfred I. had written in January 1935, a few months before his death, "that it is the duty of everyone in the world to do what is within his power to alleviate human suffering." His widow, Jessie Ball du Pont, insisted that the hospital should be founded at once without waiting for her death; therefore, the Alfred I. du Pont Institute for crippled children was able to be opened at Nemours in 1940.

What individual manufacturers, like Alfred I. du Pont, did for the people of Delaware might well have been accomplished without them. There would, almost certainly, have been parks without William Bancroft and an art museum without his nephew Joseph, who left his estate to the Wilmington Society of the Fine Arts. Even without the interest of Martha Gause, hospitals would have been founded, and provision for women's education at the college level would have been made had Emalea Warner never lived. New schools for that matter would have eventually been built without Pierre du Pont, and new roads without his cousin Coleman.

What, then, did these individuals matter? They mattered

because they speeded the process of change. Some old people received financial assistance who might otherwise have died without it. Some children were encouraged by improved educational opportunities who might otherwise never have had an opportunity to make much of their natural talents. The civic spirit and public service of individuals was of importance to Delaware in the twentieth century. Who these individuals were and what they did made a significant difference.

13

The Depression and the War

Politics in the Roosevelt Years

Like the Civil War, the Great Depression had a profound effect on the politics of Delaware. Until 1936, not one Democrat had been chosen governor of Delaware in the twentieth century, and only once, in the three-sided election of 1912, had Delaware cast its electoral votes for a Democratic candidate for president. Even in 1932, after the depression had begun, Delaware was one of only five states that preferred the Republican President, Herbert Hoover, to Franklin Roosevelt.

By 1936, however, a change had occurred, and Roosevelt carried Delaware, as he did again in 1940 and 1944. In the beginning, it was the reputation of Roosevelt himself and of his national policies that won the support of Delaware voters, not any particular attractiveness of the local Democratic party. Roosevelt's personal popularity was extraordinary. Voters viewed him as someone concerned about the common man, a president actively seeking to help people in need. It was not that Roosevelt conquered the economic depression, for it lingered until the outbreak of the Second World War. Yet Roosevelt did cure the depression in men's minds; they found both help and hope in his policies.

In the decade following 1936, the change in Delaware politics was effective only in the years of presidential elections, and though some state candidates were able to ride Roosevelt's coattails to victory or take advantage of unusual circumstances, such as a division in the ranks of their opponents, the Delaware voter in state elections normally gave Republican candidates a majority. It is likely that a good part of the difference between Roosevelt's popularity in Delaware and that of the average local Democratic candidate was accounted for by the black vote.

In 1932 Delaware Democrats had demonstrated a significant shift in their opinions, when they eliminated all reference to race from their party rules and began at last to compete with Republicans for the favor of the black voter. This was not a development altogether peculiar to Delaware, for in the North generally the Democrats were actively seeking black votes at this time. The wonder is that the Delaware Democrats had so long retained their attachment to their "lily white" party concepts of the Reconstruction era. Perhaps the success of the Democrats in the 1870s and 1880s, added to their strong disapproval of Republican vote-buying tactics of the Addicks years, had mired them in a fixed position of self-confident righteousness from which they could not easily move. At any rate, in their attitude toward the black voter the second generation of Democratic leaders, of Bayards, Saulsburys, and Wolcotts, had changed very little from their fathers of the first postbellum generation.

Not so with the third generation. By 1932 the Delaware Democratic party was willing to accept the twentieth century. The black voter and the woman voter were both valued highly, at least at election time. Women voters as a whole did not long nurse any grievance they felt against the Democratic party because its legislators had not supported the Nineteenth Amendment. However, the attitude of the Democrats toward the Fifteenth Amendment had been remembered for decades by black voters, and with good reason. Therefore the switch of the Delaware Democrats in 1932, their new eagerness to win black votes that led them, in Wilmington at least, to organize Negro Democratic clubs, did not win an immediate response as far as local candidates were concerned.

Roosevelt was something else. Blacks appreciated his concern for the third of a nation that he described as ill-housed, ill-clothed, ill-fed, and they responded to it. But they could not so quickly respond to the Democratic leaders in Delaware—or, for that matter, desert their friends in the state Republican party. The result was that Roosevelt found a following among Delaware blacks that local Democrats did not have.

Some blacks saw the advantage of encouraging competition for their vote. They took credit for the defeat of Republican Congressman Caleb R. Layton in 1922 because of their anger at his failure to support an antilynching bill in Congress. But their commitment to the Republican party was so certain that they received little in the way of those jobs or offices with which politicians customarily reward followers. As late as 1947, for instance, except for one messengership, they held none but menial jobs, like janitors, in Legislative Hall at Dover. They did slightly better in getting jobs in the Wilmington city government, where the first black, Thomas Postles, was elected to city council in 1901, and thereafter black representation was continuous. But in the days of vote-buying, it is said that less was paid for the black man's vote than for the white man's. What was true in terms of hard cash was true also in terms of the rewards of political victory.

The first woman to serve in the state legislature, Florence M. Hanby, a Brandywine Hundred Republican, was elected in 1924, but no black representative was seated until William J. Winchester, a Wilmington businessman and a Republican, won election to the state House of Representatives in 1948. There were, of course, more women voters than black voters in Delaware, but the tardiness of the advance of blacks in politics is due in part to their social, economic, and educational status, which gave them little opportunity to develop the skill and sophistication necessary for politics. An Independent Colored Republican party had been announced in 1892, but nothing came of it. Formation of a chapter of the National Association for the Advancement of the Colored People in Wilmington in 1912, did, on the other hand, mark the beginning of a drive for improvement centered among the Delaware blacks themselves—in contrast to movements for the welfare of blacks organized by sympathetic whites—though the NAACP was not segregated.

In 1934 some Delaware manufacturers—John J. Raskob, Irénée du Pont, and his brother-in-law R. R. M. Carpenter—took a prominent role in founding the American Liberty League, a national organization with state chapters, the first of these chapters being in Delaware. The Liberty League proclaimed itself a nonpartisan group to defend the Constitution and traditional American individual liberties, but to the public it seemed a propaganda agency of the wealthy devoted to opposing the innovative and experimental projects called the New Deal with which the Roosevelt administration sought to counter the depression.

Though the Liberty League took over many of the officers and financial supporters of the successful National Association

Against the Prohibition Amendment, it lacked the latter group's popular base. Even if the Liberty League's conservative philosophy had awakened a sympathetic reaction among ordinary voters, the depression had plunged so many people into desperate financial straits that they were inclined to support a government that seemed to be actively trying to relieve their distress.

The very height of the activity of the Liberty League brought the Democrats their greatest success in Delaware in the twentieth century to this time, for in 1936 they not only carried the state for Roosevelt but also elected a governor, senator, representative, and many other officials. The scope of the Democratic victory was partly attributable to a schism among their opponents; a group of independent Republicans, including several men who had once held important roles in the party, protested what they referred to as Du Pont domination of the party and put up a ticket of their own, helping defeat, among others, Senator Daniel O. Hastings, who had been Coleman du Pont's choice as his successor and was an ardent spokesman for the Liberty League on the Senate floor. The total of votes on both Republican tickets, however, was not as large as that of the Democrats.

Insofar as it pertains to Delaware, the Liberty League episode indicates that the manufacturers, generous and public-spirited as they were, had little political effect when they stopped working through the accustomed channels of political parties. They were, in essence, sold a piece of goods in the Liberty League, supporting an organization that was top-heavy with officers and sponsors but lacking in popular support.

In 1938, working again through a unified party, the Republicans regained control of the General Assembly from Democrats who ran without the advantage of a presidential election that would bring them the aid of those elements, including some blacks, with whom Roosevelt had a special popularity. Through the next decade the pattern was much the same. In the years of a presidential election, the Democrats were strong because of Roosevelt (though not strong enough to capture the governorship again until 1948); in off years the Republicans produced their customary majorities.

An observer might have thought that once Roosevelt was removed from the scene, Delaware would revert to its old Republican political pattern, but this was not so. Events of the Roosevelt years—the depression and the Second World War—brought about changes that turned Delaware from a normally Republican state into a normally Democratic one, paralleling a change that had already occurred in the nation as a whole.

The new pattern appeared in 1948, the year of the first post-war (and post-Roosevelt) presidential election. Delaware voted for a Republican presidential candidate (for Dewey over Truman) but chose Democrats to many other positions, including Elbert N. Carvel, of Laurel, as governor, the second Democrat to be elected to that position in this century. For ten years more a new pattern prevailed. Republicans dominated Delaware elections in presidential years, greatly aided by the extraordinary popularity of Dwight Eisenhower; in off-year elections Democrats were generally successful. The tendency, however, was for Democratic strength to grow and Republican strength to wane. Soon the number of registered Democrats decidedly exceeded that of registered Republicans—though many voters declined to state a party preference, inasmuch as party primaries meant very little in Delaware, and the right to participate in primary elections was the only advantage gained by listing a party preference at registration.

The Great Depression

As was true of Americans in general, Delawareans were hard hit by the depression. Factories and shops closed, in some cases permanently, and thousands of workers were unemployed. New jobs were hard to find, with even college graduates often waiting six months or a year after graduation before finding a job. Values of property and of many investments plummeted; house rents, for example, were difficult to collect. The resources of private charitable agencies and churches became so strained that in November 1932 Governor Buck called a special session of the legislature, which passed a relief act establishing a Temporary Emergency Relief Commission with an appropriation of $2 million.

Soon there was a long array of federal relief agencies at work in Delaware, among them the Works Progress Administration (WPA), which provided work relief for the needy on noncompetitive projects that ranged from cleaning trash from vacant lots to establishing an orchestra and compiling guidebooks; the National Youth Administration (NYA), which employed students in tasks set up by teachers and school administrators, such as painting bleachers at an athletic field; and the Civilian Conservation Corps (CCC), which employed young men and veterans in various conservation programs, including ditching marshes for the control of mosquitoes. In 1935 and 1936 a special income tax was levied in New Castle County for the relief of the poor, and in 1937 Delaware established an unemployment compensation system, federally funded.

The need for funds to support relief programs was an argument used by those urging repeal of prohibition laws and legalization of gambling at racetracks. In 1933 Delaware was the seventh state to ratify the Twenty-First Amendment, which repealed national prohibition. All of Delaware, however, except the city of Wilmington, had been dry before the adoption of the Eighteenth Amendment. Under terms of a local option law, permitting counties to banish the sale and consumption of alcoholic beverages by a referendum, Kent and Sussex had adopted prohibition as early as 1907. The local option law permitted Wilmington and rural New Castle County to be polled separately, and in 1917 Wilmington had turned down prohibition, while rural New Castle County joined Kent and Sussex as a dry area.

With the repeal of the Eighteenth Amendment, Delaware, on June 6, 1933, held new referenda under the local option law, and this time all four districts rejected prohibition. After a 1935 law permitted pari-mutuel betting at horse races, a nonprofit racetrack, called Delaware Park, was opened at Stanton in 1937, backed by a group of well-to-do Wilmingtonians. Gambling on the races was also introduced at the State Fair Grounds at Harrington, and several other racetracks were built later.

Despite very real hardships, Delaware suffered from the depression somewhat less than most other states. Not one major bank failed in Delaware, though a few small ones were not permitted to reopen after the banking holiday proclaimed by President Roosevelt in March 1933. There was some expansion of manufacturing in this period; Du Pont built a pigments plant at Edge Moor in 1935 and a nylon factory at Seaford in 1939, and Delaware farmers found a new revenue source in the production of broilers, young chickens weighing under three pounds.

Previously, the sale of chickens for their meat was largely a by-product of the egg business, but in 1923, at Ocean View, in Sussex County, Mrs. Wilmer Steele began producing chickens for sale in big city markets for broiling, roasting, or frying. In the next twenty years the industry grew at a phenomenal rate. Between 1934 and 1942 the number of broilers produced in Dela-

The Zwaanendael Museum, Lewes. Erected in 1931 by the state to commemorate the three hundredth anniversary of the first Dutch settlement, the building was modeled by E. William Martin, its architect, after the town hall of Hoorn, North Holland, the ancestral home of David de Vries, who planned the original settlement and led a second expedition in 1632. The name is a modern Dutch adaptation of the original name of the settlement. (Courtesy of the Historical Society of Delaware.)

ware increased by 671 percent, from 7 to 54 million, which was over one-fourth of all the commercial broiler production in the United States.

This new Delaware agricultural enterprise was centered in southeastern Sussex County, especially in the area between Millsboro and Selbyville. The moderate weather, cheap land and labor, and proximity to New York City, where there was a large market for live chickens to be ritually slaughtered under Jewish religious laws, help explain the advantages of southern Delaware in broiler production. Though these advantages declined somewhat after the industry began preparing the fowl in dressing and refrigerating plants before shipment, the start Delaware producers had over other areas encouraged them to a series of improvements in feeding, in treatment of poultry diseases, and so forth, that kept them among the leading areas in this business. By 1940 poultry had become decidedly the largest source of Delaware agricultural income, a bonanza crop rivaling and then exceeding the profits made from peaches in the previous century. Thanks to broilers, Sussex became one of the richest agricultural counties in the eastern United States.

Changes in Population

Spurred by growth of the broiler industry and construction of the nylon plant at Seaford, Sussex County grew faster than any other part of Delaware in the depression decade of the 1930s. Despite this growth, the number of white people living in rural areas declined; apparently, they were moving to the small towns and cities of Delaware. Wilmington grew in population; the 1940 census listed it as having 112,054 residents, the largest number in its history. But it was not growing as fast as the rest of the state.

Nor was New Castle County. It was probably a measure of the industrial malaise of the depression that in this decade, for the first time since 1810, New Castle County did not increase its proportion of the population of Delaware—that is, it did not grow at a faster rate than the state as a whole.

On the other hand, the state as a whole grew faster than the nation did in the depression decade—by an 11.8 percent growth in Delaware against 7.2 percent for the nation. It was the first time this had happened in the 150 years over which decennial censuses had been taken. Previously, the growth rate of Delaware, even at its highest in the 1850s, had always lagged behind the growth rate of the nation. In other words, in terms of numbers, Delaware had become increasingly less important in the nation.

The reversal of this trend in the Great Depression is mainly attributable to a precipitous decline in the national growth rate. But in the years—and decades—that followed, Delaware continued to grow faster than the nation, as was made clear by Charles Tilly in a study entitled "Recent Population Changes in Delaware," which was published in 1967 as Delaware Agricultural Experiment Station Bulletin no. 347.

The reason for this growth was the continued migration of people from other states into Delaware. In 1850, for example, 12.5 percent of Delawareans were born in other states, but this proportion rose with each succeeding census until it had risen to 45.2 percent by 1970. The explanation probably lies in the general shift of population from farms to cities. The greatest growth in Delaware was occurring in the cities, at first in Wilmington, and then in its suburbs and in smaller cities. Delaware grew, as all areas along the Boston-Washington axis grew. Rural Delaware lost population to cities, towns, and suburbs, but rural Delaware did not have much population to lose (compared with rural Pennsylvania or New Jersey, for example). Since Wilmington and its suburbs, comprising the industrial area of Delaware, lay very close to rural areas of Maryland, Pennsylvania, and New Jersey, they constantly drew population from these neighboring states as well as from rural Delaware.

Foreign immigration, on the other hand, became of little significance after approximately 1920. In that year foreign-born residents of Delaware were more numerous (19,901) than in any other census year, and they also represented a historic high proportion (8.9 percent) of the total population. Thereafter, the proportion of foreign-born declined constantly, until in 1970 it was only 2.9 percent. The *number,* as distinct from the *proportion* of the foreign-born, did not decline so constantly, showing a slight rise in the decennial census of 1950 and again in 1970 (to 15,648), though never approaching the figure of the 1920 census.

The 1920 census was a sort of watershed in terms of immigration because, soon afterward, national quota laws went into effect, limiting immigration, particularly from some of the countries where conditions might have occasioned a large emigration to the United States. The depression, in its turn, made the United States less attractive to potential immigrants than it might otherwise have been. But while immigration was at its height, in the first two decades of the twentieth century, there were interesting changes in the composition of the foreign-born population of Delaware.

Whereas in the mid-nineteenth century the two largest immigrant groups coming to Delaware were the Irish and the Germans, in the early twentieth century the Italians and the Poles were most numerous among the newcomers from abroad. A comparison of the 1900 and 1920 census figures classifying immigrants residing in Delaware according to the country of

their birth shows a considerable change. (Note that the figures
for these years represent not just recent immigrants, but the
total immigrant population, including those who arrived in
America fifty or sixty years earlier.)

In 1900 the five most numerous immigrant groups were, in
order, as follows:

1. Irish
2. Germans
3. Poles
4. English
5. Italians

In 1920, the list is different:

1. Italians
2. Poles
3. Irish
4. Germans (including Austrians and Swiss)
5. Russians.

Many of the Russian, Polish, and German immigrants, and
smaller numbers from other countries, were Jews, who consequently now comprised a significant element in the Delaware
population. Other immigrant groups included a few hundred
Swedes and Greeks, as well as a more numerous representation of
English, Scots, and Canadians, who were rather easily absorbed
into the resident population of similar background. The Irish
and Germans arriving in the twentieth century also found
themselves relatively easily made at home in neighborhoods, in
churches, and in social organizations like those that utilized
German Hall and Irish-American Hall on the east side of Wilmington. More German immigrants settled in downstate Delaware than any other immigrant group from the continent.

The Italian and Polish immigrants, settling in Wilmington
because of the availability of factory and service jobs, gradually
developed their own neighborhoods, of which Little Italy and
Browntown, on the west and southwest sides of the city, became
most significant. The Poles, who had experience in Europe
maintaining their own Roman Catholic churches, quickly constructed St. Hedwig's and St. Stanislaus in Wilmington, along
with other organizations, including a school with instruction in
Polish. The Italians, accustomed to a state church abroad, were
slower in turning to church construction; eventually, however,

their St. Anthony's became a showplace among Delaware church edifices and the center of much social life.

Recent Jewish immigrants from Slavic lands built upon and expanded the religious and social organizations founded by earlier Jewish immigrants from western and southern Germany. Orthodox Christian congregations were established by Russians, Ukrainians (listed in census records among the Russians), and Greeks, which became centers for social life as well as for worship.

The Second World War

The enormous needs of the Second World War, 1939–45, converted Delaware quickly from the doldrums of a depression economy to the busy excitement of war production. The largest industry in Delaware during the war was shipbuilding, an industry with a long history in the area but one that had been almost moribund in the 1930s. The largest shipyard belonged to the Dravo Corporation and had been established in 1927 as the Atlantic coast ship assembly and launching point of this Pittsburgh firm. Dravo employed only four hundred workers in 1940 but quickly expanded to a peak of eleven thousand, which made it decidedly the largest employer of local labor. Altogether, Dravo launched 187 craft at Wilmington during the war, including 15 destroyer escorts and many landing ships. Other Wilmington shipyards, including Pusey and Jones and Jackson and Sharp (American Car and Foundry), were also busy, as were the smaller Vinyard shipyard, at Milford, and the Seaford Shipbuilding Company.

After the shipyards, the largest local employers were the powder and chemical companies, especially Du Pont, but for the first time in any national emergency since E. I. du Pont founded this company in 1802, it manufactured no explosives in Delaware. The administrative and service departments of the Du Pont Company, however, were centered in Delaware and were remarkably active. Besides adding to its own facilities, the Du Pont Company, through its engineering department, designed and constructed fifty-four plants at thirty-two locations for the United States government, including the giant $350 million Hanford atomic energy works in Washington State. In its work for the government on atomic energy, Du Pont refused to accept either profits or patents.

The emphasis for Du Pont was once again on military explosives, though this business had amounted to less than 2 percent of Du Pont's total production in the twenty previous years. Yet the company turned out three times the amount of these explosives that it had manufactured in the First World War. In fact, Du Pont alone produced 20 percent more explosives than had been used by the United States and all the Allied governments in the war of 1914–18. Most of the Du Pont nylon production at Seaford went to such war products as military parachutes.

The Hercules Powder Company followed the same course as Du Pont, operating six government-owned plants and pioneering in the production of powder for rockets. Atlas, which manufactured polyalcohols at its Atlas Point plant, south of Wilmington, operated three government-owned explosives plants besides its own facilities. North of Claymont, the General Chemical Company, a subsidiary of Allied Chemical and Dye, produced sulphuric acid and DDT. The one explosives factory in Delaware was operated near Milford by a subsidiary of Triumph Explosives of Elkton, Maryland, and concentrated on ordnance for the navy.

The specialized industries of the Wilmington area, such as leather and vulcanized fiber plants, were largely converted to war needs. The fiber production in this area is said to have been 70 percent of world production. The steel and iron foundries. like Worth Steel, at Claymont, Lobdell's, the Edge Moor Iron Company (with plants at Edge Moor and New Castle), and the Eastern Malleable Iron Company were very busy with war work. The Bellanca Aircraft Corporation, at New Castle, made airplane equipment. International Latex, at Dover, made lifeboats, among other war supplies. Seventy-five percent of the cotton cloth produced at the Bancroft mill, on the Brandywine, went to the American armed forces, and an additional amount was sent to foreign countries as Lend-Lease supplies.

The Wilmington Marine Terminal, a public facility opened in 1923 on the south bank of the Christina River, very close to its mouth, was busy with a great variety of exports and imports, including motor trucks, foodstuffs, and aviation gasoline. To provide for workers needed for war production, new housing units were built under government contract, including Millside, at Wilmington, and George Read Village, at Newark.

Over thirty thousand Delawareans, which is more than one-tenth of the 1940 population of the state, served in the armed forces during the Second World War. Some began their service more than a year before the United States entered the war. For example, the 198th Coast Artillery Anti-Aircraft Regiment of the Delaware National Guard, then composed of slightly less than a thousand men, was inducted into United States service in September 1940 and eventually sent to the South Pacific. The remainder of the Delaware National Guard was inducted on January 27, 1941, as the 261st Separate Coast Artillery Battalion (Harbor Defense), which at that time had 327 officers and men. First stationed at Fort DuPont, outside Delaware City, it moved in the spring to a new fortress called Fort Miles that was built in the sand dunes near Cape Henlopen. A battery was erected at Fort Saulsbury, near Milford, and some men of the 261st were assigned to old Fort Delaware, on Pea Patch Island.

Besides the forts, the chief defense establishments in Delaware were three airfields. The New Castle County Airport, opened by the county government in 1941 at Hare's Corner, south of Wilmington, was converted into a major army base after Pearl Harbor. It became the center of air transport to Asia, Africa, and Europe, and at the end of the war fifteen thousand personnel returned to the United States from Paris through this base. The Dover Municipal Airport also became an army air base, used for coastal patrol, for the training of fighter pilots, and for rocket research. This base was greatly enlarged after the beginning of the Korean War, when it became a center of the Military Air Transport Service, with a personnel of about ten thousand in 1953.

A number of Delawareans served in high ranks in the military during the war, including Lt. Gen. Thomas Holcomb, commander of the Marine Corps; Lt. Gen. Eugene Reybold, commander of the Army Engineers; Vice Adm. William H. Purnell Blandy, commander of Navy ordinance; Lt. Gen. John W. O'Daniel, who saw action in campaigns from North Africa to Germany; Maj. Gen. Robert H. Pepper, a Marine officer in many Pacific island battles; and Rear Adm. John H. Brown, Jr., a submarine specialist. The famous Adm. William F. Halsey, commander of the Third Fleet, considered Delaware his home since his mother, wife, daughter, and grandchildren resided in this state. Lucile Petry Leone, director of the Cadet Nurse Corps and later assistant surgeon general, was the first woman director of a major division of the United States Public Health Service.

Two Delawareans won the Congressional Medal of Honor,

the highest citation for heroism in the armed forces: Sgt. William Lloyd Nelson, who was killed in Tunisia, and Sgt. James P. Connor, who survived after sustaining three wounds on D-Day in southern France. Altogether it is believed that there were just under 2,300 Delaware casualties in the war, including 823 dead and 70 missing.

14

The Mid-Century

The Largest Minority

The war brought labor shortages, which meant new employment opportunities for two economically depressed classes, women and blacks. Women had a chance at positions that paid better than the jobs (in domestic and secretarial work, for example) that had been theirs previously. So did blacks, whose improved economic status was augmented by the antiracist attitudes that were made relatively popular by the war against Hitler and the revulsion it helped engender against theories of racial supremacy and the dreadful actions that these theories gave rise to. Though many of the new jobs of women and blacks were lost at the war's end, some portion of their improved status was retained.

Notable changes occurred in the postwar years in the number and distribution of blacks in Delaware. The proportion of blacks had been almost constantly declining, as table 3 demonstrates:

TABLE 3

PROPORTION OF BLACKS TO TOTAL DELAWARE POPULATION, 1790–1940

Census Year	Percentage of Population
1790	22
1860	19
1900	16.6
1940	13.5

SOURCE: U.S. Census

After the war this trend was reversed, and the black population grew to 16 percent of the total in 1980. This was not a great change, but a substantial shift occurred in the location of the

223

Old College Hall, Newark. Constructed in 1833–34, this original college building on the campus of the University of Delaware was extensively remodeled in 1902 and 1917. (Courtesy of Richard Stewart, University of Delaware.)

black population within Delaware. Especially notable was the movement of blacks into Wilmington, where this element in the population rose from 11.4 percent in 1930 to 51.1 percent in 1980:

TABLE 4

PROPORTION OF BLACKS TO TOTAL WILMINGTON POPULATION, 1930–80

Census Year	Population of Wilmington	Black Population	Percentage of Blacks
1930	106,597	12,138	11.4
1940	112,504	14,329	12.7
1950	110,356	17,277	15.6
1960	95,827	25,075	26.2
1970	80,386	35,072	44.1
1980	70,195	35,858	51.1

SOURCE: U.S. Census

It is notable that the black population of Wilmington grew rapidly after 1950. However, the proportion of blacks in the population grew even more rapidly because in this same period the total population of Wilmington was declining.

This change forms a peculiar contrast to the figures for New Castle County outside Wilmington. Here the black population declined from a proportion of 11.1 percent in 1930 to 4.6 percent in 1970. Yet the total number of blacks in this area, though declining in the 1930s, more than doubled between 1940, when it was 6,117, and 1970, when it was 13,948. The proportionate decline occurred because the whites in this area increased even more rapidly to 1970; thereafter the proportion of blacks rose, to 7.4 percent in 1980. These figures demonstrate the so-called flight to the suburbs, but the fact that the number of both whites and blacks in New Castle County was growing indicates that there were economic inducements encouraging people of both races to move to New Castle County. Blacks, being generally poorer than whites, moved into some of the housing whites were vacating in Wilmington. One hundred years earlier, the boundaries of Wilmington would have been extended to take in some of the suburbs, as they had often been in the past. But in the mid-twentieth century, for various reasons, mainly political and fiscal, no boundary adjustment was made.

The number of blacks in the downstate population also grew in this period, but in Kent County the proportion of blacks declined from 19 percent in 1940 to 17 percent in 1970, probably because the rapid enlargement of the Dover Air Base brought an influx of predominantly white residents. Everywhere, downstate and upstate, the basic movement of the black population was from the farm to the city. Blacks were, to a large degree, merely duplicating a migration that had taken place among whites from fifty to a hundred years earlier.

Whites had abandoned rural life before blacks did so, and now, after 1940, whites began to abandon large cities for the suburbs. The homes and neighborhoods the whites were abandoning seemed better to the rural blacks than the homes they had in the countryside. So did the facilities, such as schools, churches, libraries, stores, and amusements, while the factory jobs available in or near the cities paid better than farm labor.

In 1945 social relations between the races in Delaware were a mixture of Southern and Northern customs, with the former prevailing downstate and the latter in the Wilmington area. Throughout Delaware schools, restaurants, theaters, and most, but not all, churches were segregated; libraries, buses, and trains were not, and blacks voted as freely as whites. The peculiarities of the situation are indicated by the fact that there were two segregated reform schools for girls in New Castle County, whereas there was but one reform school for boys of both races.

The first steps to break this behavioral pattern were slow and tentative. One of the first occurred in the realm of sports in 1943 when the Wilmington Friends School scheduled a basketball game with Howard High School, the local high school for blacks. Previously, Howard had to arrange its athletic contests with out-of-state schools, but soon a Wilmington Catholic high school, Salesianum, conducted by the Oblates of St. Francis de Sales, followed the lead of the Friends School, and public high schools for whites in the Wilmington area did likewise before long. As late as 1955, however, the Milford school board canceled a football game between Milford and Dover high schools because one Dover player, a substitute, was black.

By that time, however, Milford had become embroiled in an emotional crisis over integration in its schools. Public school segregation was required by the state constitution and was abandoned only after the federal courts voided state segregation requirements. The first steps toward integration in Delaware education were taken by the University of Delaware in 1948, when, in view of federal court decisions, blacks were admitted to all courses and curricula not duplicated at Delaware State College; the latter institution, being smaller than the university, could not offer as wide a variety of course work, especially in engineering and in graduate study. Two years later, in 1950, all restrictions on the admission of Delaware blacks to the university were dropped, after a court decision to the effect that educational opportunities at Delaware State College simply were not equal to those at the university in any curriculum. This decision is notable in that it came not from a federal court but from the Delaware chancery court, with a Delawarean, Chancellor Collins J. Seitz, presiding.

In this same year, the Salesianium High School admitted five black students, and in 1952 the Catholic parochial school system was integrated. A few white public schools were opened to blacks in 1952 after another chancery court decision to the effect that the existing segregated schools for blacks were not the equal of the white schools. The Delaware decision was quoted by the United Supreme Court in 1954 in the epochal *Brown* v.

Topeka Board of Education decision, which declared that segregated schools were illegal under the terms of the Fourteenth
Amendment.

Attempts to integrate schools in northern Delaware, undertaken at varying rates of speed in different school districts, generally proceeded smoothly. Even as far south as Dover, some
blacks were quietly admitted to the senior high school in 1954.
South of Dover, however, only in Milford was integration begun
in this year, and the result was a popular protest by whites, who
permitted a rabble rouser from the South named Bryant Bowles,
president of a group called the National Association for the
Advancement of White People, to assume public leadership of a
school boycott. Under pressure of the boycott, the Milford schools
were closed until integration was temporarily abandoned. The
school board, accused of tolerating the integration experiment,
was replaced, and a number of school employees resigned.

In 1955 the state supreme court upheld the temporary abandonment of integration in Milford, ruling that pupil registration
procedures had not been followed properly. By September of
that year one-tenth of all school students in Delaware were in
integrated classes, but in downstate Delaware integration proceeded very slowly until 1960, when the federal circuit court
of appeals turned down a Delaware plan to desegregate slowly
grade by grade over a twelve-year period. A more rapid integration was demanded and generally was achieved.

In the long run, the most difficult problems of integration
were not in downstate Delaware, where the first steps had been
taken most slowly, but in Wilmington, where desegregation had
seemed successful in the 1950s. The very success of desegregation
in Wilmington aggravated the white flight to the suburbs, which
was already under way. The whites leaving Wilmington included
a high proportion of young families with children of school age,
and the result was that the public schools in the city came to
have a high majority of black students. A large number of the
white families remaining in Wilmington who had school-age
children sent their children to parochial schools. These schools
were integrated but were preponderantly white because only a
small minority of blacks were Catholics.

The steps taken against segregation in the schools were duplicated in relation to other public facilities, such as restaurants,
hotels, and theaters. The Wilmington YWCA opened its cafeteria to all races in 1951, and the Hotel du Pont, the most pres-

tigious hotel in Delaware, declared its facilities open to all in 1953. In 1961 the Wilmington city council passed an ordinance forbidding racial bias in restaurants. Though most Wilmington motion picture theaters were opened to blacks in 1951, one theater remained segregated until 1963, when the legislature passed a Public Accommodations Law, forbidding racial discrimination.

Changing economic conditions made integration of housing and of neighborhoods a new source of bitterness in the mid-twentieth century. As long as the status of blacks was decidedly servile, they could live without opposition in close proximity to whites, as they often did in rural areas, or in cities and towns, where clusters of black housing were found scattered about, wherever jobs were available. With segregation the rule in schools and in many other facilities, blacks could live close to whites and still, to some degree, be ignored.

Desegregation of schools and other public accommodations changed things, and so perhaps did an increased economic competition between the races, encouraged by federal policies stimulating the hiring of blacks (and, though not pertinent in this regard, of women). With some exceptions, such as the old Wilmington suburb of Belvedere and a few wartime housing developments on the edge of Wilmington like Dunleith and Millside, the rush to the suburbs increased land value there to such an extent that blacks had few opportunities to acquire new housing. If they purchased property in a new development, they ran a risk of being ostracized or worse, as in the case of a black family that was forced by violence to give up a house in Collins Park in 1959.

Urban renewal plans in the 1960s led to the destruction of many old homes occupied by blacks, particularly on the east side of Wilmington, and delays in their replacement forced blacks to relocate in other parts of the city. The search for new housing in the city increased racial tensions and encouraged the white migration to the suburbs, as neighborhoods and schools hitherto predominantly white came to have an increasing black constituency.

A Council on Human Relations was established by the legislature in 1961 in an effort to ameliorate race relations and to hear complaints of inequitable treatment. Developments in race relations through these years included the admission of blacks to the National Guard in 1951 and to the state police in 1963. By appointment of the governor, the state board of education added its first black member in 1963; a similar appointment added the first black to the Board of Trustees of the University of Delaware in 1969.

The most notable development in church organization was the merger of the white and black Methodist conferences in 1965 into one body, with blacks as well as whites appointed to supervisory positions. This was an especially significant development because more Delaware blacks were Methodists than members of any other denomination, though a significant proportion of the black Methodists belonged to voluntarily segregated organizations, such as the African Methodist Episcopal (A.M.E.) Church, the African Union Methodist Protestant (A.U.M.P.) Church, and the Union American Methodist Episcopal (U.A.M.E.) Church.

In July 1967 riots broke out in a black section of Wilmington that led to seven wounds by gunshot and 250 arrests for disorderly conduct, looting, and the like, though little property damage had been done before order was restored on August 8. More serious riots occurred in April 1968, after news was heard of the assassination in Memphis of the Reverend Martin Luther King, Jr. Governor Charles L. Terry, Jr., quickly called out the National Guard and kept it on duty in Wilmington for the balance of the year, despite the request of Mayor John Babiarz that the guardsmen be removed. Black students at Delaware State College also rioted and seized the student center, issuing demands that included an expansion of courses in black studies, but Governor Terry reacted by ordering National Guard troops to clear the campus and close it down in May, several weeks before the term was due to end. The college reopened peacefully in the fall, but the Wilmington incident, said to be the longest occupation of an American city by state armed forces, became an issue in the fall 1968 elections, in which Governor Terry was narrowly defeated. Immediately after his inauguration in January 1969, the new governor, Russell Peterson, withdrew the guard from Wilmington. Later in the same year, Governor Peterson and his supporters in the legislature were responsible for passage of a Fair Housing Law and for providing money for a summer employment program to keep young people off the streets.

Blacks were not without influence in the Democratic party. The first black Democrat to serve in the state legislature had been chosen in 1952, and in the year of the King riots, 1968, a black Democrat, James Sills, was the first member of his race to win a citywide election in Wilmington when he was elected to an at-large seat in the city council. Black votes had helped elect a Democrat mayor of this city in 1956, the first such victory in twenty years. Thereafter, however, the Democrats carried Wilmington easily until 1968, when a popular and wealthy Republican candidate, former Congressman Harry G. Haskell, Jr., may have been helped to victory by black resentment of the military occupation ordered by a Democratic governor.

It is difficult to measure the effect of the riots and the military occupation on elections in 1968 and subsequent years. Blacks unquestionably turned against Governor Terry, but there was also a backlash of white anger against rioters, and Terry's re-election effort may have been lost because of a heart attack the elderly governor suffered during the campaign. It is notable that in 1968 Alabama Governor George Wallace, known for his opposition to school integration (but also appealing to the white "working-class" voter on economic grounds), carried 13 percent of the vote in Delaware as an independent candidate for president. It seems doubtful that black voters turned out at elections in sufficient numbers to make use of their potential, for in 1972 black candidates lost several Democratic primary contests in Wilmington by sizable margins, and in the fall elections that year, Governor Peterson and Mayor Haskell were both defeated by Democratic challengers.

Economic Life

The postwar period, following 1945, was a time of prosperity and growth in Delaware. In several years (for example, in 1961) Delaware ranked highest among the states in per capita income, and it always ranked well above the average in this regard. This statistic could be misleading, for a few Delawareans with immense incomes could have a substantial effect on the average, granted the small total population. Another factor determining the high per capita income was the large number of jobs available in Delaware for trained scientists and technologists, who could command high wages.

The location of Delaware, midway between New York and Washington and between Philadelphia and Baltimore, gave local industries an advantage in marketing their products. The availability of the river, as well as of railroad lines and major highways, meant that raw materials could easily be imported. The Getty (formerly Tidewater) oil refinery was moved from Bayonne, New Jersey, to Delaware City because Delaware offered tax advantages as well as the opportunity to build a new, largely automated plant at a point to which tankers could conveniently bring foreign petroleum. Because of the refinery, a number of petrochemical industries built plants on the road from New Castle to Delaware City, including Stauffer Chemical and Diamond Shamrock. A jute plant was constructed at Edge Moor to be near the river for convenience in importing.

General Motors and Chrysler built automobile assembly plants at Woodcrest and Newark, respectively, beside railroad lines. Other companies found it advisable to locate downstate, where land and labor were relatively cheap. Among them were National Cash Register, near Millsboro; International Latex and General Foods, at Dover; Leeds Travelwear, at Clayton; and Globe-Union, battery manufacturers, at Middletown.

Especially well-paid positions were created by the growth of the former explosives companies that were now major chemical manufacturers, Du Pont, Hercules, and Atlas. The growth of their nationwide operations led them to enlarge their home offices and laboratories in Wilmington. Atlas built new offices in Brandywine Hundred and a pharmaceutical plant near Glasgow. Hercules Powder Company changed its name to Hercules, Incorporated, because of the diversity of its business, enlarged its experimental station, purchased the Haveg Corporation, of Marshallton, and secured increased office space through a twenty-two-story addition, called the Hercules Tower, to the Delaware Trust Company Building in Wilmington. The Nemours Building and the Brandywine Building added to the office space of the Du Pont Company in downtown Wilmington. Besides the vastly enlarged experiment station on the Brandywine, Du Pont constructed the Louviers Building at Milford Crossroads for its engineerng department and established veterinary chemical and toxicological laboratories between Newark and Elkton, an instrumentation facility near Glasgow, and market research laboratories at Chestnut Run, west of Wilmington.

Other industries, however, shrank or disappeared, including shipbuilding, railroad-car building, cotton and woolen textiles, and morocco-leather manufacturing. Several large Delaware companies were sold. The Continental-Diamond Fibre Company, of Newark, for example, became a division of the Budd Company, then of Philadelphia (founded by a Delawarean), which discontinued fiber manufacturing and abandoned the Newark plant after a few years. The Lobdell Company sold out to United Engineering and was also soon closed down. Bancroft's, the leading Delaware textile firm, was sold to Indian Head Mills. International Latex in Dover, became part of a vast conglomerate. The most important industrial merger was that of Atlas into Imperial Chemicals Industry, a British firm that became, by this addition, larger than Du Pont. The explosives business, by now a minor part of the Atlas interests, was not merged into I.C.I.; it became the independent Atlas Powder Company, with headquarters in Texas.

The decision of the Du Pont Company to absorb Christiana Securities by exchanging Du Pont stock for that of the holding company—a plan scheduled for implementation in 1978—may lead to a lessening of the ties between Delaware's largest industry and the state. Inasmuch as members of the Du Pont family have owned Christiana Securities, which in its turn has held the largest single bloc of stock in the Du Pont Company, Christiana has served as a device for perpetuating family control of the chemical company. Although the owners of Christiana Securities will hold large amounts of Du Pont Company stock after the merger, they will do so individually, with ownership so dispersed as to lose its effectiveness. The effect may be a lessening of control of the company by residents of Delaware.

Though in these instances local control of manufacturing was weakened, there were local companies that were either newly founded or grew rapidly in the postwar years. All-American Engineering Company, of Wilmington, expanded its business. W. L. Gore and Associates, of Newark, manufactured teflon wire and built plants in Maryland, Arizona, and abroad. John W. Rollins, who began his Delaware career with an automobile agency in Lewes, founded an industrial empire in such diverse fields as outdoor advertising, waste disposal, and car rentals. Intensely interested in politics, Rollins was elected lieutenant governor in 1952 and was the chief financial supporter of the Republican party in Delaware through the 1960s.

In northern New Castle County and in the Dover area of Kent County farmers lost land to housing development. Everywhere they found it necessary to adapt to economic realities; for example, they gradually abandoned many crops, like strawberries, that required intensive, and increasingly costly, labor for harvesting. The number of farmers decreased, but the size of farms grew almost constantly, thanks to the use of agricultural machinery. Irrigation grew in popularity and permitted some expansion of farm acreage; by 1975 approximately 30 percent of Sussex farms had artificial water systems.

In farming, Sussex is the most important county, its agricultural income being roughly double that of Kent, which has a larger farm income than New Castle. Broilers remained the major source of agricultural income through the third quarter of the twentieth century, but corn and soy beans were also important crops; the acreage devoted to soy beans showed especial growth in the last few decades. Agricultural economists spoke of a "broiler–corn–soy bean complex," since the last two crops furnished feed for the poultry. Dairy products, meat (primarily pork), and vegetables (especially potatoes) maintained some importance, though the acreage devoted to vegetables declined. Several diversified agricultural businesses flourished downstate, notably those of the Cannons and Newtons at Bridgeville, and of the Townsends (the business founded by Senator Townsend) in eastern Sussex. The Townsends had a large grain business and were integrated broiler producers, with investments ranging from breeder flocks to processing plants. The Newton enterprises included a feed business (subsequently sold), retail agencies for irrigation equipment and other machinery, and the production of fruit and other crops.

As a means of transportation, automobiles gradually supplanted railroads. The Delaware Railroad abandoned passenger service at the end of 1965; the Baltimore and Ohio Railroad had taken the same step several years earlier on the portion of its tracks passing through northern Delaware. Postwar prosperity led people to travel in private motor cars, with the result that mass transit companies found it difficult to make a profit. At the same time, energy shortages suggested that wasteful use of fuel and of electric power should be limited. To encourage continued use of mass transit as well as to provide for those people who had no alternate means of traveling, the state set up the Delaware Authority for Regional Transportation (DART), which assumed responsibility for local bus service in the Wilmington area. A federal agency called Amtrak took over operation of the major passenger trains through Wilmington on the lines of the Penn Central Railroad, as the Pennsylvania Railroad was called after its merger with the New York Central. Bankruptcy of the Penn Central soon led to the operation of its lines by Conrail.

The New Castle County Airport (renamed the Greater

Wilmington Airport) had grand prospects for commercial development after most of its facilities were opened for civilian use at the end of the war. The Philadelphia International Airport, however, was only an hour by limousine from the center of Wilmington and attracted most of the northern Delaware passenger business by offering many more flights than the local airport. As a consequence, the Wilmington airport was used mostly by private planes and charter services.

Federal legislation in the depression years and economic conditions thereafter gave impetus to the growth of many labor organizations. Generally, workers in Delaware had not been organized in unions to this time. A few craft unions, like the printers, had flourished, and the Knights of Labor, a secret society with idealistic aims, had been active in the 1880s. But the Knights lost a long strike of morocco-leather workers that lasted for over six months, and thereafter they fell to pieces. Socialism had little following among Delaware workers, though there was a brief flurry of interest in 1878, chiefly among German immigrants, and occasionally socialists of one faction or another presented tickets at election times through the next century.

The most successful unions in Delaware before the depression of the 1930s were the railroad brotherhoods and the craft unions, the latter mostly united through the American Federation of Labor. The operating railroad brotherhoods were strong, but the nonoperating unions suffered by loss of a strike at the Pennsylvania Railroad shops in 1922 that lasted a year before collapsing. In 1901 a seven-week strike of machinists seeking shorter hours was settled by a compromise.

Generally, there was a minimum of violence in Delaware quarrels between labor and management. Very gradually, legislation improved the legal position of labor by such laws as a wage lien act (giving a laborer a prior claim for his money) in 1903, a child labor law in 1905, and a workmen's compensation law in 1917.

Federal laws of the 1930s encouraged the introduction and growth of industrial unions, such as the United Steel Workers, United Auto Workers, United Rubber Workers, and even the active United Mine Workers, who entered many industries, including, in Delaware, vulcanized fiber. One of the major strikes in Delaware history was that of the Teamsters Union, which successfully sought recognition from trucking companies in 1937.

By 1945, 80 percent of Delaware factory wage earners were

represented by unions in collective bargaining. After the war, there was a decline in the power of several unions paralleling the decline in industries such as shipbuilding, textile manufacturing, railroad transportation, and leather making. On the other hand, a large growth of unionization occurred in commercial and service occupations, for example, among telephone workers, cafeteria and restaurant workers, grocery clerks, teachers, and other government employees.

A dearth of agricultural labor led to increasing dependence on migrant workers, including large numbers of Puerto Ricans. Many Spanish-speaking newcomers, primarily Puerto Ricans, also settled in Wilmington, where they shared the historic misfortunes and hopes of the Irish, Germans, Poles, Italians, Jews, Ukrainians, rural blacks, and other newcomers over the past century and a half.

The most remarkable change occurring in economic life in the postwar period was the apparent cessation of manufacturing growth after almost continuous expansion for over a century. In its turn, manufacturing moved into the stage of development agriculture had already occupied. Thanks to machinery, fewer people could produce more goods. Consequently, the need for blue-collar workers decreased. Paperwork increased, as did sales and service occupations, and so repairmen, clerks, technologists, and health-related workers, such as nurses and therapists, were in demand, but factory labor seemed to be approaching the stage of growth (or of satiation) that agricultural labor had reached decades earlier.

Cultural Developments

With factories and farms no longer offering young men the opportunity of following the occupations of their fathers or of moving from farms to factories, there was an increasing need of schools to fit youth not just with reading, writing, and arithmetic, as in the distant past, but with the skills to cope with modern life, to make them adjustable to needs for computer operators, television repairmen, statisticians, and the like. Where once a small amount of such classroom instruction was offered in manual training or industrial arts and agriculture, now there was a large expansion of vocational education. The old Wilmington Trade School had been replaced in 1938 by the H. Fletcher Brown

Vocational High School, a gift of the Du Pont Company chemist and executive for whom it was named. The 1970s saw the opening of new vocational high schools both in Wilmington and in rural Delaware. At a higher level the Delaware Technical and Community College, a creation of the administration of Governor Charles Terry, offered two-year programs for high school graduates. Its first campus was opened at Georgetown in 1966, and soon other branches were established in Wilmington, Dover, and Stanton.

New colleges of nursing, of business and economics, of marine studies, and of urban affairs at the University of Delaware also offered preparation to meet special needs of the twentieth century. Two-year associate degree programs were instituted, and extension classes were offered at centers throughout the state. Graduate programs also proliferated, with the doctoral degree, never awarded before the war except as an honorary degree, now offered in a large variety of fields, of which chemical engineering was the first. The Women's College and Delaware College were combined as one coeducational institution in 1944. Whereas there never were quite a thousand undergraduates in full-time attendance on campus before the Second World War, the enrollment swelled to well over twelve thousand in the mid 1970s, not including graduate or part-time students. The campus and plant grew to keep pace with enrollment; besides study centers in Wilmington and experimental farms in southern New Castle County and at Georgetown, a marine-studies laboratory was established at Lewes.

Delaware State College underwent the same sort of growth, but on a smaller scale. It too became racially integrated; the resident student body remained largely black, but a large proportion of commuting white students also enrolled in classes. The state government did not establish a school of law or medicine at either institution despite the difficulty Delaware students found in being admitted to such schools elsewhere. To aid Delaware students forced to go out of state for training in these fields and in such others as dentistry, veterinary medicine, and architecture, the state legislature established a scholarship fund. For medical students in 1970 the state established a program called DIMER (Delaware Institute of Medical Education and Research) through which a certain number of places were reserved for Delaware students at the Jefferson Medical College in Philadelphia. The Delaware Law School, a private enterprise located in Wilmington, graduated its first class in 1975 after affiliating with Widener College, of Chester, Pennsylvania.

Other private colleges also came into being. Wilmington College, opened in 1968, offered a four-year program at its campus along the Du Pont Boulevard south of Wilmington. Brandywine College, a two-year institution primarily oriented toward business education, opened on a new campus near Talleyville in Brandywine Hundred in 1966; like the Delaware Law School, which moved to its campus, Brandywine College became affiliated with Widener College. An older institution, Goldey-Beacom College, derives from the merger of two business schools, Goldey and Beacom, in 1951. The school moved from Wilmington to a suburban location on Limestone Road in 1974 and continued expanding its program. The oldest junior college in Delaware is Wesley College, at Dover, founded by Methodists as the Wilmington Conference Academy in 1873. The name was changed in the twentieth century to Wesley Collegiate Institute, and under the direction of Henry Budd it began to offer junior college work. After a few years, it reverted to a preparatory school and from 1932 to 1942 it was closed entirely. Since its reopening in 1942 as Wesley Junior College, the institution has grown considerably in number of students and buildings. *Junior* was dropped from the name after about three decades, when a four-year program was initiated.

While these innovations were occurring at the college level, Delaware also added to its educational program for young children by instituting a statewide kindergarten system in 1968. Schools were also opened for students with hearing problems and for crippled children. Meanwhile, a Unit Allocation Act, adopted in the first administration of Governor Elbert N. Carvel, had provided an equal sum—in state appropriations—for each elementary class of twenty-five students and each secondary school class of twenty. In the years that followed, this allocation system was further refined to provide for many kinds of different classes.

As a result of the Educational Advancement Act of 1968, which went into effect the following year, the first major revision of the school system since 1921 was undertaken. Piecemeal consolidation of school districts had been taking place in the intervening years by the merger of smaller districts into larger ones, like the merger of the Cheswold District into Dover in 1949 or the merger of the Clayton District into Smyrna in 1962. By greatly increasing the number of mergers, the 1969 reorganization left just twenty-three consolidated school districts, including Wilmington; in addition to these twenty-three districts, each county comprised a vocational-technical school district, making a total of twenty-six. Another provision of this same act permitted an equalization of funds between different districts on the basis of existing differences in their opportunity to raise money locally for current operations. Hereafter, allowance could be made in state appropriations for the fact that districts with large industrial installations found it much easier to raise supplementary funds by local property taxes than districts with many children but few factories.

Since the Educational Advancement Act expressly prohibited any change in the boundaries of the Wilmington school district, by this time predominantly black, parents of children affected, who were subsequently joined by the Wilmington Board of Education, successfully challenged the school boundaries in federal district court, arguing that these boundaries preserved an unconstitutional segregated system. The United States Supreme Court affirmed the ruling of the district court in favor of the parents. As a result of this litigation, eleven northern New Castle County school districts, including Wilmington, were reorganized, and the busing of school children to achieve racial balance began.

The mid-twentieth century was also a period of increasing recognition of the value of museums as educational institutions. The Zwaanendael Museum at Lewes was constructed in 1931 to mark the tercentenary of the Dutch settlement there. The Delaware Art Museum, opened in 1938 by the Society of the Fine Arts on Kentmere Parkway in Wilmington, was notable for its collection of the work of Howard Pyle, a leading Wilmington illustrator and teacher, founder of a group of artist-illustrators known as the Brandywine school, and also a writer of note. The museum also housed the Pre-Raphaelite collection of Samuel Bancroft. A tremendous incentive to museum education followed the opening to the public in 1951 of the Henry Francis du Pont Winterthur Museum, for its remarkable collection of American domestic arts became the basis of a postgraduate program conducted cooperatively with the University of Delaware. A few years after the opening of Winterthur, which represented the personal collecting of Henry Francis du Pont, son of Sen. Henry A. du Pont, the Du Pont Company established a foundation that created a museum (called the Hagley Museum) on the site of

The Winterthur Museum. The first section of this building was erected in 1839 by Jacques Antoine Bidermann, who had married a daughter of E. I. du Pont. Extensive additions were made by Senator Henry A. du Pont and his son, Henry Francis du Pont, the collector, who opened it to the public in 1951. (Courtesy of the Henry Francis du Pont Winterthur Museum.)

old powder works on the Brandywine that had been closed since 1921. The library of Pierre du Pont was moved in 1961 from Longwood to the property of this foundation, where a modern building was constructed to house it, with significant additions, as the Eleutherian Mills Historical Library. Not far away, on the Kennett Pike, is the Museum of Natural History, founded by John du Pont. Under the auspices of the legislature and the State Archives Commission, the Delaware State Museum was created in the old Presbyterian church and some adjacent buildings in Dover. In 1970 the state created a Division of Historical and Cultural Affairs to supervise the State Archives, the State

The main Hagley Museum building, which was constructed in 1814–15 as a cotton spinning mill. Located on the Brandywine, just above the village of Henry Clay, it now contains sight-and-sound exhibits devoted to American industrial history, with emphasis on the Brandywine Valley area. (Courtesy of the Hagley Museum.)

Museum, and other state-owned properties of historic interest.

The preservation of historic buildings was closely related to the museum movement. Possibly the first important restoration was of Old Swedes Church, Wilmington. Built in 1698, the old edifice had been abandoned by its congregation in 1830, but the efforts of a few friends led to the repair and reopening of Old Swedes as a place of worship. Often, however, restored buildings were put to some new use, frequently as a museum, as was the case with the Old Town Hall of Wilmington, which in 1928 became the headquarters of the Historical Society of Delaware. Several New Castle structures were preserved, notably the old Court House, restored to its eighteenth-century condition as a result of legislative appropriations. In the village of Odessa, many buildings were restored by the philanthropist, H. Rodney Sharp, who began his career as a schoolmaster there. Woodburn, in Dover, became the governor's mansion in 1966. Two homes associated with the career of John M. Clayton were preserved, the Parson Thorne Mansion, in Milford, by the local historical society, and Buena Vista, in New Castle County, by gift from Clayton's collateral descendants, the Buck family, to the state. The home of John Dickinson in Kent County also became a state property, while the New Castle mansion of George Read, Jr., was given to the Historical Society of Delaware. The Old Brandywine Village Association began a preservation program in 1963, supported by private philanthropy. A decade later the New Castle County government acquired Rockwood, the Victorian home built in Bringhurst Woods by Joseph Shipley, who was descended from the founder of Wilmington and had made a fortune as partner in the English banking house of Brown and Shipley. In Lewes several old buildings were preserved by the local historical society. The Grand Opera House, in Wilmington, was preserved as a state center for the performing arts, and a new building, John M. Clayton Hall, on the Newark campus of the University of Delaware, frequently served as a conference center for state groups.

Historic buildings were often preserved in connection with parks. For example, before Rockwood was donated to the county, descendants of Shipley had given a stretch of his land nearby, which became known as Bringhurst Park. Like specialized schools and colleges, parks were an adjustment to the needs of the twentieth century, an attempt to preserve natural and antique environments for the benefit of families overwhelmed in their daily life by the urban or suburban scene. The New Castle County park system incorporated the splendid Wilmington city parks that owed their origin to William Bancroft's gift of an extensive tract of land along the Brandywine, and a state park system also came into being in the mid-twentieth century. Among the county and state parks are Brandywine Springs Park, on the site of a famous nineteenth-century spa near Red Clay Creek (not on the Brandywine), Lum's Pond, near the Chesapeake and Delaware Canal, Trappe Pond, in western Sussex County, and a Seashore State Park, beside the ocean between Rehoboth and Bethany. Two former fortifications became state parks: Fort Delaware, which was ceded back to the state in 1948, along with all of Pea

242 HISTORY OF DELAWARE

Patch Island, on which it lies; and part of the Fort Miles property, which became Cape Henlopen State Park after cession to the state in 1963. On the other hand, when Fort du Pont was ceded to the state in 1946, it was utilized not as a park but as a health center, to supplement such existing state facilities as the hospitals at Farnhurst and at Smyrna and the Emily Bissell Sanatorium, named for the Delaware woman who introduced in this country the use of the Christmas Seal to support anti-tuberculosis activities.

The merger of the Delaware, Memorial, and Wilmington General Hospitals in 1965 to form the 1,050-bed Wilmington Medical Center created one of the nation's largest new teaching hospitals. Postgraduate medical training is given to a house staff of over a hundred residents and interns, as well as to a smaller number of medical students who have not yet received their M.D. degrees. The aim of the program is to provide an ample supply of physicians for the state as older members of the profession die or retire. A rehabilitation hospital called Pelleport, the gift of Eugene du Pont, is also a part of the Medical Center. Two other hospitals are in Wilmington, St. Francis Hospital, a Catholic foundation, and Riverside Hospital, founded by osteopathic physicians. Downstate there are community hospitals in Dover, Milford, Lewes, and Seaford and a state institution for the mentally retarded at Stockley. The Veterans' Hospital near Elsmere is a federal facility. Despite the attention to vocational training in the mid-twentieth century, there developed a serious shortage of physicians and of some other medical specialists that was felt most seriously in rural areas. A high proportion of the newly licensed physicians in Delaware were immigrants, often from Asia or Latin America.

The Population Explosion

The most remarkable event in the history of Delaware in the mid-twentieth century was the population explosion of the 1950s. Delaware had begun growing at a faster rate than the nation in the depression decade of the 1930s, but this was partly due to the declining rate of national growth. The real surge in the growth of the Delaware population occurred in the 1940s, when it increased by 19.4 percent, but the growth rate accelerated in the next decade to 40.3 percent, higher than that of any other states except four in the West (Alaska, Nevada, California, and

Arizona) and one state in the East (Florida) that resembled a Western state in its growth. The growth rate declined to 22.8 percent in the 1960s, still high enough to rank Delaware as the eighth state in rate of growth.*

TABLE 5

Comparative Growth of the United States and Delaware, 1930–70

	Percent Increase from Previous Census	
Census Year	United States	Delaware
1930	16.0	6.9
1940	7.2	11.8
1950	14.4	19.4
1960	18.5	40.3
1970	13.3	22.8

Source: U.S. Census

The likely explanation of this phenomenon is, as suggested earlier, that Delaware population figures reflect very closely the growth of the "megalopolitan" area from Boston to Washington, since Delaware lies on the axis connecting the large urban centers of the East. Maryland has grown similarly to Delaware (surpassing Delaware in growth in the 1960s), and other states along this axis would show a similar growth rate if only their counties on or near the axis were considered.

Sussex County, which is farthest from the axis of the Megalopolis, had no sudden population explosion but continued to grow steadily and by the 1970s was the fastest growing county in Delaware. It had no large cities, for its largest communities, Seaford and Milford (the latter being partly in Kent), had less than 5,500 residents. The resort communities beside the ocean grew mainly in terms of summer population.

The great population growth of the mid-century was in New Castle and Kent, particularly in the suburbs of Wilmington and in and around Newark and Dover. By expanding its land area to include new housing developments, Dover more than doubled its population. In spite of Dover's growth, Newark, which had made its major land acquisitions earlier, maintained the rank of second largest Delaware city that it had achieved in 1950, but only because of the resident college students. Elsmere, on the

---

* Table 5 shows the recent growth rate of Delaware compared with that of the nation as a whole:

edge of Wilmington, was the fourth largest incorporated community, while Brookside Park, an unincorporated postwar housing development near Newark, ranked fifth in population, according to the 1970 census.

It is difficult to measure the population of unincorporated
areas because they have no fixed boundaries. Yet it is just such
areas that grew fastest of all. The nine incorporated communities
of New Castle County had a combined population of 118,407 in
1970, but the unincorporated suburban areas of the county had
a population twice as large as this. Delaware, once threatened
with domination by Wilmington, was now threatened with
domination by suburbia.

In 1970 most Delawareans lived in the developed areas within
fifteen miles of Wilmington but outside the Wilmington city
limits. Old suburbs, like Claymont, Holly Oak, Brack-Ex, Richardson Park, and Holloway Terrace; the newer suburbs, like
Holiday Hills, Fairfax, Wilmington Manor, Klair Estates, and
Brookside; and the incorporated communities of Bellefonte, Elsmere, New Castle, Newport, and Newark—these were the areas
that, in terms of numbers and wealth, threatened to dominate
Delaware in the 1970s.

Although many residents of suburbia commuted to jobs in
Wilmington, commerce and industry had also migrated to the
suburbs. Here were the automobile assembly plants, most of
the new facilities of the chemical companies, including some
offices, plus numerous shopping centers of varying sizes, some
featuring large department stores.

Some churches moved outside of Wilmington with their
congregations; others staying in the city sought to serve the
changing urban population. Some denominations appeared that
were new to Delaware, like the Mormons and the Missouri Synod
Lutherans, moving to the state to serve migrants from other areas
of the United States. Mennonite and Adventist churches also
generally served people who had moved to Delaware from other
states in the twentieth century. Some denominations—such as
the Bible Presbyterians, Jehovah's Witnesses, Assemblies of God,
and Pentecostals—arose through schisms in old churches or by
vigorous proselytizing. The largest denominations remained the
Catholics and the Methodists, as in the late nineteenth century,
but now with the Catholics decidedly more numerous.

Most of the Delaware population between the ages of twenty
and sixty-four in 1970 had been born elsewhere than in Dela-

ware. Only a small proportion (2.9 percent) were foreign-born; most newcomers were from states in the Northeast, such as Pennsylvania, New Jersey, and New York, with the second largest number coming from the South. A greater percentage of Delaware blacks (60 percent) than of whites (52 percent) were natives of Delaware.

The largest foreign element, counting immigrants and those who had at least one immigrant parent (11.7 percent of the total population), was composed of Italians, and the second largest group was Polish. Besides English, Irish, Scottish, German, Canadian, and Jewish elements (the last coming chiefly from eastern Europe), there were smaller but significant groups of Greeks, Russians, and other Slavic peoples, Hungarians, and Orientals, the last coming principally from the Philippines, China, and Japan. Members of the large Puerto Rican community were different from other overseas immigrants in that they were all American citizens when they came, were near enough to their homeland to return easily to visit, and, being often of racially mixed origin, were generally viewed as a group distinct from their neighbors, whether white or black.

Like the blacks, the Puerto Ricans moved into Wilmington housing vacated by the white families that had gone to new homes in the suburbs. Since the automobile made suburban living convenient for those wealthy enough to own cars and healthy enough to drive them, many of the people remaining in Wilmington were those unwilling or unable (like the poor and the elderly) to be dependent on automobiles. New high-rise apartments in Wilmington found tenants from the latter group. In a few sections of the city, like the Polish section, Browntown, or the Highlands area on the west side, a strong neighborhood pride led people to maintain or improve the quality of their housing. In other areas new housing was erected with the aid of federal funds. The administration of Mayor Thomas Maloney, elected in 1972, sought to promote improved housing by offering some abandoned houses free to those who would undertake to improve them for their own use, not as rental properties. Nevertheless, there were areas of Wilmington where empty and vandalized houses were eyesores that presented a grim scene of urban decay.

By the mid-twentieth century, Wilmington had entered a new stage in its history. Though remnants of the industrial city of the late nineteenth and early twentieth century still existed, Wilmington had become a service center, a city of offices, hospitals, and agencies. It was now the home of the public and private bureaucracy. In twentieth-century Wilmington, the bureaucrat was the dominant figure, the successor to the Wilmington merchant of the eighteenth century and to the Wilmington manufacturer of the nineteenth century. Valiant efforts to improve his city led to the creation of new parks and malls, as well as of a new civic center. Some old houses were grouped together in a restoration called Willingtown Square. The nineteenth-century customs house became the center of a group of new buildings.

15

The Suburban State

Reapportionment

While Wilmington sought through physical renewal to portray the vitality that underlay its new role in Delaware society, it was suburbia, old and new, that had the numbers, the wealth, and the educational advantages to dominate Delaware in the late twentieth century. Until 1964, however, the dead hand of the 1897 constitutional convention provided a restraint upon the full exercise of this power.

The system of apportionment established by the 1897 convention was intended to restrict the political power of Wilmington, then the most vigorous, populous, and wealthy part of Delaware. By 1964, the constitutional provision worked differently. By this date Wilmington was in decline, losing population yearly, and it was the suburbs that felt the restrictions of the constitutional apportionment of legislative seats.

In 1960, for example, one representative district in New Castle County (Brandywine Hundred) had a population of 58,228, whereas all of Kent County, with ten representatives, had only 65,651 people. Three representative districts in New Castle County (Brandywine, Christiana, and New Castle hundreds) had a total population (146,030) larger than Kent and Sussex Counties combined (138,846), which comprised twenty representative districts. Senatorial districts were similarly uneven.

The greatest disparity, however, was not between legislative districts in different counties but within New Castle County. Brandywine Hundred, with its 58,228 people, was the most populous representative district in the state, but Blackbird Hundred, also in New Castle County, with 1,643 people, was the least populous.* This discrimination against Brandywine Hun-

*POPULATION DISPARITY BETWEEN
REPRESENTATIVE DISTRICTS, 1960

TABLE 6

THE SIX MOST POPULOUS DISTRICTS

Symbol	District	Population
NC 6	Brandywine Hundred	58,228
NC 7	Christiana Hundred	47,509
NC 10	New Castle Hundred	40,293
NC 2	9th Ward and parts of 6th and 8th Wards of Wilmington	33,772
NC 5	10th, 11th, 12th, and part of 5th Ward in Wilmington	30,488
NC 8	Mill Creek Hundred	23,428

SOURCE: U.S. Census

TABLE 7

THE SIX LEAST POPULOUS DISTRICTS

Symbol	District	Population
NC 15	Blackbird Hundred	1,643
NC 14	Appoquinimink	2,534
K 6	Part of North Murderkill, South Murderkill, and Mispillion	2,626
S 8	Indian River Hundred	2,957
K 3	Kenton Hundred	3,361
NC 12	Red Lion Hundred	3,401

SOURCE: U.S. Census

dred had not been intended by members of the constitutional convention. Yet by providing that the constitution could, in effect, be amended only with the consent of the legislature, they made it very difficult to change the constitutional apportionment, because vested interests of some legislators and their constituencies would be damaged by any change.

The antiquated nature of the constitutional apportionment is further displayed by the difference between the most populous representative district (33,772) and the least populous district (5,394) in the city of Wilmington. While the inequities within Kent and Sussex were less extreme, the differences were still great, with 17,806 people in the most populous and 2,626 in the least populous district in Kent, and with 12,359 in the most populous and 2,957 in the least populous district in Sussex.

The existing inequities by no means were in favor of the rich and powerful. In fact, the most underrepresented districts were generally those that were growing most rapidly, and these were likely to be the wealthiest and to have the highest percentage of whites in their population. The constitutional apportionment tended to overrepresent the poor, the black, and the traditional elements in Delaware. It was, in a sense, a bulwark defending the old against the new, the poor against the rich, the otherwise powerless against the otherwise powerful.

Though there were factions in each party supporting and opposing this apportionment, the successful attack on it was mounted by seven New Castle County Republicans who challenged it in court (*Sincock* v. *Roman*) in 1962. Under this threat, the legislature at last sought to make a modest provision for change in the lower house, but the federal district court in 1963 struck down both the amendment and the constitutional provision. The decision was appealed to the United States Supreme Court, which in 1964 upheld the district court on the grounds that one man was entitled to the same voting power as another man.

As a result of this decision, a reapportionment law was passed in 1964, but it too was voided by the courts on grounds of gerrymandering (the creation of unequal districts so contrived as to give political advantage to those laying them out). Finally, a new state census was taken in 1967 as the basis for an apportionment law that the courts found acceptable. A further change occurred after the 1970 census, with the result that New Castle County was allotted fifteen seats in the state senate and twenty-nine in the house; Kent and Sussex each received three senate and six house seats. As before, the state was divided into single-member constituencies, but now most of these legislative districts were in the suburbs of Wilmington. The rule of the majority was established with a vengeance. Politics, like housing and shopping and even industry, had become suburbanized.

The change in apportionment that was made in the years immediately following 1964 may have been a major watershed in Delaware history. A large share of political power now rested in the hands of the wealthiest, most innovative, best educated (or, at least, most educated) portion of the population—and also upon a portion of the population that had the highest proportion of white people and probably the highest proportion of newcomers (except for the Dover area, where the air base accounted for much of the new population growth). Suburbia could not be expected to be the area that would be most careful to maintain traditional ways, particularly in politics. Just as rural Delaware may have occasionally been insensitive to the needs of the urban population of Wilmington, suburbia, in its moment of triumph, might be somewhat insensitive to the needs of both Wilmington, with its many poor and elderly, and downstate Delaware, including the residents of small towns as well as farmers and their families.

County Reorganization and Party Politics

One of the first fruits of a redistricted legislature occurred in 1965, when the New Castle County government was drastically overhauled. A county council was established, elected in councilmanic districts, into which the county was divided. Its powers were far more extensive than those of the old levy court, which it replaced, and which had little more power than to set the county tax rate and appropriate the income to agencies largely established by the legislature or by the constitution. The new county council worked with an elected county executive and with administrative departments handling such problems as finance, recreation, sanitation, and zoning. This new, responsible, streamlined county government underwent some changes in a few years, but basically it was accepted as a necessary service, especially to the large number of people residing in unincorporated suburbs, who constituted a major part of the county population. The county executive and the council now became what the mayor and city council of Wilmington had once been: the most important agency of government in Delaware after the governor and the legislature.

Subsequently Sussex County also procured a council form of government. Though the Sussex model differed from that in New Castle, the aim in both cases was to provide more strength to county government. Kent, however, rejected change and maintained its traditional government through the elected levy court.

After midcentury Delaware was, in political terms, a swing state, sometimes supporting Democrats and sometimes Republicans, prob-

The Old State House, on the Green, in Dover. Originally intended as a new Kent County courthouse, plans for this building were altered to allow space for the legislature in 1791–92. The building has been remodeled on several occasions; the most recent remodeling, intended to restore a close approximation of the original appearance, inside and out, was completed in 1976. (Courtesy of the Division of Historical and Cultural Affairs.)

ably because a large percentage of the voters were independents, committed to neither party. Through these years the electorate showed consistency in supporting certain popular candidates for high office. Notable among them in the 1950s and 1960s were J. Caleb Boggs and John J. Williams, who were able to win election and reelection even in years when the opposite party carried the state.

Caleb Boggs, a lawyer and a University of Delaware graduate, originally from Cheswold, in Kent County, was known to many admiring friends as an officer with the 198th Coast Artillery in the South Pacific during the Second World War. Immediately after the war, in 1946, he defeated a Democratic incumbent for the single Delaware seat in the United States House of Representatives, to which he was reelected in 1948 and 1950. In 1952 he defeated the popular incumbent governor, Elbert Carvel, and was reelected governor in 1956 to serve the constitutional limit of two terms. In 1960 he again defeated a popular incumbent Democrat (J. Allen Frear, Jr., who had served two terms) for a seat in the United States Senate, to which he was reelected in 1966. Altogether Boggs won seven statewide election contests, more than anyone previously in the history of Delaware.

John J. Williams, a self-educated businessman from Mills boro, in Sussex County, was also first elected to office, in his case the United States Senate, in the victorious Republican election campaign of 1946. It is remarkable that a man not well known outside his own county and never previously a candidate for elective office should have been nominated for the Senate, but apparently the Republicans had learned from divisions caused in their party in the 1930s by their spurning Sussex candidates and had determined to allow Sussex County to nominate a man of its own choice for this position.

In the Senate, Williams made a remarkable reputation both for his intrepidity in exposing graft and for his tightfistedness in regard to the expenditure of public funds. His independence so pleased Delawareans that he was reelected as long as he was willing to run for office. After four terms, he refused renomination in 1972, characteristically acting on principle, being opposed to men serving when they were past seventy, as he would have been if he had served a fifth term. His four terms in the Senate constituted the longest service in that body by any Delawarean.

Continuity in office, however, became the rule rather than the exception. John Williams's successor in the Senate, William V. Roth, Jr., also a Republican, was elected to his fourth successive term in that body in 1988, and he had already served two terms in the House of

Representatives. Joseph R. Biden, Jr. defeated Boggs, a reluctant candidate, in 1972 and like Roth was reelected to the Senate three times, beginning his fourth term in 1991. Other popular politicians included Pierre S. du Pont IV, a Republican who served three terms in the House of Representatives before being elected twice (the constitutional limit) as governor, and Harris B. McDowell, Jr. and Thomas R. Carper, Democrats, each elected to five terms in the House of Representatives.

Centralized Authority

The reorganization of the legislature in the 1960s coincided with a resurgence of Republican strength. In 1966 Republicans scored their greatest victory in Delaware in a decade, capturing control of the lower house of the General Assembly for the first time since 1952, the year of Eisenhower's first election. Apparently, the new apportionment of seats played a part in this Republican renaissance, since it gave increased representation to such Republican strongholds as Brandywine Hundred.

Then, in 1968 the Republicans scored even greater victories, winning control of both houses of the legislature and also electing a governor and a mayor of Wilmington and carrying the state for Nixon in the presidential contest. Probably the Republicans profited even in state contests from widespread dissatisfaction with the Democratic government's involvement in Vietnam, as well as from the challenge in the presidential race of a dissident Democrat, George Wallace, running on a third-party ticket. In a sense, the Republican victory was also a triumph of suburbia, for the new governor and many of the assemblymen and other elected officials represented the white-collar class that had been attracted to northern Delaware in the two most recent decades to take positions with the large corporations having central offices and laboratories there.

Russell N. Peterson, Jr., the new governor, a Du Pont Company scientist with a doctorate of philosophy in chemistry from the University of Wisconsin, had never sought elective office before but had distinguished himself by leadership in a number of civic improvement movements. The second most important executive office in Delaware was the newly created post of New Castle County executive, to which William J. Conner had been elected in 1966. Conner, a corporation lawyer, came from Minnesota; his wife, Louise Conner, was a member of the General Assembly, where she represented one of the new districts in Brandywine Hundred.

Governor Peterson, already supported by strong Republican majorities in the legislature, gained the greatest power ever known by any governor of Delaware to this time by reason of a reorganization of the executive branch of the government that had been under way for years but reached its culmination in 1971. Since 1776, when almost all power had been stripped from the governorship, there had been a steady expansion of the executive division of the state government. This increase in executive responsibilities, however, had proceeded in company with a historic tendency to avoid centralizing authority in the hands of the governor, who did not even have veto power over legislation until 1897. A plethora of commissions, agencies, and bureaus was established by successive legislatures, which often required representation of each county on a supervising commission and sometimes staggered terms and provided for representation of the minority party (by forbidding more than a simple majority of members from one party) in order to provide continuity. Since commission members usually received no compensation, these boards provided cheap supervision of state services, which fitted a state with a small population. By control of finances, the legislature retained a strong influence over these boards, which it enlarged or replaced (by what was called "ripper" legislation) to suit its will when it could persuade the governor to acquiesce or could pass the required statute over his veto.

As state business grew, the inefficiency of the commission system of government was frequently noted. In 1918 the Townsend administration hired the New York Bureau of Municipal Research to make a research study, including recommendations for reform. The recommendations were duly presented to the legislature and ignored, except for the establishment of an executive budget in 1921.

Nevertheless, some consideration of functions did occur in the years between 1918, when there were 117 administrative agencies, and 1951, when Professor Paul Dolan noted in his work *The Organization of State Administration in Delaware* the existence of 70 agencies. A Committee on the Reorganization of Government established at this time encouraged further consolidation, but in the next two decades the expansion of state business actually led to an increase in the number of commissions. Some progress was made, however, in the interest of efficiency, as when the Department of Public Welfare was created in 1951 and the Department of Labor and Industrial Relations in 1961. Three more departments were created in 1968, but the flowering of the new system came about in 1970, when full cabinet government was instituted.

Ten executive departments (State, Finance, Agriculture, Labor, Public Safety, Highways and Transportation, Health and Social Services, Natural Resources and Environmental Control, Community Affairs and Economic Development, and Administrative Services) combined the functions of approximately 140 commissions and agencies. At the head of each department was a secretary appointed by the governor and confirmed by the senate, and within each department were divisions with heads reporting to the secretary. Since each secretary reported to the governor, Delaware at last had attained a responsible, centralized administrative system, though a few commissions still existed, like the state board of education, supervising the Department of Public Instruction, which was left independent because of fear that politics might otherwise enter this agency. Other remaining commissions were largely regulatory, like the Board of Bar Examiners.

State and county merit systems for retention and promotion of employees had already been adopted under the Terry administration. Governor Terry, who, as a former chief justice, was well aware of deficiencies in the lower courts, had also utilized his party's control of the assembly in the first two years of his term to push through a long-needed reform of the magistrate system, putting the justices of the peace on salaries (instead of fees) and otherwise seeking to improve and standardize their preparation and the service they offered. Other steps toward modernizing the government had been made in the administrations of Carvel and Boggs.

The Peterson administration saw passage of much additional reform legislation, including a Fair Housing Law, previously mentioned; a Coastal Zoning Law that prohibited construction of heavy industry, including paper and steel mills and oil refineries along the river, bay, or ocean shore; and acts that lowered the voting age to nineteen, established air quality standards, and sought to modernize the parole and pardon system. A new state correctional facility was constructed near Smyrna to replace the workhouse at Greenbank. A thorough revision of the 1897 constitution, reducing its length by more than 50 percent, was proposed as an amendment and accepted twice by the legislature, but because of failure to comply with technical details of public announcement, it still needed approval, which it never received, from the 1973–75 legislature.

The very centralization of authority provided by the new administrative organization that gave Peterson greater power than his predecessors as governor also made him peculiarly liable for whatever credit or blame voters chose to apply to administration policies. Some fault was, of course, found with various details of these policies, and the administration also suffered from a fiscal crisis in 1971 when it was suddenly learned that expenditures for the past year had exceeded receipts.

Voters found the new administrative organization expensive. Despite public clamor for increased services from the state government, which had been enlarging its functions for several decades, voters were reluctant to pay the bill. Perhaps there was also some failure on the part of the activist element of the Republican party to keep in close touch with other significant elements in the community. Suburbia in the driver's seat went a little too fast for some of the passengers.

Since 1973

Reaction came swiftly. Utilizing a law allowing a defeated candidate for a party nomination to carry his candidacy to the people if supported by a significant minority (over 35 percent) in the state nominating convention, Attorney General David P. Buckson forced Governor Peterson into a contest for renomination. Buckson, who had previously served as lieutenant governor and, briefly, as governor, when Caleb Boggs resigned to enter the Senate, rallied Republican elements irritated by various parts of the Peterson program and by the blunt strength that the new administrative organization had allowed the governor to use.

Peterson won the primary, but the division it revealed in his party proved fatal in the fall election in 1972. The Democratic nominee, Sherman W. Tribbitt, another former lieutenant governor, attracted some of the same discordant elements that had supported Buckson. Like Buckson, Tribbitt came from a small town downstate and appealed to the rural voter who feared the newly strengthened executive power, particularly since reapportionment had so recently taken away his former control of the legislature.

The Tribbitt administration, like the Peterson administration, was plagued by a public demand for services that cost more than the income of the state could cover.

These services lay in three fields particularly: (1) in highways and transportation, (2) in education, and (3) in welfare. The automobile age placed responsibilities on the state for highway construction and repair and for mass transportation that were immeasurably greater than in earlier times when private business had provided railroad, streetcar, and bus service, as well as steamboats, canals, turnpikes, and even bridges. Whereas there had been no public schools whatever until 1829, people now demanded educational services from kindergarten through graduate and professional school. Welfare services had always been a public responsibility, but whereas the hundred and the county had provided what care was once given to unfortunates, this care now became a state responsibility, and the greatly enlarged population, together with the peculiar complexities of modern life, the increased life expectancy (especially for the infirm), and the recognition of personal problems that were formerly unknown or ignored—these developments magnified and complicated the problem of providing for the people's welfare.

In responding to increased needs and new demands for governmental services, Delaware avoided imposition of a general sales tax but increasingly relied on the sale of bonds, especially, but not solely, to finance construction of buildings, roads, and bridges. Bonded indebtedness of the state, which had amounted to only $3 million in 1937, rose to $428 million in 1976, when debt service—that is, scheduled payments of principal and interest—accounted for more than one-eighth of the budget. Financial advisers warned that this increase in indebtedness could not be continued with impunity.

In 1976, in the midst of a financial crisis accentuated by the near collapse of the Farmers Bank, in which the state owned a majority interest and deposited the bulk of its funds, voters turned to a du Pont to rescue them, electing as their new chief executive the namesake of the financial genius who had brought the state out of its educational "dark ages" and had found miraculous cures (primarily through the income tax) for its perennial shortage of money. Unlike his great-uncle, Pierre du Pont IV had to give first priority to the need to reduce expenditures, a task that allowed him little leeway to encourage the undertaking of new responsibilities. Under du Pont the budget was balanced, while future fiscal stability was provided by a constitutional amendment requiring that annual expenditures should not exceed 98 percent of the estimated revenue. Taxpayers received encouragement from a slight reduction in the income tax and from a new constitutional provision requiring a three-fifths majority in the legislature for raises in taxes or fees. Sale of the Farmers Bank to the Girard Company, of Philadelphia, brought needed income and severed the state's long connection with a private bank.

The most important piece of legislation adopted during the du Pont administration was the Financial Center Development Act of 1981. This statute was designed to attract large out-of-state banks to move their credit-card operations to Delaware primarily by eliminating usury laws that restricted interest charges. Its authors made this act palatable to Delaware bankers by limitations placed upon the right of the new banks to enter into a general retail business. And it was made attractive to the Delaware body politic by requirements that the new banks hire Delawareans.

The new statute was successful almost beyond belief. Led by such giants as Chase Manhattan and Morgan, more than thirty banks opened new offices in Delaware. The results, in terms of employment, were fantastic. The new banks provided so many new jobs that by the end of the decade financial services had become the second largest industry in this state both in number of employees and in total wages paid. Only the chemical industry ranked higher, while such older businesses as automobile manufacturing (Chrysler and General Motors) and the poultry industry were third and fourth.

The secondary effects of the new banking business were also great. A new wave of construction took place. Housing developments absorbed large new tracts of open land, particularly in northern New Castle County, though the new suburban housing rapidly moved southward toward the canal, near, for instance, the onetime tiny villages of Bear and Glasgow. It is an oddity that Delaware has the largest percentage of its land area devoted to urban or suburban living and business of any state. Yet it also still has the largest percentage of its land devoted to agriculture, the absence of mountains or deserts accounting for this conundrum.

Construction other than housing was also stimulated, such as schools, shops, and especially offices. Many of the banks settled in Wilmington, where a number of new highrises changed the skyline. Others moved into adjacent areas of the county, where several office parks soon appeared. One new bank, MBNA America, erected a large office complex near Ogletown, a village that vanished in the wake of highway construction. The new banking activity extended even into southern Delaware, where a Maryland bank established a credit processing office at Millsboro.

New shopping malls proliferated, each in its turn threatening to damage the prospects of an older mall. Office buildings bidding for tenants from various new enterprises were similarly overbuilt and by 1990 much of the space they offered had become redundant.

The new prosperity attracted a wave of migrants into Delaware. By 1990 barely half of Delawareans (50.6%) were natives of the state. Once again, as in the decades from 1930 to 1970, Delaware's population grew faster than the nation's. The growth (12.1%) in the 1980s did not, however, approach the very rapid growth (40.3%) in the 1950s, and there were indications that it had peaked by 1990. By this date the growth of the credit-card banks had probably reached maturity. Some banks were even induced to leave Delaware as other states altered their laws to make them more attractive.

Unemployment rates in Delaware, which had been very low in the 1980s, began to climb. A further problem in Delaware, as in the nation, was that service jobs, often low-paying, grew faster than the higher-paying jobs in manufacturing.

Some of the older factories in Delaware closed: for instance, the plants of the National Vulcanized Fibre Company (NVF), which fell into the hands of a greedy corporate wrecker. Delawareans were relieved that the Hercules Company, after considering offers to move elsewhere, was persuaded by municipal authorities to erect a new office building in Wilmington.

A significant change occurred in the ownership of the Du Pont Company in 1981. In that year it purchased a large oil company, Conoco, which had previously been the subject of a takeover bid from the Bronfmans, a Canadian family that owned a major distiller, Seagram's. As a somewhat surprising result of this acquisition, which included an exchange of Du Pont shares for those of Conoco, the Bronfmans, who had bought a large block of Conoco, became significant investors in Du Pont. Indeed the Bronfmans now became the largest shareholders in Du Pont, taking the place once occupied by the du Pont family when du Pont holdings had been concentrated through the Christiana Securities Company.

Previously the Du Pont Company had sold the dominant Delaware newspaper, the *News-Journal*, which it had acquired from Christiana Securities, to the Gannett chain, thus continuing the long process by which local enterprises passed out of local hands. Most of the retail banks of Delaware also surrendered their independence to out-of-state interests as the desirability of large capitalizations became clear. A notable exception was the Wilmington Trust Company, which extended its presence downstate by acquisition of the Sussex Trust Company.

Near the end of the twentieth century ecological questions were gaining popular attention. Hazardous waste sites and asbestos construction (particularly in schools) challenged authorities to finance their treatment or removal. A series of threats to the Coastal Zone Act were beaten off, and greenways were sought to connect parks and other public lands. Anti-development feelings were voiced, especially in opposition to the political influences of some builders whose contributions to political campaigns were thought to have undue influence on zoning of land, such as required for the multiplication and enlargement of shopping malls. In the same spirit of concern, a voluntary recycling program was instituted.

In terms of health and education new developments included a statewide paramedic service financed by the state, and a large new hospital erected in the country near Christiana by the Wilmington Medical Center with the help of bonds issued by the state, tax-free but dependent for payment on the Center. A remarkably successful and self-sustaining enterprise was the Academy of Lifelong Learning, opened by the University of Delaware as a service for seniors interested in noncredit courses. A similar venture was later started in Milford. Among other University projects were the Institute of Energy Conversion (for solar energy) and the Center for Composite Materials, both aided by some financial assistance from the federal government.

By the last quarter of the twentieth century Delaware had changed in many ways from what it was a century or two centuries ago. There still exists a difference between upstate and downstate. The one is diverse, populous, ever changing; the other is more homogeneous, less crowded, more traditional. Upstate is wealthier than downstate Delaware, as it has been since the rise of commerce in the eighteenth century. Yet upstate Delaware has now the largest pocket of poverty and the most serious problem of race relations in the state.

To some extent, the melting pot has worked well in Delaware. The colonial Swedes, Dutch, and Finns, as well as the Scotch-Irish immigrants, who were scorned and feared in the eighteenth century, have been thoroughly absorbed into the basic white

English element of the population. The large immigrant groups
of the nineteenth century, the Irish and Germans, Jews, Poles,
and Italians, as well as early twentieth century immigrants, like
the Greeks and Ukrainians, are well on the way to a similar ab-
sorption, and in some cases, it has already occurred.

Yet there is more diversity in Delaware today than in the
past—more economic diversity, more educational diversity, more
linguistic diversity, and more diversity in age because people live
longer. Though there is hardly more racial diversity now than
in the eighteenth century, conditions of modern life make people
more aware of the diversity that exists than they once were.
Suburbia is now the largest community in Delaware, but it lacks
unity. It has no town hall, no market place, no forum. Perhaps
in time its hundred housing developments will become a thousand and its dozens of shopping centers will similarly proliferate
until all of Delaware is one vast suburb. Despite the shrinkage
of its resident population, the total number of jobs in Wilmington has increased, and the city remains an urban center for most
Delawareans, especially the thousands who commute there daily
from the suburbs, but also for those who go there less often but
look to Wilmington for the services of governmental agencies,
financial institutions, and public utilities, and for their newspapers as well as for drama, art, and music. In lower Delaware
agriculture is thriving, increasing in acreage and in revenues,
though the number of farmers is still declining.

Time was when Delaware offered at least a superficial appearance of unity, when it was essentially an agrarian society united
under the banners of Federalists, and of Whigs, and then of Democrats of the unreconstructed, postbellum variety. The farm
gave way gradually to the factory, and the manufacturer took up
the burden of leadership that the country gentleman relinquished. Just as farms and farmers decreased in number, so now
factories are being abandoned and blue-collar workers are less
numerous (if more highly prized) than they once were. It is the
service occupations that are growing; perhaps the clerk and the
repairman will inherit the future.

Addenda to Fourth Edition

At the end of the twentieth century Delaware was experiencing a
period of prosperity, with unemployment low and the state's income
exceeding its expenditures. A new development in 2000 was the elec-

tion of the first woman as governor; at the same time a second African American was chosen mayor of Wilmington.

Though each county exhibited faster population growth than the nation, it was Sussex County that grew the fastest, at a rate double the growth in Delaware as a whole. New residential housing near the inner bays attracted retirees to homes near the beaches, and low-paying jobs on farms and in chicken-processing plants brought a wave of Latin-American immigrants.

Continued expansion of credit-card banks invigorated the economy of the Wilmington area, where the largest of these banks, MBNA America, had become, after Du Pont, the second largest private employer in Delaware. A new urban feature was the Riverfront, a group of shops with a stadium and exhibition hall on the Christina in southwestern Wilmington.

Some of the older businesses disappeared or declined, and even Du Pont, still an industrial giant, had divested itself of many operations and reduced its property holdings and the number of its employees. The welfare system was altered in an effort to transfer people from dependency to self-sufficiency after two years at most. Public and private charter schools were introduced with the hope that their freedom from restrictions would improve education. Fears that growth of the population and the economy would leave little open space were met by the enlargement of parks, refuges, and greenways, as well as through public funding for the purchase of development rights to existing farmlands and forests.

Little satisfaction could be found in the high rate of incarceration, cramming Delaware jails far beyond their planned capacity. An extraordinarily high cancer rate was slowly declining; air and water pollution also remained serious problems. The success achieved through the Coastal Zone Preservation Act in preserving the bay and ocean shore from refineries and other industrial developments encouraged the Delaware government in being the first state to forbid smoking in places of public resort, both indoor and outdoor, such as bars, restaurants, and athletic contests.

Announcement in 2005 of the merger of MBNA and an even larger financial institution, the Bank of America, concerned Delawareans since full details of the merger were not to be made known until 2006.

Appendix A

Presidential Candidates Carrying Delaware*

1789 George Washington[1]
1792 George Washington[2]
1796 John Adams
1800 John Adams
1804 Charles C. Pinckney
1808 Charles C. Pinckney
1812 De Witt Clinton
1816 Rufus King
1820 James Monroe
1824 William H. Crawford
      (2 votes) and John
      Quincy Adams (1 vote)
1828 John Quincy Adams
1832 Henry Clay[3]
1836 William H. Harrison
1840 William H. Harrison
1844 Henry Clay
1848 Zachary Taylor
1852 Franklin Pierce
1856 James Buchanan
1860 John C. Breckinridge
1864 George McClellan
1868 Horatio Seymour
1872 Ulysses S. Grant
1876 Samuel J. Tilden
1880 Winfield S. Hancock
1884 Grover Cleveland
1888 Grover Cleveland
1892 Grover Cleveland

1896 William McKinley
1900 William McKinley
1904 Theodore Roosevelt
1908 William H. Taft
1912 Woodrow Wilson
1916 Charles E. Hughes
1920 Warren G. Harding
1924 Calvin Coolidge
1928 Herbert Hoover
1932 Herbert Hoover
1936 Franklin D. Roosevelt
1940 Franklin D. Roosevelt
1944 Franklin D. Roosevelt
1948 Thomas E. Dewey
1952 Dwight D. Eisenhower
1956 Dwight D. Eisenhower
1960 John F. Kennedy
1964 Lyndon B. Johnson
1968 Richard M. Nixon
1972 Richard M. Nixon
1976 Jimmy Carter
1980 Ronald Reagan
1984 Ronald Reagan
1988 George Bush
1992 William J. Clinton
1996 William J. Clinton
2000 Albert Gore
2004 John Kerry

---

* Delaware has been entitled to only three electoral votes except for the period from 1812 to 1820 inclusive, when it was entitled to four votes. In 1816, however, only three Delaware electors cast their votes.
1. In 1789, the Delaware electors were chosen by popular vote, one being picked in each county.
2. From 1792 to 1828 inclusive, the electors were chosen by the legislature.
3. Since 1832 the electors have been chosen by popular vote on a statewide ballot.

Appendix B

Presidents and Governors of Delaware*

John McKinly	1777	*Charles Thomas*	1823–24
Thomas McKean[1]	1777	Samuel Paynter	1824–27
George Read	1777–78	Charles Polk	1827–30
Caesar Rodney	1778–82	David Hazzard	1830–33
John Dickinson	1782–83	Caleb P. Bennett	1833–36
John Cook	1783	*Charles Polk*	1836–37
Nicholas Van Dyke	1783–86	Cornelius P. Comegys	1837–41
Thomas Collins	1786–89	William B. Cooper	1841–45
Jehu Davis	1789	Thomas Stockton	1845–46
Joshua Clayton	1789–96	*Joseph Maull*	1846
Gunning Bedford, Sr.	1796–97	*William Temple*	1846–47
Daniel Rogers	1797–99	William Tharp	1847–51
Richard Bassett	1799–1801	William H. Ross	1851–55
James Sykes	1801–2	Peter F. Causey	1855–59
David Hall	1802–5	William Burton	1859–63
Nathaniel Mitchell	1805–8	William Cannon	1863–65
George Truitt	1808–11	Gove Saulsbury[2]	1865–71
Joseph Haslet	1811–14	James Ponder	1871–75
Daniel Rodney	1814–17	John P. Cochran	1875–79
John Clark	1817–20	John W. Hall	1879–83
Jacob Stout	1820–21	Charles C. Stockley	1883–87
John Collins	1821–22	Benjamin T. Biggs	1887–91
Caleb Rodney	1822–23	Robert J. Reynolds	1891–95
Joseph Haslet	1823	Joshua H. Marvil	1895

---

* Under the first constitution, 1776–92, the chief executive was called "the president," and the official title of the state was "the Delaware State." Joshua Clayton was the last president and the first governor.

1. Italics indicate an acting executive, who was not elected president or governor but assumed the position when it was vacated by the death, resignation, or (in the case of McKinly) capture of the properly elected official.

2. Gove Saulsbury completed Cannon's term and then served a full term after his own election.

William T. Watson	1895–97	Elbert N. Carvel	1949–53
Ebe W. Tunnell	1897–1901	J. Caleb Boggs	1953–60
John Hunn	1901–5	*David P. Buckson*	1960–61
Preston Lea	1905–9	Elbert N. Carvel	1961–65
Simeon S. Pennewill	1909–13	Charles L. Terry, Jr.	1965–69
Charles R. Miller	1913–17	Russell W. Peterson, Jr.	
John G. Townsend, Jr.	1917–21		1969–73
William D. Denney	1921–25	Sherman W. Tribbitt	1973–77
Robert P. Robinson	1925–29	Pierre S. du Pont IV	1977–85
C. Douglass Buck	1929–37	Michael N. Castle	1985–93
Richard C. McMullen	1937–41	Dale E. Wolf	1993
Walter W. Bacon	1941–49	Thomas R. Carper	1993–2001
		Ruth Ann Minner	2001–

Appendix C

United States Senators from Delaware

Richard Bassett	1789–93	Thomas Clayton	1837–47
George Read	1789–93[1]	Richard H. Bayard	1841–45
John Vining	1793–98	John M. Clayton	1845–49
Henry Latimer	1795–1801	Presley Spruance	1847–51
Joshua Clayton	1798–99	John Wales	1849–53
William H. Wells	1799–1804	James A. Bayard	1851–64
Samuel White	1801–9	John M. Clayton	1853–56
James A. Bayard	1805–13	Joseph P. Comegys	1856–57
Outerbridge Horsey	1810–21	Martin W. Bates	1857–59
William H. Wells	1813–17	Willard Saulsbury	1859–71
Nicholas Van Dyke	1817–23	George Read Riddle	1864–67
Caesar A. Rodney	1822–23[2]	James A. Bayard	1867–69
Nicholas Van Dyke	1824–26	Thomas F. Bayard	1869–85
Thomas Clayton	1824–27	Eli Saulsbury	1871–89
Daniel Rodney	1826–27	George Gray	1885–99[4]
Henry M. Ridgely	1827–29	Anthony Higgins	1889–95[5]
Louis McLane	1827–29	Richard R. Kenney	1897–1901[6]
John M. Clayton	1829–36	J. Frank Allee	1903–7
Arnold Naudain	1830–36	L. Heisler Ball	1903–5[7]
Richard H. Bayard	1836–39[3]	Henry A. du Pont	1906–17

1. A vacancy existed from Read's resignation on September 18, 1793, until 1795. When the legislature neglected to fill it, Governor Clayton appointed Kensey Johns, Sr., but the Senate would not seat him.
2. In 1823 when Van Dyke's term ended and Rodney resigned to accept a diplomatic appointment, the General Assembly did not fill the vacancies immediately.
3. There was a vacancy from September 19, 1839, when Bayard resigned to become chief justice of Delaware, until January 19, 1841, when he returned to the Senate.
4. Vacancy, 1899–1903.
5. Vacancy, 1895–97.
6. Vacancy, 1901–1903.
7. Vacancy, 1905–1906. These vacancies occurred during the Addicks era of Delaware politics.

Harry A. Richardson	1907–13	James H. Hughes	1937–43
Willard Saulsbury	1913–19	James M. Tunnell	1941–47
Josiah O. Wolcott	1917–21	C. Douglass Buck	1943–49
L. Heisler Ball	1919–25	John J. Williams	1947–71
T. Coleman du Pont	1921–22	J. Allen Frear, Jr.	1949–61
Thomas F. Bayard	1922–29	J. Caleb Boggs	1961–73
T. Coleman du Pont	1925–28	William V. Roth, Jr.	1971–2001
Daniel O. Hastings	1928–37	Joseph R. Biden, Jr.	1973–
John G. Townsend, Jr.	1929–41	Thomas R. Carper	2001

Appendix D

United States Representatives in Congress from Delaware*

John Vining	1789–93	John B. Penington	1887–91
John Patten	1793–94	John W. Causey	1891–95
Henry Latimer	1794–95	Jonathan S. Willis	1895–97
John Patten	1795–97	L. Irving Handy	1897–99
James A. Bayard	1797–1803	John H. Hoffecker	1899–1900
Caesar A. Rodney	1803–05	Walter O. Hoffecker	1900–01
James M. Broom	1805–07	L. Heisler Ball	1901–03
Nicholas Van Dyke	1807–11	Henry A. Houston	1903–05
Henry M. Ridgely	1811–15	Hiram R. Burton	1905–09
Thomas Cooper	1813–17	William H. Heald	1909–13
Thomas Clayton	1815–17	Franklin Brockson	1913–15
Louis McLane	1817–27	Thomas W. Miller	1915–17
Willard Hall	1817–21	Albert F. Polk	1917–19
Caesar A. Rodney	1821–22	Caleb R. Layton	1919–23
Daniel Rodney	1822–23	William H. Boyce	1923–25
Kensey Johns, Jr.	1827–31	Robert G. Houston	1925–33
John J. Milligan	1831–39	Wilbur L. Adams	1933–35
Thomas Robinson, Jr.	1839–41	J. George Stewart	1935–37
George B. Rodney	1841–45	William F. Allen	1937–39
John W. Houston	1845–51	George S. Williams	1939–41
George Read Riddle	1851–55	Philip A. Traynor	1941–43
Elisha D. Cullen	1855–57	Earle D. Willey	1943–45
William G. Whiteley	1857–61	Philip A. Traynor	1945–47
George P. Fisher	1861–63	J. Caleb Boggs	1947–53
William Temple	1863	Herbert Warburton	1953–55
Nathaniel B. Smithers		Harris B. McDowell, Jr.	
	1863–65		1955–57
John A. Nicholson	1865–69	Harry G. Haskell, Jr.	1957–59
Benjamin T. Biggs	1869–73	Harris B. McDowell, Jr.	
			1959–67
James R. Lofland	1873–75	William V. Roth, Jr.	1967–71
James Williams	1875–79	Pierre S. du Pont, IV	1971–77
Edward L. Martin	1879–83	Thomas B. Evans, Jr.	1977–83
Charles B. Lore	1883–87	Thomas R. Carper	1983–93
		Michael N. Castle	1993–

* From 1813 to 1823 Delaware was entitled to two members of the House of Representatives.

Appendix E

Population and Land Area of the State, the Counties, and Wilmington

Population

Census Year	Total	New Castle	Kent	Sussex	Wilmington
1790	59,096	19,688	18,920	20,488	. . . . . .
1800	64,273	25,361	19,554	19,358	. . . . . .
1810	72,674	24,429	20,495	27,750	. . . . . .
1820	72,749	27,899	20,793	24,057	. . . . . .
1830	76,748	29,720	19,913	27,115	. . . . . .
1840	78,085	33,120	19,872	25,093	8,367
1850	91,532	42,780	22,816	25,936	13,979
1860	112,216	54,797	27,804	29,615	21,258
1870	125,015	63,515	29,804	31,696	30,841
1880	146,608	77,716	32,874	36,018	42,478
1890	168,493	97,182	32,664	38,647	61,431
1900	184,735	109,697	32,762	42,276	76,508
1910	202,322	123,188	32,721	46,413	87,411
1920	223,003	148,239	31,023	43,741	110,168
1930	238,380	161,032	31,841	45,507	106,597
1940	266,505	179,562	34,441	52,502	112,504
1950	318,085	218,879	37,870	61,336	110,356
1960	446,292	307,446	65,651	73,195	95,827
1970	548,104	385,856	81,892	80,356	80,386
1980	594,338	398,115	98,219	98,004	70,195
1990	666,168	441,946	110,993	113,229	71,526
2000	783,600	500,265	126,697	156,638	72,664

SOURCE: United States Census figures.

Land Area

1,982 sq. mi.   438 sq. mi.   594 sq. mi.   950 sq. mi.   12.9 sq. mi.

SOURCE: *Dimensions on Delaware: A Statistical Abstract for 1977* (Dover, 1978), p. 30.

Appendix F

Comparative Growth of the United States and Delaware, 1790–2000

| | Percentages of Population Growth | |
	United States	Delaware
1790 to 1800	35.1	8.8
1800 to 1810	36.4	13.1
1810 to 1820	33.1	0.1
1820 to 1830	33.5	5.5
1830 to 1840	32.7	1.7
1840 to 1850	35.9	17.2
1850 to 1860	35.6	22.6
1860 to 1870	22.6	11.4
1870 to 1880	30.2	17.3
1880 to 1890	25.5	14.9
1890 to 1900	20.7	9.6
1900 to 1910	21.0	9.5
1910 to 1920	15.0	10.2
1920 to 1930	16.2	6.9
1930 to 1940	7.3	11.8
1940 to 1950	14.5	19.4
1950 to 1960	18.5	40.3
1960 to 1970	13.3	22.8
1970 to 1980	11.4	8.4
1980 to 1990	10.0	12.1
1990 to 2000	13.2	17.6

SOURCE: U.S. Census

Appendix G

Birthplace of Delaware Residents, 1850–2000

Year	Born in Delaware		Born Elsewhere in United States		Born Outside United States		Total Population of Delaware
	Number	Percentage	Number	Percentage	Number	Percentage	Number
1850	72,523	79.2	11,455	12.5	5,253	5.7	91,532
1860	84,869	75.6	18,182	16.2	9,165	8.2	112,216
1870	94,754	75.8	21,125	16.9	9,136	7.3	125,015
1880	110,643	75.5	26,497	18.1	9,468	6.5	146,608
1890	119,917	71.2	35,415	21.0	13,161	7.8	168,493
1900	129,546	70.1	41,379	22.4	13,810	7.5	184,735
1910	137,131	67.8	47,699	23.6	17,492	8.6	202,322
1920	142,963	64.1	60,139	27.0	19,901	8.9	223,003
1930	155,585	65.3	65,770	27.6	17,025	7.1	238,380
1940	171,219	64.2	80,373	30.2	14,913	5.6	266,505
1950	194,185	61.0	108,495	34.1	15,405	4.8	318,085
1960	242,287	54.3	189,355	42.4	14,650	3.3	446,292
1970	284,167	51.8	248,278*	45.3	15,648	2.9	548,104
1980	306,588	51.6	263,443	44.3	18,829	3.2	594,338
1990	334,209	50.2	309,684	46.5	22,275	3.3	666,168
2000	378,840	48.3	347,954	44.4	56,806	7.2	783,600

SOURCE: U.S. Census

NOTE: The birthplace of some residents in occasional years is listed as unknown.

*Includes Puerto Ricans.

Appendix H

Number and Proportion of Nonwhites in the Population for Specified Areas of Delaware, 1930–2000

Year	Wilmington		Remainder of New Castle County		Kent County		Sussex County		Delaware	
	Number	Percentage	Number	Percentage	Number	Percentage	Number	Percentage	Number	Percentage
1930	12,138	11.4	6,386	11.1	6,616	20.8	7,522	16.5	32,662	13.7
1940	14,329	12.7	6,117	9.1	6,531	19.0	8,899	16.9	35,876	13.5
1950	17,277	15.6	8,586	7.9	6,947	18.3	11,397	18.6	44,207	13.9
1960	25,075	26.2	11,346	5.4	10,004	15.2	15,540	21.2	61,965	13.9
1970	35,072	44.1	13,948	4.6	13,161	17.1	17,665	21.2	79,846	14.9
1980	38,532	54.9	28,757	8.8	19,961	20.3	19,271	19.7	106,521	17.9
1990	41,395	57.9	45,152	12.2	23,693	21.3	20,834	18.4	131,074	19.7
2000	46,853	64.5	87,602	20.5	33,591	26.5	30,781	19.7	198,827	25.4

SOURCE: U.S. Census. The Census Bureau has revised some of these figures slightly.

Appendix I

Population of Delaware Counties, with Growth Rates, 1790–2000

Year	New Castle County			Kent County			Sussex County		
	Number	Percent Change from Previous Census	Percentage of Delaware Population	Number	Percent Change from Previous Census	Percentage of Delaware Population	Number	Percent Change from Previous Census	Percentage of Delaware Population
1790	19,688	...	33.3	18,920	...	32.0	20,488	...	34.7
1800	25,351	28.8	39.4	19,554	3.4	30.4	19,358	− 5.5	30.1
1810	24,429	− 3.7	33.6	20,495	4.8	28.2	27,750	43.3	38.2
1820	27,899	14.2	38.3	20,793	1.5	28.6	24,057	−13.3	33.1
1830	29,720	6.5	38.7	19,913	− 4.2	25.9	27,115	12.7	35.3
1840	33,120	11.4	42.4	19,872	− 0.2	25.4	25,093	− 7.5	32.1
1850	42,780	29.2	46.7	22,816	14.8	24.9	25,936	3.4	28.3
1860	54,797	28.1	48.8	27,804	21.9	24.8	29,615	14.2	26.4
1870	63,515	15.9	50.8	29,804	7.2	23.8	31,696	7.0	25.4
1880	77,716	22.4	53.0	32,874	10.3	22.4	36,018	13.6	24.6
1890	97,182	25.0	57.7	32,664	− 0.6	19.4	38,647	7.3	22.9
1900	109,697	12.9	59.4	32,762	0.3	17.7	42,276	9.4	22.9
1910	123,188	12.3	60.9	32,721	− 0.1	16.2	46,413	9.8	22.9
1920	148,239	20.3	66.5	31,023	− 5.2	13.9	43,741	− 5.8	19.6
1930	161,032	8.6	67.6	31,841	2.6	13.3	45,507	4.0	19.1
1940	179,562	11.5	67.4	34,441	8.2	12.9	52,502	15.4	19.7
1950	218,879	21.9	68.8	37,870	10.0	11.9	61,336	16.8	19.3
1960	307,446	40.5	68.9	65,651	73.3	14.7	73,195	19.3	16.4
1970	385,856	25.5	70.4	81,892	24.7	14.9	80,356	9.8	14.7
1980	398,115	3.2	67.0	98,219	19.9	16.5	98,004	22.0	16.5
1990	441,946	11.0	66.3	110,993	13.0	16.7	113,229	15.5	17.0
2000	500,265	13.2	63.8	126,697	14.1	16.2	156,638	38.3	20.0

Bibliographical Essay

Bibliographies and Comprehensive Histories of Delaware

The best bibliography is by H. Clay Reed and Marion Björnson Reed and entitled *A Bibliography of Delaware through 1960* (1966). The reference staff of the Hugh M. Morris Library of the University of Delaware has prepared a supplementary *Bibliography of Delaware, 1960–1974* (1976), including typed theses and dissertations (a category not listed by the Reeds).

The best single work on Delaware also bears the name of H. Clay Reed, who was editor of a two-volume collaborative work entitled *Delaware: A History of the First State* (1947). A third volume, published under the same title, consists of eulogistic biographies and was not edited by Professor Reed. The most comprehensive work on Delaware, in two mammoth volumes, is entitled *History of Delaware, 1609–1888* (1889), written by J. Thomas Scharf and others. A mine of information, it has sections on every village and every hundred, but, unfortunately, its facts are not always accurate and it seldom offers any analysis or interpretation of the myriad of facts that it presents. To replace the almost useless index published in Scharf, the Historical Society of Delaware, with financial help from the Colonial Dames, has published a comprehensive *Index to the History of Delaware, 1609–1888* (1976) in three volumes, edited by Gladys M. Coghlan and Dale Fields.

Henry C. Conrad's three-volume *History of the State of Delaware* (1908) is largely a copy of Scharf, though the Conrad work is more attractively presented and has a better index. J. M. McCarter and B. F. Jackson edited an early *Historical and Biographical History of Delaware* (1882), and much later Wilson Lloyd Bevan and E. Melvin Williams edited a four-volume *History of Delaware, Past and Present* (1929), which contains little of value except for biographical data. J. M. Runk and Company published a two-volume *Biographical and Genealogical History of the State of Delaware* (1899) that is sometimes useful. *A History of Delaware* (1928), by Walter A. Powell, was the first complete chronological account in one volume.

Delaware: A Guide to the First State (1938, 1948, and, wholly revised by Jeannette Eckman, 1955), prepared by the Federal Writers' Project, is both informative and accurate. Its long introduction was for many years used as a textbook of Delaware history. Its organization is topical rather than chronological, as is the format of a new volume, *Delaware: A Bicentennial History* (1977), by Carol E. Hoffecker, part of *The States and the Nation* Series of Bicentennial histories sponsored by the Association for State and Local History with a grant from the National Humanities Foundation. This book is a highly competent interpretive history that is also first-rate scholarship.

Since it first appeared in 1946, *Delaware History,* a semiannual magazine published by the Historical Society of Delaware, has been the chief medium for articles on the subject indicated by its title. Previously, the Historical Society issued occasional *Papers,* beginning in 1879 and continuing to 1940. These are frequently found bound in seven volumes. Unfortunately, there is no cumulative index to the *Papers* or to *Delaware History* magazine.

Readings in Delaware History (1973), edited by Carol E. Hoffecker, is a useful compilation of previously published articles and of extracts from books. *Delaware: A Students' Guide to Localized History* (1965 and later reprintings), by John A. Munroe, is a short, chronological account. Katherine Pyle's *Once upon a Time in Delaware* (1911, 1927), though not always factually accurate, is a pleasant recounting for children of various stories from Delaware history. In *Forgotten Heroes of Delaware* (1969), W. Emerson Wilson has collected a series of biographical sketches he originally wrote for the Wilmingon *Morning News. Delaware and the Eastern Shore* (1922) is a collection of essays, charming but not always accurate, by Edward N. Vallandigham. *A History of Kent County, Delaware* (1976) and *The History of Sussex County, Delaware* (1976) were both written by Harold B. Hancock for the Bicentennial observance. On July 1, 1976, the *Delaware News* (Selbyville) and *Delaware Coast Press* (Lewes and Rehoboth) published as an insert "The History of Sussex County" by Dick Carter, a good summation of information, profusely illustrated and with historical accounts of each hundred.

Betty Harrington Macdonald's *Historic Landmarks of Delaware and the Eastern Shore* (1963), edited by Jeannette Eckman, is a collection of sketches, with brief, appropriate essays on each structure shown; a new Bicentennial edition with some textual changes appeared in 1976. *Historic Houses and Buildings of Delaware* (1962), by Harold Donaldson Eberlein and Cortlandt V. D. Hubbard, is a collection of photographs, plus textual description. In his *Early Architects of Delaware* (1932), George Fletcher Bennett presents many photographs, as well as a collection of architectural drawings.

The Early Colonial Period

The works of C. A. Weslager illuminate many segments of the colonial history of Delaware. His *Delaware's Buried Past* (1944; rev. ed., 1968) is an account of archaeological discoveries regarding the life of prehistoric man in Delaware. It may be supplemented by the *Bulletins* (1933–   ) and *Papers* (1939–   ) of the Archaeological Society of Delaware and by *Archeolog,* a publication of the Sussex County Historical and Archaeological Society, as well as by Weslager's study *The Delaware Indians* (1972), which traces the history of these people from their legendary arrival on the Delaware to their present settlements in Canada and Oklahoma. The same author's accounts of Indians in *Red Men on the Brandywine* (1953), *The Nanticoke Indians* (1948), and "The Indians of the Eastern Shore of Maryland and Virginia" (in *The Eastern Shore of Maryland and Virginia,* edited by Charles B. Clark, vol. 1 [1950]) are also useful, as is his *Brief Account of the Indians of Delaware* (1953). Weslager and A. R. Dunlap compiled a study entitled *Indian Place-Names in Delaware* (1950). A new transation of the *Walum Olum,* the legends of the Delawares, was published in Indianapolis in 1954.

The greatest authority on New Sweden was Amandus Johnson, whose major work *The Swedish Settlements on the Delaware,* in two volumes (1911–12), is still unrivaled. Johnson edited two other valuable works, *The Instruction for Johan Printz* (1930) and Peter Lindeström's *Geographia Americae* (1925), based on Lindeström's visit to New Sweden in 1654. Israel Acrelius's *History of New Sweden,* translated and edited by William M. Reynolds (1874), carries the history of the Delaware Swedes into the eighteenth century. It was originally published in Stockholm in 1759 under a title translated as *Description of the Former and Present Condition of the Swedish Churches in What Was Called New Sweden.* Jeannette Eckman's *Crane Hook on the Delaware, 1667–1699* (1958) is an account of a Swedish settlement in the early English period. John H. Wuorinen, *The Finns on the Delaware, 1638–1655* (1938), studies a significant portion of the immigrants to New Sweden. C. A. Weslager's *The Log Cabin in America* (1969) deals with a major cultural contribution of New Sweden to America.

In *The Dutch and the Swedes on the Delaware, 1609–1664* (1930), Christopher Ward has made a lively story of the pre-English European settlements. Francis Vincent covers approximately the same period in *A History of . . . Delaware* (1870), intended only as the first volume of a work that was never completed. Albert Cook Myers collected documents for a somewhat longer period in his *Narratives of Early Pennsylvania, West New Jersey, and Delaware, 1630–1707* (1912). B. Fernow edited *Documents Relating to the History of the Dutch and Swedish Settlements on the Delaware River* (1877) as volume 12 of the series entitled *Documents Relating to the Colonial History of the State of New-York.* The first three volumes in this series also contain documents relating to Delaware, but the translations in this series are said to be faulty and the selection haphazard. A new edition is being prepared by Charles T. Gehring, a student of the Dutch language, and one volume has appeared, covering records for the period 1664–82; its title is somewhat confusing, *New York Historical Manuscripts: Dutch, Volumes XX–XXI, Delaware Papers (English Period)* (1977).

Willem Usselinx, Founder of the Dutch and Swedish West India Companies (1877) by J. Franklin Jameson is a short biography of one of the instigators of European colonization, while David Peterson de Vries, who helped plan the Zwaanendael settlement, has left an autobiography (originally published at Hoorn in 1655) that has been partially published in English translation as *Voyages from Holland to America, A.D. 1632 to 1644* (1853, 1857). A. R. Dunlap has compiled a useful list in *Dutch and Swedish Place-Names in Delaware* (1956). In *De Halve Maen* 39 (January 1965) and 40 (April 1965), Simon Hart published articles on "The City-Colony of New Amstel on the Delaware." Another valuable work relating to the Dutch in Delaware is C. A. Weslager's *Dutch Explorers, Traders and Settlers in the Delaware Valley, 1609–1664* (1961).

The history of the Delaware counties in the seventeenth century after their conquest by the English is related in the "Historical Notes" by Benjamin M. Nead, published in a volume identified on the title page as *Charter to William Penn*, etc., but commonly referred to as the *Duke of Yorke's Book of Laws* (1879), edited by Staughton George, Benjamin M. Nead, and Thomas McCamant. A larger part of the same century is covered by *The English on the Delaware. 1610–1682* (1967), still another work by C. A. Weslager.

The Eighteenth Century

The Collected Essays of Richard S. Rodney on Early Delaware (1975), compiled by George H. Gibson, is probably the most useful secondary work on the English colonial period. Benjamin Ferris, *A History of the Original Settlements on the Delaware* (1846), carries the larger story only to 1682, but the most valuable portion of this book is a long appendix on the history of Wilmington, primarily in the eighteenth century. "The Burning of the Whorekill, 1673," by Leon de Valinger, Jr., a good short article, appeared in the *Pennsylvania Magazine of History and Biography* 74 (1950).

Two compilations of miscellaneous materials by C. H. B. Turner, *Some Records of Sussex County, Delaware* (1909) and *Rodney's Diary and Other Delaware Records* (1911), deal primarily with the eighteenth century, although the Daniel Rodney diary indicated in the title of the second volume is from the early nineteenth century. A recent publication is *The Milford, Delaware, Area before 1776, Antecedents of Today's Milfordians—Their Origins and Lives* (1976), by E. Dallas Hitchens. *Delaware Historic Events* (1946) is a compilation of essays, largely on the colonial period, by Edward W. Cooch. *New Castle on the Delaware,* edited in early editions (1936, 1937, 1950) by Jeannette Eckman and more recently (1973) by Anthony Higgins, was the first guidebook to be completed by the Federal Writers' Project; it is an excellent introduction to the colonial capital of the Delaware counties.

The Bounds of Delaware by Dudley Lunt (1947) summarizes the long quarrel over boundary lines; the location of the Maryland boundary is clarified by William H. Bayliff in his pamphlet The Maryland-Delaware and Maryland-Pennsylvania Boundaries (2d ed., 1959). Leon de Valinger, Jr.'s Colonial Military Organization in Delaware and M. M. Daugherty's Early Colonial Taxation in Delaware are useful pamphlets published in celebration of the tercentenary (1938) of the first permanent European settlement. John H. Powell, in The House on Jones Neck (1955), presents a splendid essay on Samuel Dickinson's establishment of a home in Kent County.

The best study of a religious denomination in Colonial Delaware is Nelson W. Rightmyer's The Anglican Church in Delaware (1947). Volume 5 of William Stevens Perry, ed., Historical Collections Relating to the American Colonial Church (1878) is devoted to Delaware, but Delaware material is also to be found in volumes 2 and 4, pertaining to Pennsylvania and Maryland respectively. Morgan Edwards, "Materials towards a History of the Baptists in the Delaware State," written in the eighteenth century but published in the Pennsylvania Magazine of History and Biography (vol. 9) in 1885, is a valuable historical document in itself. There are too many histories of individual churches to permit listing; a useful compilation of facts is Frank R. Zebley's The Churches of Delaware: A History (1937).

A chapter entitled "A Nondescript Colony on the Delaware" in Lawrence H. Gipson's The British Isles and the American Colonies: The Northern Plantations, 1748–1754 (1960) describes the Lower Counties in the mid-eighteenth century. The most recent account of the entire period from Hudson's voyage of discovery through the Revolution is John A. Munroe's Colonial Delaware: A History (1978), which contains a long, annotated bibliography. An excellent short account, designed primarily for young readers, is H. Clay Reed's The Delaware Colony (1970), which is good reading for any age.

The Revolutionary Era

Federalist Delaware, 1775–1815 (1954), by John A. Munroe, is a scholarly study of the period indicated in the title. Harold B. Hancock's Liberty and Independence: The Delaware State during the American Revolution (1976) is a good popular account of roughly the same period. Hancock's The Loyalists of Revolutionary Delaware (1977) is a vastly enlarged and revised edition of his earliest publication, The Delaware Loyalists (1940).

The three most useful books on the three men who represented Delaware in Congress at the beginning of the Revolution are George H. Ryden, ed., Letters to and from Caesar Rodney, 1756–1784 (1933); William T. Read, Life and Correspondence of George Read (1870); and John M. Coleman, Thomas McKean: Forgotten Leader of the

Revolution (1975). Coleman's study goes only to 1780; it can be supplemented by articles by G. S. Rowe, such as "A Valuable Acquisition in Congress: Thomas McKean, Delegate from Delaware to the Continental Congress, 1774–1783," in *Pennsylvania History* 38 (1971). A short, vivid biography entitled *Caesar Rodney: Patriot,* by William P. Frank, was published in 1975. Another short account of the independence movement is given in John A. Munroe, *Delaware Becomes a State* (1953). No satisfactory life has yet appeared of John Dickinson, though there are several good articles concerning him in the serial publications of the Historical Society of Delaware. Charles J. Stillé's *The Life and Times of John Dickinson, 1732–1808* (1891) is inadequate. *The Political Writings of John Dickinson* was published in two volumes in 1801; a new edition of *Writings of John Dickinson,* edited by Paul Leicester Ford, never got beyond one volume of political writings to 1774, published in 1895. Bernard Bailyn published an excellent essay on Dickinson in his *Pamphlets of the American Revolution, 1750–1776,* vol. 1 (1965), and two other good essays by John H. Powell, entitled "A Certain Great Fortune and Piddling Genius" and "The Day of American Independence," appear in that author's collected essays, called *General Washington and the Jack Ass, and Other American Characters, in Portrait* (1969).

A *Calendar of Ridgely Family Letters, 1742–1899, in the Delaware State Archives,* edited and compiled by Leon de Valinger, Jr., and Virginia E. Shaw, and published in three volumes (1948–1961), contains a wealth of information about the Revolutionary period and on through the mid-nineteenth century. Some of this material is also used in *The Ridgelys of Delaware and Their Circle* (1949), by Mabel Lloyd Ridgely, which emphasizes Revolutionary and Federal times. Another Kent Countian is described by William B. Hamilton, in his *Thomas Rodney, Revolutionary and Builder of the West* (1953), which also is printed as the introduction to his *Anglo-American Justice on the Frontier: Thomas Rodney and His Territorial Cases* (1953).

Two of the most important contemporary documents are *The Life, Experience, and Gospel Labors of the Rt. Rev. Richard Allen* (reprint, 1960), the autobiography of a onetime Kent County slave, and *Timoleon's Biographical History of Dionysius, Tyrant of Delaware,* edited by John A. Munroe (1958), a scathing political history of the Revolution directed against George Read and written by James Tilton. The latter work is reprinted from *Delaware Notes* 31 (1958). Hilda Justice has compiled many useful documents about a noted Kent County abolitionist in her work entitled *Life and Ancestry of Warner Mifflin: Friend, Philanthropist, Patriot* (1905).

The best account of Delaware troops in the Revolution is Christopher Ward's *The Delaware Continentals, 1776–1783* (1941). The major military encounter on Delaware soil is described by Edward W. Cooch in his *Battle of Cooch's Bridge,* (1940). Many Delaware military and naval records of the period are printed in *Delaware Archives* (1911–16), issued by the Public Archives Commission in five volumes. Military developments in Delaware are recounted in Charles

E. Green, *Delaware Heritage: The Story of the Diamond State in the Revolution* (1975) and in Charles J. Truitt, *Breadbasket of the Revolution: Delmarva in the War for Independence* (1975). A good article on an important map of this period is Lawrence C. Wroth, "Joshua Fisher's Chart of Delaware Bay and River," which appeared in the *Pennsylvania Magazine of History and Biography* 74 (1950). Elizabeth Waterson's *Churches in Delaware during the Revolution* (1925) is a general survey. A booklet entitled *Coffee Run, 1772–1960* (1960) contains several articles on the beginnings of Catholicism in Delaware. More information can be found in a series of articles on "Catholicity in the Three Lower Counties" by Charles H. Esling, published in *Records of the American Catholic Historical Society of Philadelphia* in 1887 and in 1896–98. The growth of Methodism in Revolutionary Delaware is described in Robert W. Todd, *Methodism of the Peninsula* (1886) and in E. C. Hallman, *The Garden of Methodism* (1948). Francis Asbury's journal is rich in references to Delaware; see particularly the first volume of Asbury's *Journal and Letters,* edited by Elmer E. Clark et al. in three volumes (1958).

Two excellent monographs, though their subjects are quite diverse, are H. Clay Reed's "The Delaware Constitution of 1776," published in *Delaware Notes* 6 (1930), and John A. H. Sweeney's *Grandeur on the Appoquinimink: The House of William Corbit at Odessa* (1959). "James Tilton's Notes on the Agriculture of Delaware in 1788," edited by R. O. Bausman and John A. Munroe and published in *Agricultural History* 20 (1946), is a valuable survey by an intelligent contemporary observer.

James T. Lemon's "Urbanization and the Development of Eighteenth-Century Southeastern Pennsylvania and Adjacent Delaware," in the *William and Mary Quarterly* 24 (1967), is a valuable article. Dorothy L. Hawkins's "James Adams, the First Printer of Delaware," in *Papers of the Bibliographical Society of America* 28, pt. 1 (1934) and Evald Rink's *Printing in Delaware, 1761–1800* (1969) are good accounts of the beginnings of publishing in Delaware. *Bancroft Woodcock, Silversmith* (1976) is the title of a study by Roland H. Woodward.

The Nineteenth Century

Elizabeth Donnan edited *Papers of James A. Bayard, 1796–1815* (1915); another collection of Bayard's had already been published in 1901 by the Historical Society of Delaware. Morton Borden's *The Federalism of James A. Bayard* (1955) is limited to the congressional career of its subject. John A. Munroe, *Louis McLane: Federalist and Jacksonian* (1973), explores the long career in politics and business of this former law student of Bayard's, with attention to Delaware politics in the period when McLane was active. No adequate biography of John M. Clayton is available, though there is a careful study of his diplomatic career by Mary W. Williams in *The American Secretaries of State and Their Diplomacy*, vol. 6 (1928), edited by Samuel F. Bemis, and a lengthy and eulogistic *Memoir* by Joseph P. Comegys, published in 1882 as part of *Papers of the Historical Society of Delaware*. In the same series appeared the brief *Bombardment of Lewes by the British* (1901), by William M. Marine, which is still a useful history of the 1813 engagement. *Brandywine Village* (1974), by Carol E. Hoffecker, is an account of the milling community that foreshadowed the industrialization of Delaware in the nineteenth century. Greville and Dorothy Bathe, in their *Oliver Evans: A Chronicle of Early American Engineering* (1935), study the life of the most famous of Delaware millwrights and inventors. Henry Seidel Canby, in *Family History* (1945), tells of his progenitors among the Brandywine millers, and in *The Brandywine* (1941) he sketches some of the historic developments along this stream.

There are many publications relating to the most successful of the Brandywine industrialists, the Du Ponts; a basic work is the *Life of Eleuthère Irénée du Pont from Contemporary Correspondence*, translated and edited by Bessie G. du Pont, in eleven volumes (1923), consisting, except for an introduction, wholly of letters. Ambrose Saricks's *Pierre Samuel Du Pont de Nemours* (1965) is an excellent biography of the statesman who brought the du Ponts to America. *E. I. du Pont, Botaniste: The Beginning of a Tradition* (1972), by Norman B. Wilkinson, studies one aspect of the life of the founder of the powder mills, as well as noting the continuing botanic interest of his children. Bessie G. du Pont is the author of *E. I. du Pont de Nemours and Company* (1920), a useful short account of the company's first century. *The Garesché, De Bauduy, and Des Chapelles Families* (1963) by Dorothy Holland, a work partly genealogical, includes many letters and much information concerning French families of the Wilmington area. A two-volume *Life of Alexis Irénée du Pont* (1945), edited by Allan J. Henry, includes a diary of the Rev. Samuel C. Brincklé, as well as many letters.

Elizabeth Montgomery's *Reminiscences of Wilmington* (1851, 1872), is a classic of Delawareana. The standard history of Wilmington is Anna T. Lincoln's *Wilmington, Delaware: Three Centuries under Four Flags, 1609–1937* (1937), basically a chronicle. Carol E. Hoffecker's *Wilmington, Delaware: Portrait of an Industrial City, 1830–1910* (1974) is much more sophisticated within a more limited scope. *The Age of Confidence; Life in the Nineties* (1934), by Henry Seidel Canby, is an impressionistic portrait of Wilmington during the author's boyhood. The *Diaries of Phoebe George Bradford, 1832–1839* (1976), edited by W. Emerson Wilson, throws light on the society of an earlier Wilmington.

The development of several communities along the Christina River is described in C. A. Weslager's *Delaware's Forgotten River* (1947), and his *Brandywine Springs* (1949) relates the history of a spa. One of the best histories of a downstate community is the recent *Sixteen Miles from Anywhere, A History of Georgetown, Dela-*

ware (1976), by William J. Wade. Among other community histories, *A History of Milford* (1962), edited by John Kuhlmann, Virginia F. Cullen's *History of Lewes, Delaware* (1956), and Ella Weldin Johnson's *Story of Newport* (1963) are relatively recent. *The Evolution of Lewes Harbor* (1972), by John C. Kraft and Robert L. Caulk, is an interesting study by geologists.

Ralph L. Gray's *The National Waterway* (1967) is an excellent history of the Chesapeake and Delaware Canal from 1769, when plans were made for it, to 1965. The middle years of an old Delaware business are described by Harold Livesay in "The Lobdell Car Wheel Company," in *Business History Review* 42 (1968). Another old Delaware institution is described in an anecdotal history, *The Farmers Bank, 1807–1957* (1957), by Dudley C. Lunt, who is also the author of *Tales of the Delaware Bench and Bar* (1963) and of a history of the elite Wilmington Club. "Murder at Delaware College," by Richard C. Quick, published in *Delaware Notes* 31 (1958), is an excellent account of one of the most famous crimes in Delaware history. H. Clay Reed's "Student Life at Delaware College, 1834–1859," in vol. 8 (1934) of the same publication furnishes background.

David B. Tyler, in *The American Clyde* (1958), has related the history of iron and steel shipbuilding along the shores of the Delaware from 1840 to the first World War, and the same author is responsible for *The Bay and River Delaware* (1955), a pictorial survey of maritime history. Kenneth R. Martin's *Delaware Goes Whaling, 1833–1845* (1974) is an account of the adventures of Wilmington whalers. James E. Marvil has made two contributions to maritime history, his *Sailing Rams* (1961, 1974), a history of ships built in Sussex County, and his *Pilots of the Bay and River Delaware and Lewes Lore* (1965).

No thorough study of slavery or of blacks in Delaware has appeared in print, but there are several theses on the subject listed in the new supplemental *Bibliography of Delaware, 1960–1974*, referred to above, and several articles on the subject have appeared in *Delaware History* magazine. James Newton and Harold Hancock are preparing a book of readings in the history of blacks in Delaware that should be very useful. Meanwhile, a vivid picture of some aspects of slavery may be found in the autobiographical *Narrative of Some Remarkable Incidents in the Life of Solomon Bayley, Formerly a Slave in the State of Delaware* (1825), and in William Still, *The Underground Rail Road* (1872), there are interviews with former slaves in Delaware. A short essay by John A. Munroe, "The Negro in Delaware," appeared in the *South Atlantic Quarterly* 56 (1957). Another short article is "Not Quite Men: The Free Negroes in Delaware in the 1830s," by Harold B. Hancock, in *Civil War History* 17 (1971).

The *Narrative and Confessions of Lucretia P. Cannon* (1841), which describes the career of a notorious slave kidnapper, was reprinted in about 1936, and Ted Giles has written a biography called *Patty Cannon: Woman of Mystery* (1965). George Alfred Townsend used her as the central figure in his exciting novel of slave days in

Delaware and the Eastern Shore entitled *The Entailed Hat; or, Patty Cannon's Times* (1884 and many reprintings). *George Alfred Townsend* (1946) by Ruthanna Hindes is a brief biography of the novelist and journalist, a native of Delaware. Augustus H. Able III later published a short sketch of Townsend in *Delaware Notes 25* (1952). An essay on Thomas Garrett, the abolitionist, by Thomas E. Drake, appears in *Friends in Wilmington, 1738–1938* (1938).

Fort Delaware (1957) by W. Emerson Wilson and *Delaware Stays in the Union* (1955) by John S. Spruance are short, inexpensive pamphlets that furnish background to Civil War history. Harold Hancock's *Delaware during the Civil War* (1961) is an excellent political history. *Delaware in the Civil War* (1962), edited by W. Emerson Wilson, contains several essays by different authors, predominantly on military history. *Admiral Samuel Francis Du Pont: A Selection from His Civil War Letters* (1969), edited by John D. Hayes in three volumes, is a superb collection of data from the papers of the leading Delaware naval officer.

Norman B. Wilkinson, *The Brandywine Home Front During the Civil War* (1966), depicts the war's impact on life along the Brandywine. H. Clay Reed's "Lincoln's Compensated Emancipation Plan and Its Relation to Delaware," in *Delaware Notes 7* (1931), is a pioneering article of value. *United States Bonds; or, Duress by Federal Authority* (1874), by Isaac W. K. Handy, is a Presbyterian minister's account of his incarceration at Fort Delaware. There is a chapter on Delaware in *The Secession Movement in the Middle Atlantic States* (1973) by William C. Wright. Emalea Pusey Warner's *Childhood Memories of the Civil War Years* (1939) is a brief reminiscence by an important Delawarean.

The best work on the immediate postbellum years in Delaware is an essay by Harold B. Hancock, "Reconstruction in Delaware," in *Radicalism, Racism, and Party Realignment: The Border States during Reconstruction* (1969), edited by Richard O. Curry. The outstanding Delaware statesman of this period is the subject of two books by Charles C. Tansill, *The Congressional Career of Thomas F. Bayard, 1865–1885* (1946) and *The Foreign Policy of Thomas F. Bayard, 1885–1897* (1949), but neither gives much attention to Delaware.

The History of Education in Delaware (1893), by Lyman P. Powell, is a pioneering study, followed by Stephen Weeks, *History of Public School Education in Delaware* (1917). A charming reminiscence of Delaware College was written by George Morgan under the title of "Sunny Days at Dear Old Delaware, 1871–1875" and published in *Delaware Notes 8* (1934). Morgan's friend Edward N. Vallandigham wrote *Fifty Years of Delaware College, 1870–1920* (ca. 1921).

Charles Heber Clark, using the pen name Max Adeler, wrote comic tales of New Castle life under the title *Out of the Hurly-Burly; or, Life in an Odd Corner* (1874), a best-seller in its day. The last section of *Rambles and Reflections* (1892), a travel book by Thomas J. Clayton, is devoted to Brandywine Hundred, where he made his home. *Annals of a Village in Kent County, Delaware* (1934) is a brief reminiscence by Walter A. Powell of Dover in the mid-nineteenth century. John Janvier Black's *Forty Years in the Medical Profession* (1900) is mainly devoted to summarizing the medical knowledge of his day.

Under the Old Flag (1912), by James Harrison Wilson, is a two-volume autobiography, mainly military. A chapter of David F. Healy's recent *U.S. Expansionism* (1970) is devoted to General Wilson. The five volumes of *Debates and Proceedings* of the 1896–1897 constitutional convention, reported by Charles G. Guyer and Edmond C. Hardesty, which were not published until 1958, are a rich source of political and social history.

Possibly excepting George A. Townsend, the most distinguished Delaware writer of the nineteenth century was Robert Montgomery Bird, whose dramas were reprinted in *The Life and Dramatic Works of Robert Montgomery Bird* (1919), by Clement E. Foust; a second biography is Mary Mayer Bird's *Life of Robert Montgomery Bird* (1945). William W. Smithers wrote *The Life of John Lofland* (1894), a biography of an eccentric poet known as "the Milford bard."

The Twentieth Century

The best work on the subject is *Government of Delaware* (1976), by Paul Dolan and James R. Soles, which replaces the older *Government and Administration of Delaware* (1956), by Paul Dolan. Dolan's *Organization of State Administration in Delaware* (1951) is also a classic. Cy Liberman and James Rosbrow wrote a guide to government called *The Delaware Citizen* (1952), which went through several editions. *The Delaware Corporation* (1937) by Russell C. Larcom and *The Income Tax in Delaware* (1944) by R. Jean Brownlee deal with these special subjects, though they are now somewhat out of date.

The relations between the Du Ponts and Delaware concerned a study group sponsored by Ralph Nader; its findings appeared in a volume entitled *The Company State* (1973) by James Phelan and Robert Pozen, but the authors' knowledge of Delaware history was acquired quickly and is distinctly limited. An earlier example of muckraking is John K. Winkler's *The Du Pont Dynasty* (1935), and a more recent example is Gerald C. Zilg's *Du Pont: Behind the Nylon Curtain* (1974), which is factually undependable. Between November 1934 and January 1935, *Fortune* magazine ran a series of three interesting articles on the Du Pont family, the Du Pont Company, and the influence of both on Delaware. Other fairly recent books of varying merit on the family or company are William S. Dutton, *Du Pont: One Hundred and Forty Years* (1942); William H. Carr, *The Du Ponts of Delaware: A Fantastic Dynasty* (1964); Max Dorian, *Du*

Ponts: From Gunpowder to Nylon (1962) ; and Marc Duke, *The du Ponts: Portrait of a Dynasty* (1976).

"The American Liberty League, 1934–1940" by Frederick Rudolph, in the *American Historical Review* 56 (1950), is a good scholarly article on the involvement of John J. Raskob, R. R. M. Carpenter, and several Du Ponts in a crusade against the New Deal. Though it has flaws, Marquis James's biography *Alfred I. du Pont: The Family Rebel* (1941) is a superior work. An excellent and thorough study, limited to one facet—though the major one—of the subject's many interests, is *Pierre S. du Pont and the Making of the Modern Corporation* (1971), written by Alfred D. Chandler and Stephen Salsbury. A graceful, short eulogy of one of P. S. Du Pont's colleagues is *Harry Fletcher Brown: An Essay in Appreciation* (1960), by John A. Perkins and Robeson Bailey.

An article by Charles P. Wilson, "Organized Labor: How Effective Is It?" in *Delaware Today* 13 (November 1975), is one of the few studies of the relation of organized labor to Delaware politics. A study of the political relationship of the leading farmers' organization, entitled *History of the Delaware State Grange and the State's Agriculture, 1875–1975* (1975), by Joanne Passmore and others, is a book-length study, covering a much longer period than Wilson's essay. Many valuable studies of different aspects of agricultural history have been printed as Bulletins of the University of Delaware Agricultural Experiment Station, like R. O. Bausman's *Economic Survey of the Broiler Industry in Delaware* (1943), which was Bulletin no. 242.

Bulletin no. 347 of the same series was Charles Tilly's *Recent Changes in Delaware Population* (1962), a useful work. C. Harold Brown and J. Kevin O'Connor prepared a study entitled *Population in Delaware* (1965), which was widely distributed as a mimeographed publication, as was *Race and Residence in Wilmington, Delaware* (1965), by Charles Tilly, Wagner D. Jackson, and Barry Kay. Jerome Holland, usually with associates, was the author of a number of studies of the black population. Two valuable studies dealing with crime and punishment are *Red Hannah: Delaware's Whipping Post* (1947) and *The New Castle County Workhouse* (1940), both by Robert G. Caldwell. A. O. H. Grier's *This Was Wilmington* (1945) is a collection of newspaper articles. *The Horse on Rodney Square* (1977), by Lee Reese, is an anecdotal history of Wilmington, particularly of its "society"; it contains priceless stories of leading Wilmingtonians and of the institutions of their city in the first four decades of this century. The title describes *A Time to Remember, 1920–1960: Picture Story of Forty Years in the History of Northern New Castle County, Delaware* (1962), by Charles Silliman, who has written accounts of several institutions, including the Delaware Hospital, Christ Church (Christiana Hundred), and the Delaware Trust Company.

The student interested in a particular church should examine the card catalog in any leading scholarly library, such as the State

Archives (Hall of Records), in Dover, the Historical Society in Wilmington, or the University of Delaware, in Newark. Business histories are not quite as common as church histories, but a good collection of those that exist may be found in the Eleutherian Mills Historical Library, in Christiana Hundred. *The District: A History of the Philadelphia District, U.S. Army Corps of Engineers, 1866–1971* (ca. 1975) by Frank E. Snyder and Brian H. Guss is profusely illustrated and covers a longer period than its title indicates, with especially interesting material on the first Delaware Breakwater at Lewes, a major project, and on additions and supplementary works.

Richard V. Elliott's *Last of the Steamboats: The Saga of the Wilson Line* (1970) is an illustrated narrative of a Philadelphia-Wilmington river connection. *New Castle, Delaware, 1651–1939* (1939), is a handsome volume composed of Bayard Wootten's photographs and brief textual additions by Anthony Higgins. The history of Richardson Park, a trolley-car suburb, is related in C. A. Weslager's *The Richardsons of Delaware* (1957). A phenomenon of the twentieth century, though with earlier origins, the popularization of the ocean shore, is described in Dan Terrell's recent history of Rehoboth Beach, *Room for One More Sinner* (1974). Dorothy Williams Pepper's *Folklore of Sussex County, Delaware* (1976), is an initial exploration of a field of Delaware folk culture that has been given little attention in the past.

The two volumes on *Delaware's Role in World War II* (1955), by William H. Conner and Leon de Valinger, Jr., are a valuable compendium of facts. Father Thomas J. Peterman, in *Priests of a Century* (1971), has compiled biographical data on Roman Catholic clergy of the Diocese of Wilmington.

All I Have Seen (1976) is the autobiography of the retired Episcopal Bishop Arthur McKinstry. William D. Lewis presents an engaging series of essays in *The University of Delaware: Ancestors, Friends, and Neighbors,* which comprised most of vol. 34 (1961) of *Delaware Notes.* Charles E. Green offers useful data on Masonic lodges and their leadership in his *History of the M. W. Grand Lodge of Ancient Free and Accepted Masons of Delaware* (1956).

The illustrators and other artists of the so-called Brandywine School have been receiving much attention recently from writers, as in Henry C. Pitz's *The Brandywine Tradition* (1969). *Howard Pyle: Writer, Illustrator, Founder of the Brandywine School* (1975) is by the same author; an earlier study entitled *Howard Pyle: A Chronicle* (1925) was by Charles D. Abbott. Pyle's most famous successors, N. C. Wyeth and his children, live across the state line in Pennsylvania. Theodore Bolton published an article entitled "The Book Illustrations of Felix Octavius Carr Darley," a predecessor of Pyle who lived at Claymont, in the *Proceedings of the American Antiquarian Society,* vol. 61 (1952).

A Final Note

No mention has been made in this bibliography of individual essays in H. Clay Reed's *Delaware: A History of the First State,* both in order to save space and because it is assumed that anyone seriously interested in Delaware history must examine its table of contents in the first volume and the excellent index in the second. Such articles as those by Elizabeth C. Goggin on public welfare, Jeannette Eckman on constitutional changes, John W. Christy on the Presbyterians, and Harold B. Hancock on agriculture and manufacturing should not be neglected.

Similarly, individual articles in *Delaware History* magazine have not been cited here. In the thirty years since its initiation in 1946 this semiannual journal has published a large number of important articles, as well as many valuable documents. It is sad that there is as yet no cumulative index to this journal, but the student of history may find citations of individual articles in the Reed and Reed bibliography or in its new supplement. To mention only a few items, the articles pertaining to the history of African-Americans by Harold B. Hancock, Harold Livesay, Amy McNulty Heller, and Jacqueline Jones Halstead; the memoirs of Christopher L. Ward and John C. Higgins; various diaries; John Powell's study of Dickinson as president of the Delaware State; and Ernest Moyne's biography of John Haslet deserve attention.

Nor has this selective bibliography cited the valuable dissertations, theses, and other unpublished papers that are available to students in many Delaware repositories, but primarily at the Hugh M. Morris Library of the University of Delaware, which has purchased or been given copies of many theses written elsewhere. Among such unpublished materials available at the Morris Library are Hugh Gibb's study of the Delaware Railroad, Harold Hancock's master's thesis on John Edward Addicks, and studies of political change in Delaware by David Peltier and Richard Mumford, of the free black by Gary Dean, and of social responsibility by William Kerr. Unless circulated widely in mimeographed form, such items are not listed in the Reed and Reed bibliography, but they are included in the supplement prepared by the Morris Library reference staff at the University of Delaware.

The interested student should also be aware of the existence at the Wilmington Institute Free Library of two Delaware indexes on catalog cards, one biographical and one topical. Made years ago, these indexes occasionally turn up obscure references in books otherwise not indexed or in newspaper clippings placed in a vertical file.

Recent Publications

A notable recent publication is the long-anticipated life of Dickinson, entitled *John Dickinson, Conservative Revolutionary* (1983), by Milton E. Flower. Other good recent biographies include G. S. Rowe's *Thomas McKean: The Shaping of an American Republicanism* (1978) and Thomas J. Peterman's well-researched study of the first Catholic bishop of Wilmington—*The Cutting Edge:*

The Life of Thomas A. Becker (1982). Mary Sam Ward's *Delaware Women Remembered* (1977) is a useful collective biography, and Eugene S. Ferguson has written a short, authoritative study of *Oliver Evans: Inventive Genius of the American Industrial Revolution* (1980). In editing *The Correspondence between Samuel Bancroft, Jr., and Charles Fairfax Murray, 1892–1916* (1980), Rowland Elzea has portrayed the activity of Delaware's first important art collector.

John D. Gates's *The Du Pont Family* (1979) and Leonard Mosley's *Blood Relations: The Rise and Fall of the du Ponts of Delaware* (1980) add to the lengthy list of works on this subject, while Philip J. Wingate, in his *The Colorful Du Pont Company* (1982), supplies an insider's view of men and developments in the dye industry.

A second volume of *Delaware Papers* has appeared (1981) in the series of *New York Historical Manuscripts: Dutch,* edited by Charles Gehring; this volume covers the years 1648–64, whereas the previous volume covered a later period, 1664–82. A short essay by James B. Jackson, *The Early Settlement and Founding of Kent County, Delaware, 1671–1683* (1983), breaks fresh ground, as does an essay by Pearl G. Herlihy [Daniels], "The Evolution of Delaware Cartography to 1800—Early Maps," in *Transactions of the Delaware Academy of Science* 6 (1976): 163–88. Charles A. Silliman in *The Episcopal Church in Delaware, 1785–1954* (1982) takes up where Nelson Rightmyer's earlier book stops.

Jeffrey A. Raffel has written about racial integration in the schools in his *Politics of School Desegregation: The Metropolitan Remedy in Delaware* (1980). There is a chapter on Delaware in Richard Kluger's *Simple Justice: The History of Brown v. Board of Education and Black America's Struggle for Equality* (1976). Along with this should be read Louis L. Redding's "Desegregation in Higher Education in Delaware," *Journal of Negro Education* 27 (1958): 253–59. For the history of blacks in an earlier period, see Elizabeth Moyne Homsey's "Free Blacks in Kent County, Delaware, 1790–1830," *Working Papers from the Regional Economic History Research Center* (Eleutherian Mills-Hagley Foundation) 3 (1980): 31–57.

There is a chapter on the Delaware federal district court in Stephen B. Presser's *Studies in the History of the United States Courts of the Third Circuit* (1982). Harold Hancock has produced histories of Seaford (1981), with Madeline Dunn Hite; of Milton (1982), with Russell McCabe; and of Laurel (1983). Toni Young's *The Grand Experience* (1976), an account of the opera house, now restored, in Wilmington, is a contribution to cultural history.

Since the second edition a major documentary publication has appeared in two volumes, the minutes of the Delaware house of assembly from 1770 to 1792 and of the constitutional conventions of 1776 and 1791–92. Edited by Claudia L. Bushman, Harold Hancock, and Elizabeth M. Homsey, these volumes include brief biographical sketches of the legislators. The earliest Delaware legislators, who met with those of Pennsylvania to 1701, are described in detail in *Lawmaking and Legislators in Pennsylvania: A Biographical Dictionary,* vol. 1, *1682–1709,* edited by Craig W. Horle, et al. (1991). Brief accounts of all the colonial assemblymen are in Bruce A. Bendler, *Colonial Delaware Assemblymen, 1682–1776* (1989). *Records of the Courts of Sussex County, Delaware, 1677–1710,* edited by Craig W. Horle, has just been published.

C. A. Weslager has recently written several colonial histories: *The Swedes and Dutch at New Castle* (1987), *New Sweden on the Delaware, 1638–1655* (1988), and *A Man and His Ship: Peter Minuit and the Kalmar Nyckel* (1989). Bernard L. Herman's *Architecture and Rural Life in Central Delaware, 1700–1800* (1987) covers a wide period.

New biographies include Dick Carter, *Clearing New Ground: The Life of John G. Townsend, Jr.* (1983); Joseph F. Wall, *Alfred I. du Pont: The Man and His Family* (1990); and Norman B. Wilkinson, *Lammot du Pont and the American Explosives Industry, 1850–1884* (1984). The governors are given particular attention in Roger A. Martin's *History of Delaware through Its Governors* (1984).

Two new studies focussed on women are Gloria F. Hull, *Give Us Each Day: The Diary of Alice Dunbar-Nelson* (1984) and Betty-Bright Low and J. Hinsley, *Sophie du Pont: A Young Lady in America: Sketches, Diaries, and Letters, 1823–1833* (1987).

Education and religion are the subject of three full and documented studies: John A. Munroe, *The University of Delaware: A History* (1984); Robert J. Taggart, *Private Philanthropy and Public Education: Pierre S. du Pont and the Delaware Schools, 1890–1940* (1988); and William H. Williams, *The Garden of American Methodism: The Delmarva Peninsula, 1769–1820* (1982). In *"Invisible" Strands in African Methodism* (1983) Lewis V. Baldwin studies two churches of local origin from 1805 to 1980.

Twentieth-century developments are discussed in Carol E. Hoffecker, *Corporate Capital: Wilmington in the Twentieth Century* (1983); David A. Hounshell and John K. Smith, Jr., *Science and Corporate Strategy: Du Pont R & D, 1902–1980* (1988); and David Dyer and David B. Sicilia, *Labors of a Modern Hercules: The Evolution of a Chemical Company* (1990). A related study is Robert F. Burk's *The Corporate State and the Broker State: The du Ponts and American National Politics, 1925–1940* (1990).

The last decade of the twentieth century produced many useful volumes relating to the history of Delaware and its people. On the earliest European settlers *New Sweden in America* (1994), edited by Carol E. Hoffecker and three colleagues, is a collection of essays deserving careful attention. *The 1693 Census of the Swedes on the Delaware* (1993), by Peter Craig, a genealogical study, should not be neglected by historians.

William H. Williams' *Slavery and Freedom in Delaware, 1639–1865*, and Patience Essah's *A House Divided: Slavery and Emancipation in Delaware, 1638–1865* (both 1996) discuss an important but neglected subject. *A History of African Americans of Delaware and Maryland's Eastern Shore*, edited by Carole Marks (2d ed., 1998), contains essays of varying quality. Other ethnic groups are studied in *Catholics in Colonial Delmarva*, by Thomas Peterman (1996) and *Becoming American, Remaining Jewish*, by Toni Young (1999), which is restricted to Wilmington in the years 1879–1924. Elements of social life in southern Delaware are portrayed in *The Stolen House*, by Bernard Herman (1992).

Biographies are prominent among the new books. Carol E. Hoffecker employs a biographical approach to her study of *Federal Justice in the First State: A History of the United States District Court for the District of Delaware* (1992), and the same prolific scholar is the author of *Honest John Williams* (2000). Other biographies include Julian Winslow's on Samuel Maxwell Harrington (1994), Robert Barnes and Judith Pfeiffer on Everett Johnson (1999), Matthew Hermes on Wallace Carothers (1996), Seymour Toll on Judge John Biggs, Jr. (1993), and Charles W. Cheape on Walter Carpenter (1995). Ruth Lord wrote of her father and his spectacular creation in *Henry F. du Pont and Winterthur* (1998). Autobiographies include Russell Peterson's *Rebel with a Conscience* (1999), Jack Smyth's *From Diamonds to Headlines* (1996), and J. Saunders Redding's *Troubled in Mind* (1991), a reprinted account of the author's early years in Wilmington, with a brief life by Annette Woolard. The Delaware Heritage

Commission, publisher of the Redding book, has also issued short studies of governors Elbert Carvel, Charles Terry, Russell Peterson, and Sherman Tribbitt.

In celebration of the hundredth anniversary of the present state constitution Harvey B. Rubenstein edited *The Delaware Constitution of 1897*, a group of commissioned essays (1997). Two other valuable political studies are Roger Martin's *Memoirs of the Senate* (1995) and William Boyer's *Governing Delaware* (2000).

Recent contributions to educational history include Carol E. Hoffecker's *Beneath Thy Guiding Hand* (1994), a history of women at the University of Delaware, and Lloyd W. Kline's *History of Goldey-Beacom College* (1993). George J. Frebert explored a new subject in *Delaware Aviation History* (1998).

Even more recent books are Carol E. Hoffecker, *Democracy in Delaware: The Story of the First State's General Assembly* (2004); Randy J. Holland and Helen L. Winslow, eds., *Delaware's Supreme Court, Golden Anniversary, 1961–2001* (2001); Margaret M. Mulrooney, *Black Powder, White Lace: The du Pont Irish and Cultural Identity in Nineteenth-Century America* (2002); and T. J. Reed, W. Andrew McKay, and Anthony R. Wade, *Untying the Political Knot: Delaware During the War Between the States* (2001).

Index